Pro Docker

Deepak Vohra

Apress®

Pro Docker

ISBN-13 (pbk): 978-1-4842-1829-7

ISBN-13 (electronic): 978-1-4842-1830-3

Managing Director: Welmoed Spahr
Lead Editor: Michelle Lowman
Technical Reviewer: Massimo Nardone
Editorial Board: Steve Anglin, Pramila Balan, Louise Corrigan, Jonathan Gennick, Robert Hutchinson, Celstin Suresh John, Michelle Lowman, James Markham, Susan McDermott, Matthew Moodie, Jeffrey Pepper, Douglas Pundick, Ben Renow-Clarke, Gwenan Spearing
Coordinating Editor: Mark Powers
Compositor: SPi Global
Indexer: SPi Global
Artist: SPi Global

Distributed to the book trade worldwide by Springer Science+Business Media New York, 233 Spring Street, 6th Floor, New York, NY 10013. Phone 1-800-SPRINGER, fax (201) 348-4505, e-mail orders-ny@springer-sbm.com, or visit www.springeronline.com. Apress Media, LLC is a California LLC and the sole member (owner) is Springer Science + Business Media Finance Inc (SSBM Finance Inc). SSBM Finance Inc is a Delaware corporation.

For information on translations, please e-mail rights@apress.com, or visit www.apress.com.

Apress and friends of ED books may be purchased in bulk for academic, corporate, or promotional use. eBook versions and licenses are also available for most titles. For more information, reference our Special Bulk Sales–eBook Licensing web page at www.apress.com/bulk-sales.

Any source code or other supplementary material referenced by the author in this text is available to readers at www.apress.com/9781484218297. For additional information about how to locate and download your book's source code, go to www.apress.com/source-code/. Readers can also access source code at SpringerLink in the Supplementary Material section for each chapter.

Contents at a Glance

Contents

About the Author

Deepak Vohra is a consultant and a principal member of the NuBean.
com software company. Deepak is a Sun-certified Java programmer and
Web component developer.He has worked in the fields of XML, Java
programming, and Java EE for over seven years. Deepak is the coauthor of
Pro XML Development with Java Technology (Apress, 2006). Deepak is also
the author of the *JDBC 4.0* and *Oracle JDeveloper for J2EE Development,
Processing XML Documents with Oracle JDeveloper 11g, EJB 3.0 Database
Persistence with Oracle Fusion Middleware 11g,* and *Java EE Development
in Eclipse IDE* (Packt Publishing). He also served as the technical reviewer
on *WebLogic: The Definitive Guide (O'Reilly Media, 2004)* and *Ruby
Programming for the Absolute Beginner* (Cengage Learning PTR, 2007).

About the Technical Reviewer

Massimo Nardone holds a Master of Science degree in Computing Science from the University of Salerno, Italy. He worked as a PCI QSA and Senior Lead IT Security/Cloud/SCADA Architect for many years and currently works as Security, Cloud and SCADA Lead IT Architect for Hewlett Packard Enterprise. He has more than 20 years of work experience in IT including Security, SCADA, Cloud Computing, IT Infrastructure, Mobile, Security and WWW technology areas for both national and international projects. Massimo has worked as a Project Manager, Cloud/SCADA Lead IT Architect, Software Engineer, Research Engineer, Chief Security Architect, and Software Specialist. He worked as visiting lecturer and supervisor for exercises at the Networking Laboratory of the Helsinki University of Technology (Aalto University). He has been programming and teaching how to program with Perl, PHP, Java, VB, Python, C/C++ and MySQL for more than 20 years. He holds four international patents (PKI, SIP, SAML and Proxy areas).

He is the author of *Pro Android Games* (Apress, 2015).

Massimo dedicates his work on this book to Roberto Salvato, Roberto Franzese and Michele Romano, who are like brothers to him and are always there when he needs them.

CHAPTER 1

■ ■ ■

Hello Docker

Docker is an open standards platform for developing, packaging and running portable distributed applications. Using Docker, developers and sysadmins may build, ship and run applications on any platform such as a PC, the cloud, data center or a virtual machine. Getting all the required dependencies for a software application including the code, the runtime libraries, and the system tools and libraries is often a challenge when developing and running an application. Docker simplifies the application development and execution by packaging all the required software for an application including the dependencies into a single software unit called a Docker image that may be run on any platform and environment.

What makes Docker images unique and different from virtual appliances, which are also software images (virtual machine images), is that while each virtual machine image runs on a separate guest OS, the Docker images run within the same OS kernel. Docker software runs in an isolated environment called a Docker container that includes its own filesystem and environment variables. Docker containers are isolated from each other and from the underlying OS.

A Docker container for a software application includes all that is required to run the software, and files may be copied from the host OS to a Docker container if required. As an application could require other software to develop a linked application, Docker containers may be linked, which makes the environment variables and software from another Docker container available to a Docker container.

Docker makes use of a Dockerfile to build an image. A Dockerfile consists of all the instructions such as what software to download, which commands to run, which network ports to expose, which files and directories to add to the filesystem, and which environment variables to set. A Docker image may be made an executable by providing an entrypoint. A Docker image may be built by providing a Dockerfile, or pre-built Docker images may be downloaded from the Docker Hub (`https://hub.docker.com/`). The complete instruction set supported by Dockerfile can be found at *http://docs.docker.com/engine/reference/builder/*.

In this chapter, we shall install the Docker engine on Linux, download a Hello World Docker image, and run a Docker container for a Hello World application. We have used Linux because some of the other software we have used, such as Apache Hadoop, is supported (both in development and production) only on Linux. We have used two commonly used distributions of Linux, Red Hat 7 and Ubuntu 14, but any of the supported installations (`https://docs.docker.com/v1.8/installation/`) could be used.

Running the Docker Hello World Application

Downloading a Docker Image

Running an Application in a Docker Container

Listing Running Docker Containers

Accessing the Application Output on Command Line

Accessing the Application Output in a Browser

Stopping a Docker Container

Removing a Docker Container

Removing a Docker Image

Stopping the Docker Service

Setting the Environment

We shall use Amazon EC2 instances based on Linux for deploying Docker and Docker images. Linux is required to support 64 bit software. We have made use of two different 64 bit (required) Amazon Machine Images (AMIs):

1. Ubuntu Server 14.04 LTS (HVM), SSD Volume Type - ami-d05e75b8 64 bit

2. Red Hat Enterprise Linux version 7.1 (HVM), EBS General Purpose (SSD) Volume Type (ami-12663b7a) 64 bit

An Amazon EC2 instance based on the Ubuntu AMI is shown in Figure 1-1.

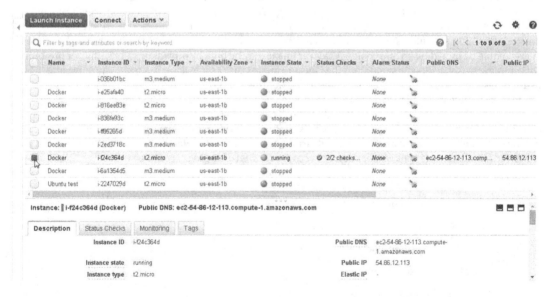

Figure 1-1. *Amazon EC2 Instance Based on Ubuntu AMI*

To connect to an Amazon EC2 instance, the public IP address is used. The public IP address may be obtained from the EC2 Console as shown in Figure 1-2.

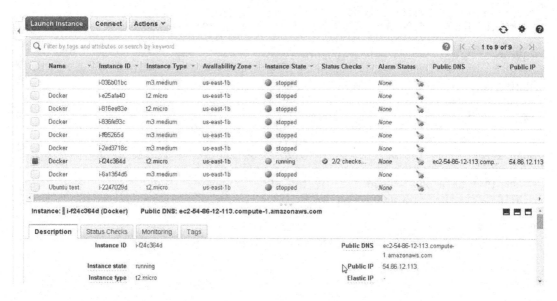

Figure 1-2. *Obtaining the Public IP Address*

Connect to an Amazon EC2 Ubuntu instance using SSH and the public IP address with the following command in which docker.pem is the private key format (.pem) generated by Amazon EC2.

```
ssh -i "docker.pem" ubuntu@54.86.12.113
```

The Ubuntu instance gets connected to as shown in Figure 1-3.

```
ubuntu@ip-172-30-1-190: ~                                    _ □ ×
File  Edit  View  Search  Terminal  Help
[root@localhost ~]# ssh -i "docker.pem" ubuntu@54.86.12.113
Welcome to Ubuntu 14.04.3 LTS (GNU/Linux 3.13.0-66-generic x86_64)

 * Documentation:  https://help.ubuntu.com/

 System information as of Fri Oct 23 16:09:08 UTC 2015

 System load:  0.0              Processes:            143
 Usage of /:   76.2% of 7.74GB  Users logged in:     0
 Memory usage: 17%              IP address for eth0:    172.30.1.190
 Swap usage:   0%               IP address for docker0: 172.17.42.1

 Graph this data and manage this system at:
   https://landscape.canonical.com/

 Get cloud support with Ubuntu Advantage Cloud Guest:
   http://www.ubuntu.com/business/services/cloud

12 packages can be updated.
6 updates are security updates.


Last login: Fri Oct 23 16:09:08 2015 from d75-157-54-139.bchsia.telus.net
ubuntu@ip-172-30-1-190:~$ []
```

Figure 1-3. *Connecting to Ubuntu Instance on Amazon EC2 from Local Host*

If a Red Hat AMI is used the command to connect to the Amazon EC2 instance is slightly different. Instead of the user "ubuntu" use the "ec2-user" user. For example, connect to the Linux instance using the following command in which docker.pem is the private key format (.pem) generated by Amazon EC2.

```
ssh -i "docker.pem" ec2-user@54.175.182.96
```

The RHEL 7.1 instance gets connected to as shown in Figure 1-4.

```
[root@localhost ~]# ssh -i "docker.pem" ec2-user@54.175.182.96
[ec2-user@ip-172-30-1-61 ~]$ █
```

Figure 1-4. *Connecting to RHEL Instance*

Run the following command to find if the Linux architecture supports 64 bit software.

```
uname -r
```

The x86_64 in the output as shown in Figure 1-5 indicates that 64 bit is supported.

```
[root@localhost ~]# ssh -i "docker.pem" ec2-user@54.175.182.96
[ec2-user@ip-172-30-1-61 ~]$ uname -r
3.10.0-229.el7.x86_64
[ec2-user@ip-172-30-1-61 ~]$ █
```

Figure 1-5. *Finding Architecture Support*

Installing Docker on Red Hat 7

Two different methods for installing Docker on Red Hat are available: install with yum or install with script. Installing with yum requires a user to add the yum repo, which could be more involved than the script option. We have used the Docker installation script to install Docker.

As a user with sudo or root privileges, update the local repository packages with the following command.

```
sudo yum update
```

Run the Docker installation script to install Docker Engine.

```
curl -sSL https://get.docker.com/  | sh
```

Docker Engine gets installed as shown in Figure 1-6.

```
[ec2-user@ip-172-30-1-80 ~]$ curl -sSL https://get.docker.com/ | sh
+ sudo -E sh -c 'sleep 3; yum -y -q install docker-engine'
warning: /var/cache/yum/x86_64/7Server/docker-main-repo/packages/docker-engine-1
.8.2-1.el7.centos.x86_64.rpm: Header V4 RSA/SHA1 Signature, key ID 2c52609d: NOK
EY
Public key for docker-engine-1.8.2-1.el7.centos.x86_64.rpm is not installed
Importing GPG key 0x2C52609D:
 Userid    : "Docker Release Tool (releasedocker) <docker@docker.com>"
 Fingerprint: 5811 8e89 f3a9 1289 7c07 0adb f762 2157 2c52 609d
 From      : https://yum.dockerproject.org/gpg

If you would like to use Docker as a non-root user, you should now consider
adding your user to the "docker" group with something like:

  sudo usermod -aG docker ec2-user

Remember that you will have to log out and back in for this to take effect!

[ec2-user@ip-172-30-1-80 ~]$ █
```

Figure 1-6. *Installing Docker Engine*

Before starting the Docker service, you should modify the docker.service file to disable the Docker start timeout. The docker.service file is in the /usr/lib/systemd/system directory, which has permissions set. Either run a sudo command or copy the file to a directory which does not have permissions set. For example, copy the docker.service to the root directory with the following command.

```
cp /usr/lib/systemd/system/docker.service .
```

Open the docker.service file in vi editor.

```
vi docker.service
```

Alternatively open the docker.service file as sudo.

```
sudo vi /usr/lib/systemd/system/docker.service
```

Add the following line to docker.service in the [Service] header.

```
TimeoutStartSec=0
```

The updated docker.service is shown in Figure 1-7.

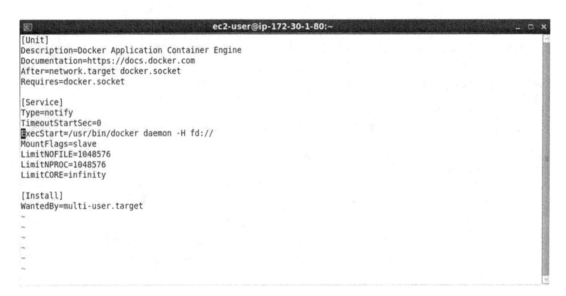

Figure 1-7. *Updated docker.service*

If the docker.service was copied to another directory copy the file back to the /usr/lib/systemd/system directory with the following command.

```
sudo cp docker.service  /usr/lib/systemd/system/docker.service
```

Flush changes to load the new configuration.

```
sudo systemctl daemon-reload
```

All the options for installing Docker on Red Hat are discussed at http://docs.docker.com/engine/installation/rhel/.

Uninstalling Docker

This section may be skipped if Docker is to be made use of in this chapter and later chapters. To uninstall Docker, run the following command to list the Docker engines installed.

```
yum list installed | grep docker
```

Remove the Docker engine and Docker directory with the following commands.

```
sudo yum -y remove docker-engine.x86_64
rm -rf /var/lib/docker
```

Installing a Specific Docker Version

To install a specific version of Docker download and install the rpm for the version. For example, install Docker 1.7.0 as follows.

```
curl -O -sSL https://get.docker.com/rpm/1.7.0/centos-6/RPMS/x86_64/
docker-engine-1.7.0-1.el6.x86_64.rpm
sudo yum localinstall --nogpgcheck docker-engine-1.7.0-1.el6.x86_64.rpm
```

Installing Docker on Ubuntu

Docker is supported on the following versions of Ubuntu: Ubuntu Wily 15.10, Ubuntu Vivid 15.04, Ubuntu Trusty 14.04 (LTS) and Ubuntu Precise 12.04 (LTS). Regardless of version, Docker requires a 64 bit OS with a minimum Linux kernel version of 3.10. To find the kernel version, run the following command in Ubuntu terminal.

```
uname -r
```

The kernel version output is 3.13, as shown in Figure 1-8, which is fine to install Docker.

```
ubuntu@ip-172-30-1-190:~$ uname -r
3.13.0-48-generic
ubuntu@ip-172-30-1-190:~$
```

Figure 1-8. *Outputting Kernel Version*

Before installing the Docker engine on Ubuntu, update the apt sources starting with the following commands.

```
sudo apt-key adv --keyserver hkp://pgp.mit.edu:80 --recv-keys
58118E89F3A912897C070ADBF76221572C52609D
```

In the "Update your apt sources" (*http://docs.docker.com/engine/installation/ubuntulinux/*) Section 6. requires you to update the /etc/apt/sources.list.d/docker.list based on the Ubuntu version. The Ubuntu distribution may be found with the following command.

```
lsb_release -a
```

For Ubuntu Trusty, the following line was added to the /etc/apt/sources.list.d/docker.list file.

```
sudo deb https://apt.dockerproject.org/repo ubuntu-trusty main
```

Run the following commands after updating the /etc/apt/sources.list.d/docker.list file.

```
sudo apt-get update
sudo  apt-get purge lxc-docker*
sudo  apt-cache policy docker-engine
```

Install the pre-requisites for Ubuntu with the following commands.

```
sudo apt-get update
sudo apt-get install linux-image-generic-lts-trusty
```

Reboot the system.

```
sudo reboot
```

After the host system reboots, install Docker with the following commands.

```
sudo apt-get update
sudo apt-get install docker-engine
```

Starting the Docker Service

Regardless of the Linux distribution, start the Docker service with the following command.

```
sudo service docker start
```

Docker gets started via systemctl as indicated by the OK message in Figure 1-9.

```
[ec2-user@ip-172-30-1-80 ~]$ sudo systemctl daemon-reload
[ec2-user@ip-172-30-1-80 ~]$ sudo service docker start
Starting docker (via systemctl):                    [  OK  ]
[ec2-user@ip-172-30-1-80 ~]$ ▊
```

Figure 1-9. *Starting Docker Service*

Finding the Docker Service Status

To verify the status of the Docker service run the following command.

```
sudo service docker status
```

If the Docker service is running, the message Active: **active (running)** should be output as shown in Figure 1-10.

```
[ec2-user@ip-172-30-1-61 ~]$ sudo service docker status
docker.service - Docker Application Container Engine
   Loaded: loaded (/usr/lib/systemd/system/docker.service; enabled)
   Active: active (running) since Mon 2015-10-12 14:43:46 EDT; 9min ago
     Docs: https://docs.docker.com
 Main PID: 724 (docker)
   CGroup: /system.slice/docker.service
           └─724 /usr/bin/docker daemon -H fd://

Oct 12 14:43:46 ip-172-30-1-61.ec2.internal docker[724]: time="2015-10-12T14:...
Oct 12 14:43:46 ip-172-30-1-61.ec2.internal docker[724]: time="2015-10-12T14:...
Oct 12 14:43:46 ip-172-30-1-61.ec2.internal docker[724]: time="2015-10-12T14:...
Oct 12 14:43:46 ip-172-30-1-61.ec2.internal docker[724]: time="2015-10-12T14:...
Oct 12 14:43:46 ip-172-30-1-61.ec2.internal docker[724]: time="2015-10-12T14:...
Oct 12 14:43:46 ip-172-30-1-61.ec2.internal docker[724]: time="2015-10-12T14:...
Oct 12 14:43:46 ip-172-30-1-61.ec2.internal docker[724]: time="2015-10-12T14:...
Oct 12 14:43:46 ip-172-30-1-61.ec2.internal docker[724]: time="2015-10-12T14:...
Oct 12 14:43:46 ip-172-30-1-61.ec2.internal docker[724]: time="2015-10-12T14:...
Oct 12 14:43:46 ip-172-30-1-61.ec2.internal systemd[1]: Started Docker Applic...
Hint: Some lines were ellipsized, use -l to show in full.
[ec2-user@ip-172-30-1-61 ~]$ █
```

Figure 1-10. *Finding Docker Service Status*

Running a Docker Hello World Application

To test Docker, run the Hello World application with the following docker run command.

```
sudo docker run hello-world
```

The docker run command is introduced in a later section. If the hello-world application runs fine, the output in Figure 1-11, which was generated on Red Hat 7, should be generated.

```
[ec2-user@ip-172-30-1-80 ~]$ sudo service docker start
Starting docker (via systemctl):                    [  OK  ]
[ec2-user@ip-172-30-1-80 ~]$ sudo docker run hello-world
Unable to find image 'hello-world:latest' locally
latest: Pulling from library/hello-world
535020c3e8ad: Pull complete
af340544ed62: Pull complete
Digest: sha256:a68868bfe696c00866942e8f5ca39e3e31b79c1e50feaee4ce5e28df2f051d5c
Status: Downloaded newer image for hello-world:latest

Hello from Docker.
This message shows that your installation appears to be working correctly.

To generate this message, Docker took the following steps:
 1. The Docker client contacted the Docker daemon.
 2. The Docker daemon pulled the "hello-world" image from the Docker Hub.
 3. The Docker daemon created a new container from that image which runs the
    executable that produces the output you are currently reading.
 4. The Docker daemon streamed that output to the Docker client, which sent it
    to your terminal.

To try something more ambitious, you can run an Ubuntu container with:
 $ docker run -it ubuntu bash

Share images, automate workflows, and more with a free Docker Hub account:
 https://hub.docker.com

For more examples and ideas, visit:
 https://docs.docker.com/userguide/

[ec2-user@ip-172-30-1-80 ~]$ █
```

Figure 1-11. *Running hello-world Application*

On Ubuntu, run the same command for hello-world.

sudo docker run hello-world

The "Hello from Docker" message gets output as shown in Figure 1-12.

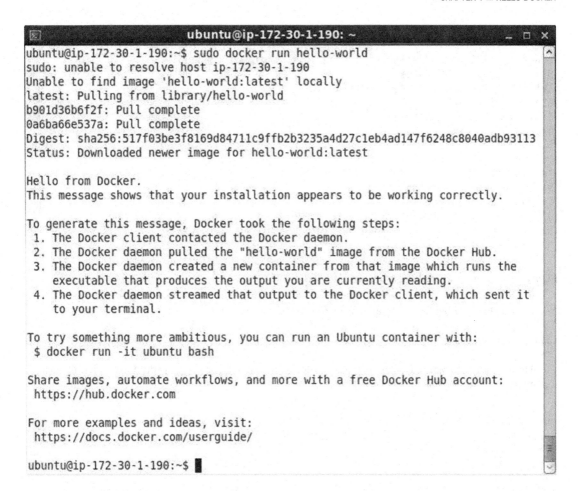

Figure 1-12. *Running hello-world on Ubuntu*

Downloading a Docker Image

When we ran the hello-world application using the docker run command, the Docker image hello-world got downloaded and a Docker container for the HelloWorld application started. A Docker image may be downloaded automatically when a Docker container for the Docker image is started, or the Docker image may be downloaded separately. The docker pull command is used to download a Docker image. For example, run the following command to download the Docker image tutum/hello-world, which is a different HelloWorld application packaged as a Docker image.

```
sudo docker pull tutum/hello-world
```

The Docker image is pre-built and is not required to be built. Docker image tutum/hello-world:latest gets downloaded as shown in Figure 1-13. The suffix :latest is a label for the Docker image specifying the image version, and by default the latest version gets downloaded.

```
ubuntu@ip-172-30-1-190:~$ sudo service docker status
docker start/running, process 896
ubuntu@ip-172-30-1-190:~$ sudo docker pull tutum/hello-world
Using default tag: latest
latest: Pulling from tutum/hello-world
e8ab10ad658e: Pull complete
4fbc1b79196a: Pull complete
b4aed9498114: Pull complete
6afabb57d3b2: Pull complete
00615b0849a1: Pull complete
fde01e38127f: Pull complete
5f98efe94a4e: Pull complete
5f75a51d4b66: Pull complete
Digest: sha256:bae77beaf4c2938d80e6745c788327dcacbcdad15e048980538f61ef8beca394
Status: Downloaded newer image for tutum/hello-world:latest
ubuntu@ip-172-30-1-190:~$ []
```

Figure 1-13. *Downloading tutum:hello-world:latest*

List the downloaded Docker images using the following command.

```
sudo docker images
```

The tutum/hello-world Docker image gets listed as shown in Figure 1-14 in addition to other images that might have been installed previously.

```
ubuntu@ip-172-30-1-190:~$ sudo docker images
REPOSITORY             TAG             IMAGE ID          CREATED
VIRTUAL SIZE
couchbase              latest          ff61ecf3bacb      6 days ago
371.3 MB
tutum/hello-world      latest          5f75a51d4b66      5 months ago
17.33 MB
ubuntu@ip-172-30-1-190:~$ █
```

Figure 1-14. *Listing Docker Images*

Running an Application in a Docker Container

The docker run command is used to run a process, which is another term for an application, in a separate container. The syntax for the docker run command is as follows.

```
docker run [OPTIONS] IMAGE[:TAG|@DIGEST] [COMMAND] [ARG...]
```

The only required command parameter is a Docker image. A Docker container may be started in a detached mode (or background) or foreground mode. In detached mode the process's stdin, stdout and stderr streams are detached from the command line from which the docker run command is run. To start a container in detached mode, set –d=true or just –d. The default mode is the foreground mode in which the container starts in the foreground, and the stdin, stdout and stderr streams are attached to the host command line console. The –name option may be used to specify a name for the Docker container. The

-p option is used to specify a port for the process running in the container. As an example, start a Docker container for the tutum/hello-world image in detached mode using the -d parameter, with container name as helloapp and port on which the application runs as 80 using the -p parameter.

```
sudo docker run -d -p 80 --name helloapp tutum/hello-world
```

The Docker container gets started as shown in Figure 1-15.

```
ubuntu@ip-172-30-1-190:~$ sudo docker run -d -p 80 --name helloapp tutum/hello-w
orld
82171f7ade462aa940f7176ea92d0a095409d42285a0b62bfa83be82ffbc57b0
```

Figure 1-15. *Running an Application in a Docker Container*

An interactive shell or terminal (tty) may be started to run commands applied to the process running in a container. An interactive terminal is started with the -i and -t command parameters used together or combined as -it. For a complete syntax of the docker run command, refer to *http://docs.docker.com/engine/reference/run/*.

Listing Running Docker Containers

To list running Docker container run the following command.

```
sudo docker ps
```

The helloapp container gets listed as shown in Figure 1-16. A container id is also assigned to the container. In all docker commands such as docker stop, docker start either the container name or the container id may be used.

```
ubuntu@ip-172-30-1-190:~$ sudo docker ps
CONTAINER ID        IMAGE               COMMAND                 CREATED
    STATUS              PORTS                 NAMES
82171f7ade46        tutum/hello-world   "/bin/sh -c 'php-fpm "   34 seconds ago
    Up 33 seconds       0.0.0.0:32768->80/tcp   helloapp
ubuntu@ip-172-30-1-190:~$
```

Figure 1-16. *Listing only the Docker Containers that are Running*

In the PORTS column, the external port allocated to the process running on port 80 in the container is listed as 32768. When accessing the helloapp application from outside the container, the 32768 port has to be used (not port 80). The external port may also be listed using the docker port command.

```
sudo docker port 82171f7ade46
```

The port 32768 gets listed as shown in Figure 1-17. The 0.0.0.0 host IP Address implies all IP Addresses on the local machine.

```
ubuntu@ip-172-30-1-190:~$ sudo docker port 82171f7ade46 80
0.0.0.0:32768
ubuntu@ip-172-30-1-190:~$ █
```

Figure 1-17. *Listing Port*

To list all Docker containers, running or exited, run the following command.

```
sudo docker ps -a
```

Accessing the Application Output on Command Line

The curl tool may be used to connect to the host and port on which the helloapp is running. Run the following command to access the application on external port 32768.

```
curl http://localhost:32768
```

The HTML generated by the helloapp gets output in the host as shown in Figure 1-18.

```
ubuntu@ip-172-30-1-190:~$ curl http://localhost:32768/
<html>
<head>
        <title>Hello world!</title>
        <link href='http://fonts.googleapis.com/css?family=Open+Sans:400,700' re
l='stylesheet' type='text/css'>
        <style>
        body {
                background-color: white;
                text-align: center;
                padding: 50px;
                font-family: "Open Sans","Helvetica Neue",Helvetica,Arial,sans-s
erif;
        }

        #logo {
                margin-bottom: 40px;
        }
        </style>
</head>
<body>
        <img id="logo" src="logo.png" />
        <h1>Hello world!</h1>
        <h3>My hostname is 82171f7ade46</h3>        </body>
</html>
ubuntu@ip-172-30-1-190:~$ █
```

Figure 1-18. *Output from helloapp Application*

Accessing the Application Output in a Browser

However, accessing an application that generates HTML output using a curl tool is not always the best method. In this section we shall access the `helloapp` in a browser. If the browser is on the same machine as the host running the Docker container, the url `http://localhost:32768` may be used to display the application output. But if the browser is on a different host as in the example used in this chapter, the public DNS of the Amazon EC2 instance must be used to access the application. The public DNS may be obtained from the Amazon EC2 Console as shown in Figure 1-19.

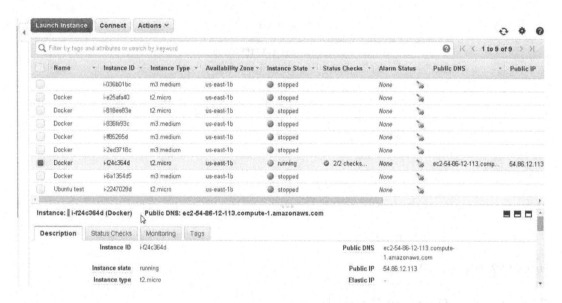

Figure 1-19. *Finding Public DNS*

Using the public DNS, access the `helloapp` in a remote browser, which could be running on Windows OS, with the URL `http://ec2-54-86-12-113.compute-1.amazonaws.com:32768/`. The output generated by the application running in the Docker container `helloapp` gets displayed in the browser as shown in Figure 1-20.

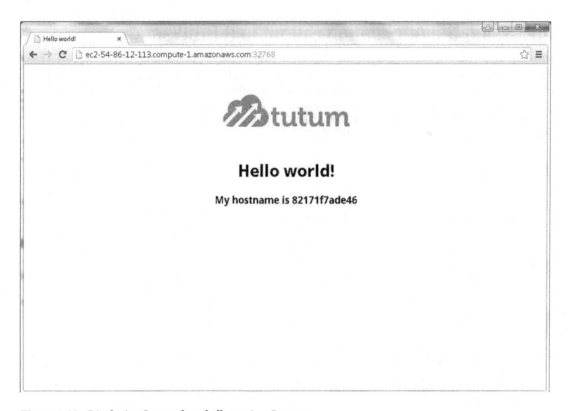

Figure 1-20. *Displaying Output from helloapp in a Browser*

Stopping a Docker Container

A Docker container may be stopped with the docker stop command. For example, stop the helloapp container with the following command.

```
sudo docker stop helloapp
```

The Docker container gets stopped. Subsequently run the docker ps command to list the running containers. The helloapp container does not get listed as shown in Figure 1-21.

```
ubuntu@ip-172-30-1-190:~$ sudo docker stop helloapp
helloapp
ubuntu@ip-172-30-1-190:~$ sudo docker ps
CONTAINER ID        IMAGE               COMMAND             CREATED
STATUS              PORTS               NAMES
ubuntu@ip-172-30-1-190:~$ 
```

Figure 1-21. *Stopping a Container*

Removing a Docker Container

A Docker container may be removed with the docker rm command. For example, remove the helloapp container with the following command.

```
sudo docker rm helloapp
```

A Docker container must be stopped before removing the container.

Removing a Docker Image

To remove a Docker image, run the docker rmi command. For example, run the following command to remove the Docker image tutum/hello-world.

```
sudo docker rmi tutum/hello-world
```

All containers accessing a Docker image must be stopped and removed before a Docker image can be removed. Sometimes some incompletely downloaded Docker images could get listed with the docker images command. Such Docker images do not have a name assigned to them and instead are listed as <>. All such dangling images may be removed with the following command.

```
sudo docker rmi $(sudo docker images -f "dangling=true" -q)
```

As indicated in the output in Figure 1-22, multiple Docker images get removed.

```
ubuntu@ip-172-30-1-190:~$ sudo docker rmi $(sudo docker images -f "dangling=true
" -q)
Deleted: d02b48686af0eeb6ac5b22c78df4493b3a50e99c98f4cf4a4452ad1ab968d85f
Deleted: b9e0df4394839f2f474af56294e163aa8de7e41c321eb697d3487e231ef3a015
Deleted: 61c9f33b4ccee13666b55a00b27803c0a32ad764ec961a717c4c90249ed87fb4
Deleted: 6cc920ef2ab61d96b976680de2f977c318bed511b81d63ecdb44201b22083810
Deleted: 151412b3996cc4f5865f51708da0e9bf88977930b9b9663f02b96eba04aed811
Deleted: ecf0db68805f1c65163be5f791394f0ebf35a04c1033c15477afd49f24fc93ee
Deleted: 94669ea371331cfe58e90e7d275d7c4afb6037d70f9ceb279188536d91a0a710
Deleted: b73d97ec6a2a56a9523d8689ccaf02f54876ddfe2ad9b9f7654adefe006c2b74
Deleted: 1d073211c498fd5022699b46a936b4e4bdacb04f637ad64d3475f558783f5c3e
Deleted: 5a4526e952f0aa24f3fcc1b6971f7744eb5465d572a48d47c492cb6bbf9cbcda
Deleted: 99fcaefe76ef1aa4077b90a413af57fd17d19dce4e50d7964a273aae67055235
Deleted: c63fb41c2213f511f12f294dd729b9903a64d88f098c20d2350905ac1fdbcbba
```

Figure 1-22. *Removing Dangling Docker Images*

Stopping the Docker Service

To stop a Docker service, run the following command.

```
sudo service docker stop
```

The Docker service may be started again with the following command.

```
sudo service docker start
```

Alternatively, a running Docker service may be restarted with the following command.

```
sudo service docker restart
```

Summary

In this chapter we introduced the Docker engine. We installed Docker on two Linux distributions: Red Hat 7 and Ubuntu, but Docker may also be installed on other Linux distributions. For supported Docker installation operating systems, refer to *http://docs.docker.com/v1.8/installation/*. We discussed downloading a Docker image, running a Docker container using a Docker image, accessing the Docker container application from a remote browser, and stopping and removing a Docker container and a Docker image. In the next chapter, we shall run Linux in a Docker container.

CHAPTER 2

■ ■ ■

Installing Linux

Installing Linux is a task most developers and all Linux administrators are familiar with. Several Linux distributions are available including Red Hat Linux, Ubuntu, openSuse and Oracle Linux. Some of the options for installing Linux include using the Amazon Linux AMIs, ISO images and virtual machine images. Linux could also be installed using a Docker image. Several Docker images for Linux distributions are available from the Docker public repository (https://hub.docker.com/). In this chapter we will install Oracle Linux using a Docker image.

> Setting the Environment
>
> Downloading the Docker Image
>
> Listing Docker Images
>
> Running a Container in Detached Mode
>
> Running a Container in Foreground
>
> Listing Docker Containers
>
> Finding Oracle Linux Container Information
>
> Listing the Container Processes
>
> Starting an Interactive Shell
>
> Creating a Container
>
> Stopping a Container
>
> Removing a Container

Setting the Environment

The following software is required for this chapter:

> -Docker (version 1.8.x used)
>
> -Docker Image for Oracle Linux
>
> -Host Linux OS (Amazon EC2 AMI used)

For Host OS we have used the Red Hat Enterprise Linux 7.1 (HVM), SSD Volume Type - ami-12663b7a on Amazon EC2. Login to the Amazon EC2 instance using the following command; the IP address (54.165.251.73) will be different for different users and may be obtained as explained in Appendix A.

```
ssh -i "docker.pem"  ec2-user@54.165.251.73
```

Install Docker as explained in Chapter 1. Start Docker with the following command.

```
sudo service docker start
```

An OK message indicates that Docker has started. To confirm that Docker has started run the following command.

```
sudo service docker status
```

If the Active: label has the **active (running)** value as shown in Figure 2-1, Docker has started and is ready to deploy applications in Docker containers.

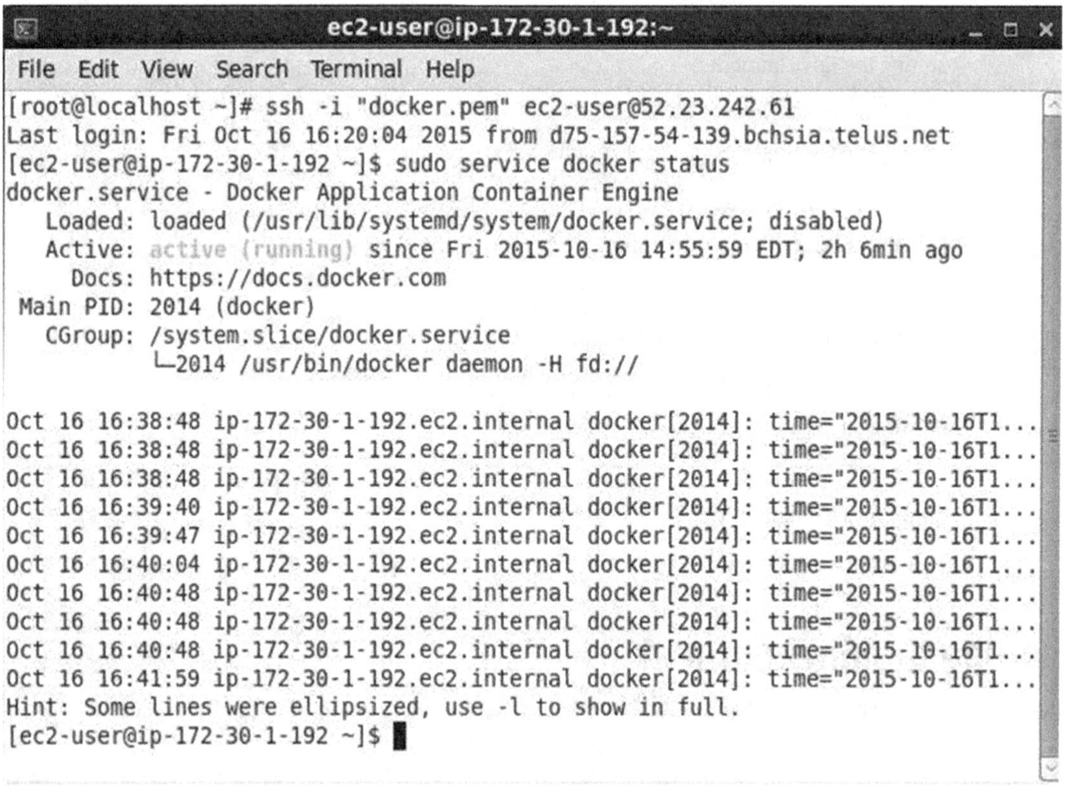

Figure 2-1. *Finding Docker Status*

Downloading the Docker Image

We have used the Docker image oraclelinux available from the Docker Hub Repository (https://hub.docker.com/_/oraclelinux/). Download the latest version of the oraclelinux Docker image with the following command.

```
sudo docker pull oraclelinux
```

Docker images are tagged to the image name to differentiate the variants (or versions) of the image. For example, to download the oraclelinux 6.6 version, run the following command.

```
sudo docker pull oraclelinux:6.6
```

To download the oraclelinux 7 version run the following command.

```
sudo docker pull oraclelinux:7
```

The Docker images for oraclelinux 6.6 and 7 versions get downloaded as indicated by the output in Figure 2-2.

```
[ec2-user@ip-172-30-1-192 ~]$ sudo docker pull oraclelinux:6.6
6.6: Pulling from library/oraclelinux
f359075ce4d8: Already exists
be320e81e49b: Already exists
e87e65fe4000: Already exists
Digest: sha256:63085b5ebc89c4d537254adf6be3b54b6029f450dcfb605974b0f2f73d98d88e
Status: Image is up to date for oraclelinux:6.6
[ec2-user@ip-172-30-1-192 ~]$ sudo docker pull oraclelinux:7.0
7.0: Pulling from library/oraclelinux
2b2532654289: Pull complete
707f44423637: Pull complete
f359075ce4d8: Already exists
Digest: sha256:a104c349bdb5153373ae979247df91b12a0ec6742a1d83f575ed237a5ff61dff
Status: Downloaded newer image for oraclelinux:7.0
```

Figure 2-2. *Downloading Docker Images*

Listing Docker Images

The Docker images downloaded and available to run applications may be listed with the following command.

```
sudo docker images
```

The two oraclelinux images; versions 6.6 and 7 are listed as shown in Figure 2-3. The TAG column lists the version (or variant) of the image.

```
[ec2-user@ip-172-30-1-192 ~]$ sudo docker images
REPOSITORY          TAG                 IMAGE ID            CREATED
VIRTUAL SIZE
mongo               latest              910678a338ed        2 days ago
261.6 MB
couchbase           latest              bace3bc64d06        2 days ago
371.2 MB
cassandra           latest              b87e7f05a105        2 days ago
362.6 MB
oraclelinux         6.6                 e87e65fe4000        4 weeks ago
157.7 MB
oraclelinux         7.0                 707f44423637        4 weeks ago
197.2 MB
[ec2-user@ip-172-30-1-192 ~]$ █
```

Figure 2-3. *Listing Docker Images*

Running a Container in Detached Mode

The docker run command is used to run a process in a container. The docker run command may be run in *detached mode* or *attached mode*. In detached mode the container is detached from the command line and the I/O is done through networking and shared volumes. The following command syntax would run a Docker container in a detached mode as indicated by the –d option. The –name option sets the name of the container.

```
sudo docker run -d  --name <container-name> <image-name>
```

The –i –t options if specified with the -d option do not start an interactive terminal or shell. For example run the following command to start a container in detached mode with name oraclelinux using the oraclelinux Docker image with tag 6.6.

```
sudo docker run -i -t  -d  --name oraclelinux6 oraclelinux:6.6
```

Even though the –i and –t options are specified, the container runs in detached mode as shown in Figure 2-4.

```
[ec2-user@ip-172-30-1-192 ~]$ sudo docker run -i -t -d --name oraclelinux6 oracl
elinux:6.6
861058a1eddd40521d3c4b15b34e33a5389f5b7c63c058b2cc4641e788972665
```

Figure 2-4. *Starting Docker Container in Detached Mode*

In detached mode, the Docker container is detached from the STDIN, STDOUT and STDERR streams. The -rm option cannot be used in the detached mode. For docker run command syntax detail, refer to https://docs.docker.com/engine/reference/run/.

Running a Container in Foreground

To run a Docker container in attached mode, omit the -d option.

```
sudo docker run  <image-name>
```

In attached mode, a container process is started and attached to all the standard streams (STDIN, STDOUT and STDERR). The –name option may also be used in attached mode to specify a container name. To start an interactive terminal, use the –i and –t options, which allocates a tty to the container process. The –rm option if specified cleans up the container resources including the filesystem allocated the container after the container has exited. Run the following command to run a container process using the oraclelinux:7.0 Docker image; the –name option specifies a name to the container, the –i –t options start an interactive terminal (tty) and the –rm option cleans up the container after the container has exited.

```
sudo docker run -i -t -rm -name oraclelinux7 oraclelinux:7.0
```

The Docker container process using the oracleinux image starts and attaches to an interactive shell or tty as shown in Figure 2-5.

```
[ec2-user@ip-172-30-1-192 ~]$ sudo docker run -i -t --rm --name oraclelinux7 ora
clelinux:7.0
[root@edeb5ffb295d /]# []
```

Figure 2-5. *Starting Docker Container in Attached Mode*

A container name must be unique. If a container with the same name as a running container is started, an error is generated as indicated in Figure 2-6.

```
[ec2-user@ip-172-30-1-192 ~]$ sudo docker run -i -t --rm --name oraclelinux7 ora
clelinux:7.0
Error response from daemon: Conflict. The name "oraclelinux7" is already in use
by container edeb5ffb295d. You have to delete (or rename) that container to be a
ble to reuse that name.
```

Figure 2-6. *Container Name must be Unique*

Listing Docker Containers

Docker containers can be running or not running. Run the following command to list Docker containers that are running.

```
sudo docker ps
```

The only running containers, oraclelinux:6.6 and oraclelinux:7.0, get listed as shown in Figure 2-7. The STATUS column indicates whether the container is "Up" and running or "Exited". The CONTAINER ID column lists the container ID.

```
[ec2-user@ip-172-30-1-192 ~]$ sudo docker ps
CONTAINER ID         IMAGE               COMMAND             CREATED
  STATUS               PORTS               NAMES
edeb5ffb295d         oraclelinux:7.0     "/bin/bash"         About a minute ago
  Up About a minute                       oraclelinux7
861058a1eddd         oraclelinux:6.6     "/bin/bash"         5 minutes ago
  Up 5 minutes                            oraclelinux6
```

Figure 2-7. *Listing Running Docker Containers*

To list all containers running or exited, run the following command.

```
sudo docker ps -a
```

The containers that have exited also get listed as shown in Figure 2-8.

```
[ec2-user@ip-172-30-1-192 ~]$ sudo docker ps -a
CONTAINER ID         IMAGE              COMMAND            CREATED
  STATUS                      PORTS            NAMES
4a453d3ebe8d         oraclelinux:6.6    "/bin/bash"              2 minutes ago
  Exited (137) 30 seconds ago             orcl6
edeb5ffb295d         oraclelinux:7.0    "/bin/bash"              8 minutes ago
  Up 8 minutes                            oraclelinux7
861058a1eddd         oraclelinux:6.6    "/bin/bash"              12 minutes ago
  Up 12 minutes                           oraclelinux6
a037a210d3f2         couchbase          "/entrypoint.sh couch"   2 hours ago
  Exited (0) 37 minutes ago               couchbasedb
d965cbf2ad18         cassandra          "/docker-entrypoint.s"   22 hours ago
  Exited (143) 22 hours ago               cassandradb3
3629909b411b         cassandra          "/docker-entrypoint.s"   22 hours ago
  Exited (143) 22 hours ago               cassandradb2
dfade563f871         cassandra          "/docker-entrypoint.s"   23 hours ago
  Exited (143) 22 hours ago               cassandradb
68fe88ca79fe         mongo              "/entrypoint.sh mongo"   26 hours ago
  Exited (0) 26 hours ago                 mongodb
[ec2-user@ip-172-30-1-192 ~]$ █
```

Figure 2-8. *Listing All Docker Containers*

Finding Oracle Linux Container Information

Information about a container can be listed with the docker inspect command. Run the following command to list information about container oraclelinux7.

```
sudo docker  inspect oraclelinux7
```

The container detail gets listed in JSON format as shown in Figure 2-9.

```
                    ec2-user@ip-172-30-1-192:~                    _ □ ✗

 File  Edit  View  Search  Terminal  Help
[ec2-user@ip-172-30-1-192 ~]$ sudo docker inspect oraclelinux7
[
{
    "Id": "edeb5ffb295d932965c1cd035a537997971225bb9ae5423d6a1d783c3f76aaf1",
    "Created": "2015-10-16T21:09:11.557976047Z",
    "Path": "/bin/bash",
    "Args": [],
    "State": {
        "Running": true,
        "Paused": false,
        "Restarting": false,
        "OOMKilled": false,
        "Dead": false,
        "Pid": 4332,
        "ExitCode": 0,
        "Error": "",
        "StartedAt": "2015-10-16T21:09:11.826495545Z",
        "FinishedAt": "0001-01-01T00:00:00Z"
    },
    "Image": "707f44423637017b4f15e4c0ef303cb2bffa754cab7b555f2c2d164ba9bc33c7",
    "NetworkSettings": {
        "Bridge": "",
        "EndpointID": "3f144652abc36fb4278c7668ee37e785b296ccc1ce73b18456d45f91b
c43c5a7",
        "Gateway": "172.17.42.1",
        "GlobalIPv6Address": "",
        "GlobalIPv6PrefixLen": 0,
        "HairpinMode": false,
        "IPAddress": "172.17.0.5",
        "IPPrefixLen": 16,
        "IPv6Gateway": "",
```

Figure 2-9. *Output from docker inspect*

Listing the Container Processes

List the processes that a container is running with the docker top command. The following command lists the processes run by the oraclelinux6 container.

```
sudo docker top oraclelinux6
```

The UID and PID are among the columns listed for the processes as shown in Figure 2-10.

```
[ec2-user@ip-172-30-1-192 ~]$ sudo docker top oraclelinux6
UID                 PID                 PPID                C
STIME               TTY                 TIME                CMD
root                4135                2014                0
17:05               pts/2               00:00:00            /bin/bash
root                4441                2014                0
17:11               pts/4               00:00:00            bash
[ec2-user@ip-172-30-1-192 ~]$ █
```

Figure 2-10. *Listing Container Processes*

Starting an Interactive Shell

The interactive shell or tty may be started when the container process is started with the docker run command using the attached mode and the -i -t options to indicate an interactive terminal.

```
sudo docker run -i -t --rm <image-name>
```

Run the following command to run a container for the oraclelinux:7.0 image and start a tty terminal.

```
sudo docker run -i -t --rm –name oraclelinux7 oraclelinux:7.0
```

An interactive shell gets started and the container process gets attached to the terminal as shown in Figure 2-11.

```
[ec2-user@ip-172-30-1-192 ~]$ sudo docker run -i -t --rm --name oraclelinux7 ora
clelinux:7.0
[root@edeb5ffb295d /]# []
```

Figure 2-11. *The interactive shell gets started when a Docker container is started in Attached Mode*

If a container process has already been started in detached mode using the -d option, the interactive terminal may be started with the following command syntax.

```
docker exec -i -t <container> bash
```

The -i and -t options could be combined into -it. Run the following command to start a tty for the oraclelinux6 container.

```
sudo docker exec –it oraclelinux6 bash
```

An interactive tty gets started as shown in Figure 2-12.

```
[ec2-user@ip-172-30-1-192 ~]$ sudo docker exec -it oraclelinux6 bash
[root@861058a1eddd /]#
```

Figure 2-12. *Starting an Interactive Terminal for a Docker Docker Container running in Detached Mode*

Whether the tty is started when a container process is started using the -rm, -it options or subsequently using the preceding command, container commands may be run in the interactive shell. Commands run in an interactive shell are directed at the software or application that is running in the container. For example, if the Docker container is running Oracle Linux, the tty commands are for the Oracle Linux platform. For example, output the Oracle release using the following command.

```
cat /etc/oracle-release
```

The Oracle Linux Server release 7.0 gets listed as shown in Figure 2-13.

```
[root@1a402fa196a0 /]# cat /etc/oracle-release
Oracle Linux Server release 7.0
[root@1a402fa196a0 /]#
```

Figure 2-13. *Outputting Oracle Release*

Run some other Linux commands to create a directory, set the permissions on the directory, and list the files and directories.

```
mkdir /orcl
chmod 777 /orcl
ls -l
```

The /orcl directory gets created and gets listed as shown in Figure 2-14.

```
@861058a1eddd:/                          _ □ ✕

File  Edit  View  Search  Terminal  Help

[ec2-user@ip-172-30-1-192 ~]$ sudo docker exec -it oraclelinux6 bash
[root@861058a1eddd /]# cat /etc/oracle-release
Oracle Linux Server release 6.6
[root@861058a1eddd /]# mkdir /orcl
[root@861058a1eddd /]# chmod 777 /orcl
[root@861058a1eddd /]# ls -l
total 76
dr-xr-xr-x.   2 root root  4096 Jun 15 22:35 bin
dr-xr-xr-x.   3 root root  4096 Jun 15 22:35 boot
drwxr-xr-x.   5 root root   380 Oct 16 21:05 dev
drwxr-xr-x.  49 root root  4096 Oct 16 21:05 etc
drwxr-xr-x.   2 root root  4096 Nov  1  2011 home
dr-xr-xr-x.   7 root root  4096 Jun 15 22:35 lib
dr-xr-xr-x.   7 root root 12288 Jun 15 22:35 lib64
drwxr-xr-x.   2 root root  4096 Nov  1  2011 media
drwxr-xr-x.   2 root root  4096 Nov  1  2011 mnt
drwxr-xr-x.   2 root root  4096 Nov  1  2011 opt
drwxrwxrwx.   2 root root  4096 Oct 16 21:12
dr-xr-xr-x. 144 root root     0 Oct 16 21:05 proc
dr-xr-x---.   3 root root  4096 Jul 10 21:31 root
dr-xr-xr-x.   2 root root  4096 Jun 15 22:35 sbin
drwxr-xr-x.   2 root root  4096 Nov  1  2011 selinux
drwxr-xr-x.   2 root root  4096 Nov  1  2011 srv
dr-xr-xr-x.  13 root root     0 Oct 16 18:25 sys
drwxrwxrwt.   2 root root  4096 Nov  1  2011 tmp
drwxr-xr-x.  13 root root  4096 Jun 15 22:34 usr
drwxr-xr-x.  17 root root  4096 Jun 15 22:34 var
[root@861058a1eddd /]# █
```

Figure 2-14. *Listing Files and Directories*

Run the exit command to exit the interactive shell as shown in Figure 2-15.

```
[root@1a402fa196a0 /]# exit
exit
[ec2-user@ip-172-30-1-192 ~]$ sudo docker ps
```

Figure 2-15. *Running the exit Command*

Creating a Container

The docker create command is used to create a container. Run the following command to create a container called orcl6 for the oraclelinux:6.6 image. Even though the -i -t options are specified, an interactive shell does not get started.

```
docker create -i -t --name orcl6 oraclelinux:6.6 /bin/bash
```

To start the Docker container orcl6 and an interactive shell for the orcl6 container, run the docker start command. The -a and -i options attach the current shell's standard input, standard output and standard error streams to those of the container. All signals are forwarded to the container.

```
sudo docker start -a -i orcl6
```

The Docker container orcl6 and an interactive shell get started as shown in Figure 2-16.

```
[ec2-user@ip-172-30-1-192 ~]$ sudo docker create -i -t --name orcl6 oraclelinux:
6.6 /bin/bash
4a453d3ebe8df5d16948a89c1736d0eb1fa5297d531661496588bd0895576bf1
[ec2-user@ip-172-30-1-192 ~]$ sudo docker start -a -i orcl6
[root@4a453d3ebe8d /]# 
```

Figure 2-16. *Starting an Interactive Shell with docker start*

Stopping a Container

To stop a running container, run the docker stop command. Run the following command to stop the orcl6 container.

```
sudo docker stop orcl6
```

The orcl6 container gets stopped as shown in Figure 2-17.

```
[ec2-user@ip-172-30-1-192 ~]$ sudo docker stop orcl6
orcl6
```

Figure 2-17. *Stopping a Docker Container*

Subsequently, the docker ps -a command should list the orcl6 container as "Exited" as shown in Figure 2-18.

```
[ec2-user@ip-172-30-1-192 ~]$ sudo docker ps -a
CONTAINER ID        IMAGE                  COMMAND            CREATED
    STATUS                      PORTS              NAMES
4a453d3ebe8d        oraclelinux:6.6        "/bin/bash"        2 minutes ago
    Exited (137) 30 seconds ago                    orcl6
```

Figure 2-18. *Listing an Exited Container*

Removing a Container

To remove a container, run the docker rm command. The container first must be stopped before removing, or the docker rm command will not remove the container. Run the following command to remove the orcl6 container.

```
sudo docker rm orcl6
```

The orcl6 container gets removed as shown in Figure 2-19.

```
[ec2-user@ip-172-30-1-192 ~]$ sudo docker rm orcl6
orcl6
[ec2-user@ip-172-30-1-192 ~]$ █
```

Figure 2-19. *Removing A Docker Container*

Summary

In this chapter we installed Oracle Linux in a Docker container. We discussed how to download the Docker image and run a container process. We also discussed using the different image tags, starting an interactive shell, the different modes of running a container, and starting, stopping and removing a container. In the next chapter we shall discuss running Oracle database in a Docker container.

CHAPTER 3

■ ■ ■

Using Oracle Database

Oracle Database is the most commonly used relational database. Relational databases are based on a fixed schema with the basic unit of storage being a table. Docker Hub has several Docker images for Oracle Database in the Public repository. In this chapter we shall use a Docker image for Oracle Database to install and use the database on Linux. This chapter has the following sections.

>Setting the Environment

>Starting Oracle Database

>Listing Container Logs

>Starting SQL* Plus

>Creating a User

>Creating a Database Table

>Removing Oracle Database

Setting the Environment

The following software is required for this chapter.

>-Docker Engine (version 1.8 used)

>-Docker Image for Oracle Database

We have used an Amazon EC2 instance with Red Hat Linux 7 as the OS. First, SSH login to the Amazon EC2 instance. The IP Address would be different for different users.

```
ssh -i "docker.pem" ec2-user@54.175.172.33
```

Find the status of the Docker engine.

```
sudo service docker status
```

If the Docker engine is not running, start the Docker service.

```
sudo service docker start
```

Download the sath89/oracle-xe-11g Docker image.

```
sudo docker pull sath89/oracle-xe-11g
```

The latest image of sath89/oracle-xe-11g gets downloaded as shown in Figure 3-1.

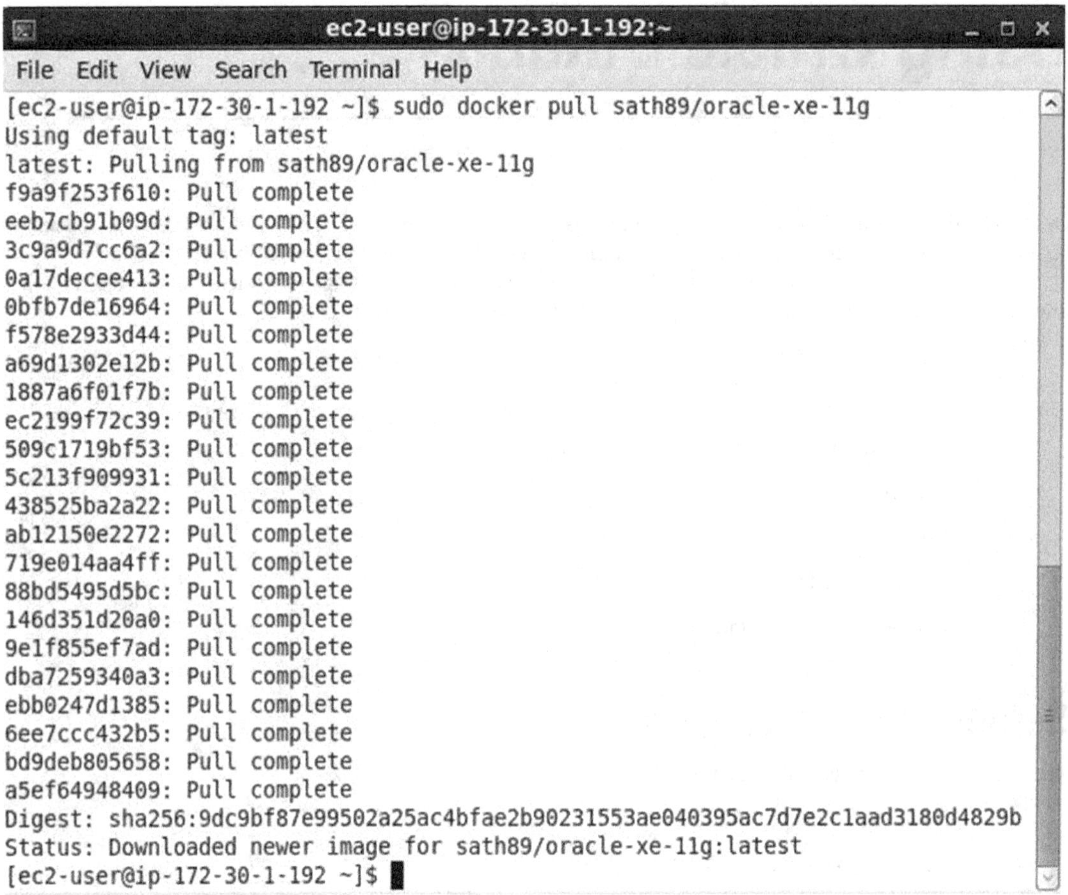

```
ec2-user@ip-172-30-1-192:~                              _ □ ×

File  Edit  View  Search  Terminal  Help
[ec2-user@ip-172-30-1-192 ~]$ sudo docker pull sath89/oracle-xe-11g
Using default tag: latest
latest: Pulling from sath89/oracle-xe-11g
f9a9f253f610: Pull complete
eeb7cb91b09d: Pull complete
3c9a9d7cc6a2: Pull complete
0a17decee413: Pull complete
0bfb7de16964: Pull complete
f578e2933d44: Pull complete
a69d1302e12b: Pull complete
1887a6f01f7b: Pull complete
ec2199f72c39: Pull complete
509c1719bf53: Pull complete
5c213f909931: Pull complete
438525ba2a22: Pull complete
ab12150e2272: Pull complete
719e014aa4ff: Pull complete
88bd5495d5bc: Pull complete
146d351d20a0: Pull complete
9e1f855ef7ad: Pull complete
dba7259340a3: Pull complete
ebb0247d1385: Pull complete
6ee7ccc432b5: Pull complete
bd9deb805658: Pull complete
a5ef64948409: Pull complete
Digest: sha256:9dc9bf87e99502a25ac4bfae2b90231553ae040395ac7d7e2c1aad3180d4829b
Status: Downloaded newer image for sath89/oracle-xe-11g:latest
[ec2-user@ip-172-30-1-192 ~]$ █
```

Figure 3-1. *Downloading Docker Image for Oracle Database*

List the Docker images.

```
sudo docker images
```

The sath89/oracle-xe-11g image gets listed as shown in Figure 3-2.

```
[ec2-user@ip-172-30-1-192 ~]$ sudo docker images
REPOSITORY                    TAG          IMAGE ID         CREATED
          VIRTUAL SIZE
mongo                         latest       910678a338ed     2 days ago
          261.6 MB
sath89/oracle-xe-11g          latest       a5ef64948409     2 days ago
          792.3 MB
couchbase                     latest       bace3bc64d06     2 days ago
          371.2 MB
cassandra                     latest       b87e7f05a105     2 days ago
          362.6 MB
oraclelinux                   6.6          e87e65fe4000     4 weeks ag
o         157.7 MB
oraclelinux                   7.0          707f44423637     4 weeks ag
o         197.2 MB
wscherphof/oracle-xe-11g-r2   latest       d4f75d4d9566     13 months
ago       2.811 GB
[ec2-user@ip-172-30-1-192 ~]$ █
```

Figure 3-2. *Listing Docker Images*

Starting Oracle Database

Next, start an Oracle Database instance in a Docker container with the docker run command. Specify the 8080 port for the Oracle Application Express admin console and the 1521 port for the Oracle Database listener. Specify the container name with the –name option.

```
docker run --name orcldb -d -p 8080:8080 -p 1521:1521 sath89/oracle-xe-11g
```

Oracle Database gets started in a Docker container as shown in Figure 3-3.

```
[ec2-user@ip-172-30-1-192 ~]$ sudo docker run -d -p 8080:8080 -p 1521:1521 sath8
9/oracle-xe-11g
d8fb6c478d14af5bbd40a5ea7ab953ff456484511bd67c20be34a1815cd383c8
[ec2-user@ip-172-30-1-192 ~]$ █
```

Figure 3-3. *Starting Oracle Database in a Docker Container*

List the Docker containers with the following command.

```
sudo docker ps
```

The orcldb container gets listed as shown in Figure 3-4.

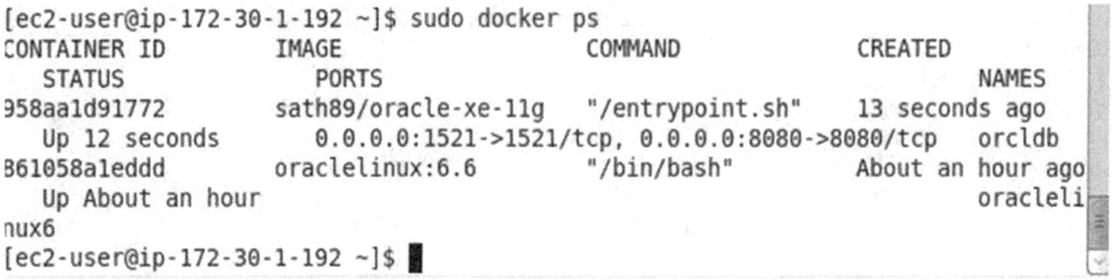

```
[ec2-user@ip-172-30-1-192 ~]$ sudo docker ps
CONTAINER ID        IMAGE                    COMMAND            CREATED
    STATUS              PORTS                                       NAMES
958aa1d91772        sath89/oracle-xe-11g     "/entrypoint.sh"    13 seconds ago
    Up 12 seconds       0.0.0.0:1521->1521/tcp, 0.0.0.0:8080->8080/tcp    orcldb
B61058a1eddd        oraclelinux:6.6          "/bin/bash"         About an hour ago
    Up About an hour                                             oracleli
nux6
[ec2-user@ip-172-30-1-192 ~]$ █
```

Figure 3-4. *Listing Docker Containers that are Running*

The Oracle Database hostname, port, SID, user name and password are as follows.

```
hostname: localhost
port: 1521
sid: xe
username: system
password: oracle
```

Listing Container Logs

To list the container logs, run the docker logs command.

```
sudo docker logs -f c0fa107a43d2
```

The container logs get listed as shown in Figure 3-5. The Oracle Database logs include the database initialization and configuration.

```
ec2-user@ip-172-30-1-192:~                          _  □  ×

File  Edit  View  Search  Terminal  Help
[ec2-user@ip-172-30-1-192 ~]$ sudo docker logs -f c0fa107a43d2
ls: cannot access /u01/app/oracle/oradata: No such file or directory
Database not initialized. Initializing database.
Setting up:
processes=500
sessions=555
transactions=610
If you want to use different parameters set processes, sessions, transactions en
v variables and consider this formula:
processes=x
sessions=x*1.1+5
transactions=sessions*1.1

Oracle Database 11g Express Edition Configuration
-------------------------------------------------
This will configure on-boot properties of Oracle Database 11g Express
Edition.  The following questions will determine whether the database should
be starting upon system boot, the ports it will use, and the passwords that
will be used for database accounts.  Press <Enter> to accept the defaults.
Ctrl-C will abort.

Specify the HTTP port that will be used for Oracle Application Express [8080]:
Specify a port that will be used for the database listener [1521]:
Specify a password to be used for database accounts.  Note that the same
password will be used for SYS and SYSTEM.  Oracle recommends the use of
different passwords for each database account.  This can be done after
initial configuration:
Confirm the password:

Do you want Oracle Database 11g Express Edition to be started on boot (y/n) [y]:
Starting Oracle Net Listener...Done
```

Figure 3-5. *Listing Docker Container Log*

A more detailed Docker container log is as follows.

```
[ec2-user@ip-172-30-1-192 ~]$ sudo docker logs -f c0fa107a43d2
Database not initialized. Initializing database.
Setting up:
processes=500
sessions=555
transactions=610
If you want to use different parameters set processes, sessions, transactions env variables
and consider this formula:
processes=x
sessions=x*1.1+5
transactions=sessions*1.1
```

```
Oracle Database 11g Express Edition Configuration
--------------------------------------------------
This will configure on-boot properties of Oracle Database 11g Express
Edition.  The following questions will determine whether the database should
be starting upon system boot, the ports it will use, and the passwords that
will be used for database accounts.  Press <Enter> to accept the defaults.
Ctrl-C will abort.

Specify the HTTP port that will be used for Oracle Application Express [8080]:
Specify a port that will be used for the database listener [1521]:
Specify a password to be used for database accounts.  Note that the same
password will be used for SYS and SYSTEM.  Oracle recommends the use of
different passwords for each database account.  This can be done after
initial configuration:
Confirm the password:

Do you want Oracle Database 11g Express Edition to be started on boot (y/n) [y]:
Starting Oracle Net Listener...Done
Configuring database...Done
Starting Oracle Database 11g Express Edition instance...Done
Installation completed successfully.
Database initialized. Please visit http://#containeer:8080/apex to proceed with
configuration
Oracle Database 11g Express Edition instance is already started

Database ready to use. Enjoy! ;)

[ec2-user@ip-172-30-1-192 ~]$
```

Starting SQL* Plus

Start an interactive shell using the following command. The container ID would most likely be different.

```
sudo docker exec -it c0fa107a43d2 bash
```

For more detail on bash refer to http://www.gnu.org/software/bash/manual/bash.html#Bash-Startup-Files. Run the following command in the tty. The terms "tty", "interactive shell" and "interactive terminal" have been used interchangeably.

```
sqlplus
```

When prompted for a user-name as shown in Figure 3-6, specify "system".

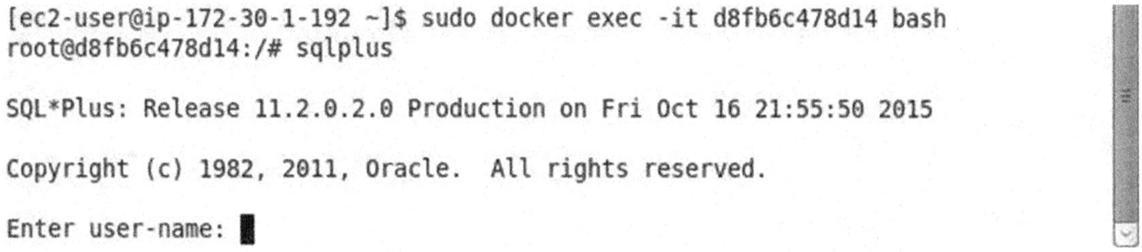

```
[ec2-user@ip-172-30-1-192 ~]$ sudo docker exec -it d8fb6c478d14 bash
root@d8fb6c478d14:/# sqlplus

SQL*Plus: Release 11.2.0.2.0 Production on Fri Oct 16 21:55:50 2015

Copyright (c) 1982, 2011, Oracle.  All rights reserved.

Enter user-name: ▮
```

Figure 3-6. *Starting SQL*Plus*

When prompted for a password, specify "oracle". A connection gets established with Oracle Database 11g Express. SQL*Plus gets started and the SQL> prompt gets displayed as shown in Figure 3-7.

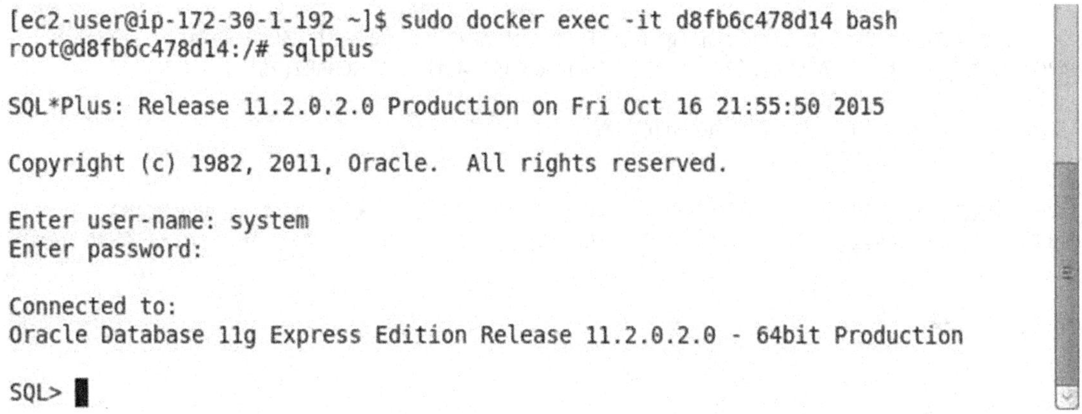

```
[ec2-user@ip-172-30-1-192 ~]$ sudo docker exec -it d8fb6c478d14 bash
root@d8fb6c478d14:/# sqlplus

SQL*Plus: Release 11.2.0.2.0 Production on Fri Oct 16 21:55:50 2015

Copyright (c) 1982, 2011, Oracle.  All rights reserved.

Enter user-name: system
Enter password:

Connected to:
Oracle Database 11g Express Edition Release 11.2.0.2.0 - 64bit Production

SQL> ▮
```

Figure 3-7. *SQL*Plus Shell Prompt*

We used the container id to start the interactive tty terminal. Alternatively, the container name may be used as follows.

```
sudo docker exec -it orcldb bash
```

Creating a User

To create a user called OE with unlimited quota on SYSTEM tablespace and password as "OE", run the following command.

```
SQL> CREATE USER OE QUOTA UNLIMITED ON SYSTEM IDENTIFIED BY OE;
Grant the CONNECT and RESOURCE roles to the OE user.
GRANT CONNECT, RESOURCE TO OE;
```

User "OE" gets created and the roles get granted as shown in Figure 3-8.

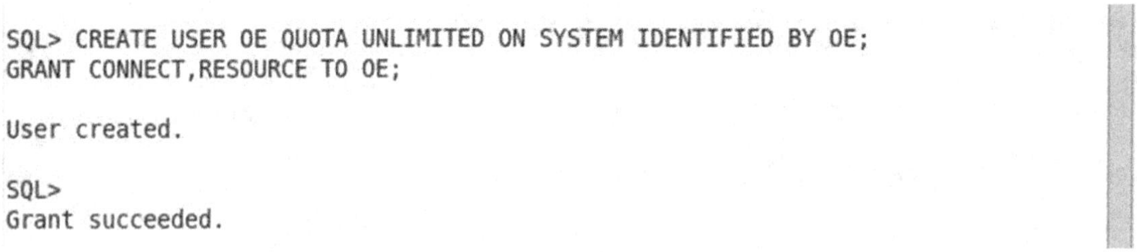

```
SQL> CREATE USER OE QUOTA UNLIMITED ON SYSTEM IDENTIFIED BY OE;
GRANT CONNECT,RESOURCE TO OE;

User created.

SQL>
Grant succeeded.
```

Figure 3-8. *Creating User OE*

Creating a Database Table

Create a database called called "Catalog" in the "OE" schema with the following SQL statement.

```
SQL> CREATE TABLE OE.Catalog(CatalogId INTEGER PRIMARY KEY,Journal VARCHAR2(25),Publisher
VARCHAR2(25),Edition VARCHAR2(25),Title VARCHAR2(45),Author VARCHAR2(25));
```

Table "Catalog" gets created as shown in Figure 3-9.

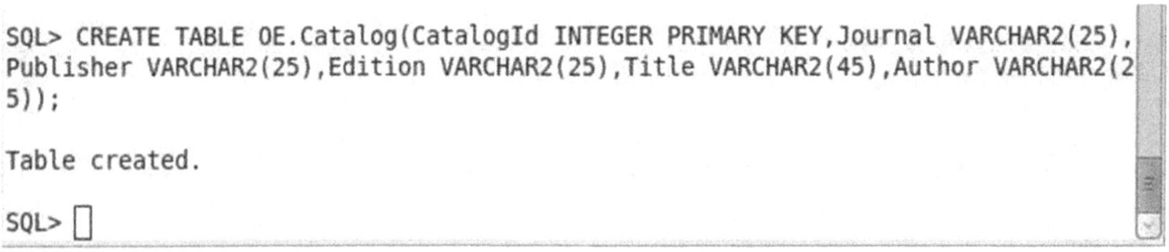

```
SQL> CREATE TABLE OE.Catalog(CatalogId INTEGER PRIMARY KEY,Journal VARCHAR2(25),
Publisher VARCHAR2(25),Edition VARCHAR2(25),Title VARCHAR2(45),Author VARCHAR2(2
5));

Table created.

SQL>
```

Figure 3-9. *Creating Oracle Database Table OE.Catalog*

Add data to the Catalog table with the following INSERT SQL statement.

```
SQL> INSERT INTO OE.Catalog VALUES('1','Oracle Magazine','Oracle Publishing','November
December 2013','Engineering as a Service','David A. Kelly');
```

One row of data gets added as shown in Figure 3-10.

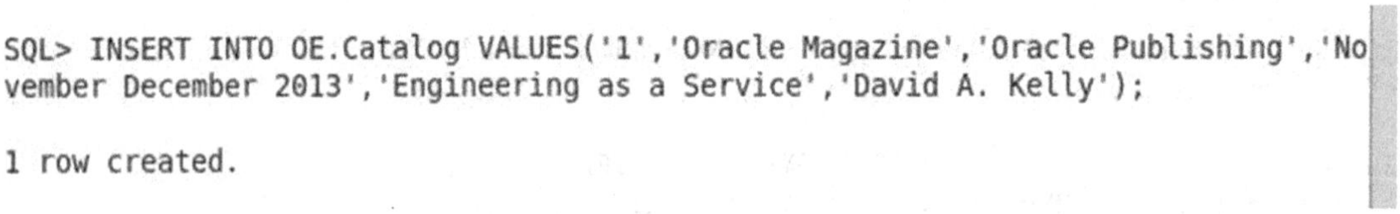

```
SQL> INSERT INTO OE.Catalog VALUES('1','Oracle Magazine','Oracle Publishing','No
vember December 2013','Engineering as a Service','David A. Kelly');

1 row created.
```

Figure 3-10. *Adding Data to OE.Catalog Table*

Run a SQL query with the following SELECT statement.

```
SQL> SELECT * FROM OE.CATALOG;
```

The one row of data added gets listed as shown in Figure 3-11.

```
SQL> SELECT * FROM OE.CATALOG;

 CATALOGID JOURNAL                      PUBLISHER
---------- ------------------------ -------------------------
EDITION                   TITLE
------------------------- -------------------------------------------
AUTHOR
-------------------------
         1 Oracle Magazine               Oracle Publishing
November December 2013     Engineering as a Service
David A. Kelly
```

Figure 3-11. *Running a SQL Query*

To exit from SQL*Plus, specify the exit command as shown in Figure 3-12.

```
SQL> exit
Disconnected from Oracle Database 11g Express Edition Release 11.2.0.2.0 - 64bit
 Production
root@c0fa107a43d2:/# █
```

Figure 3-12. *Exiting SQL*Plus*

Removing Oracle Database

To remove the container running the Oracle Database instance, run the following docker rm command.

```
sudo docker rm c0fa107a43d2
```

To remove the Docker image sath89/oracle-xe-11g, run the following command.

```
sudo docker rmi sath89/oracle-xe-11g
```

The Docker container and image get removed as shown in Figure 3-13.

```
[ec2-user@ip-172-30-1-192 ~]$ sudo docker rm c0fa107a43d2
c0fa107a43d2
[ec2-user@ip-172-30-1-192 ~]$ sudo docker rmi sath89/oracle-xe-11g;
Untagged: sath89/oracle-xe-11g:latest
Deleted: 64ba943f4946a3708406cd85bfdedcfe92db6c88390cc28610624e88dadffec8
Deleted: 129333db1a2bccf888380860cdc657c676284895d2183c5f0a79e1d42b165d71
Deleted: 3deda6a7eb42960b7644d6f40ba6cd4f372d66e79d5ed8efc3c342aa7466204c
Deleted: 3f115617bdbbf1262cdc9d6d5a251b97500b30dbb6e0f57f77907261d7bd8f2d
Deleted: ea069a6319bc52509d9fd396649804925a5a1b9eacec42504b98f8d9c814affd
Deleted: c7dd68b919effacb9889cde331b727e3d424fc969586e6576db01f816390cfc6
Deleted: 1ca1d4664e455015c91d2b5d84380b38f264d326ce8b905e6c1e056560a9aca2
Deleted: 1c0948b818253d845e5bf8d610eeaaca70165801f88c4ffd902e1d75d20527dc
Deleted: 9a32c4a673dcf0d7c322b27d9ad641e3856f0fc1411ab37aab0efe3d8347e3c5
Deleted: 5cb89504dc26dc126623a92585ae81ab32b6230980ccfb9a5b0743c682758ec3
Deleted: 451173061496e3dbcaedab9c1cbca836b2e61a2868ca10aba3542af0e753d951
Deleted: b2840dc7b7e9095fb6d1527a2067d37d7708bebcc697715df1d91d8788581ba1
Deleted: 61c9e7b435e700c08b5e3803c37bcfdffea4218723e09e2a1f47a9b58440e404
Deleted: c55cb1f33d2b44539acfe2630f55c965b56d9c9146e97215d2af0721b8822eb4
Deleted: 21b6bd3f7d2c2ebabbc449b3e7a0e24f57963be53907138b0b58193706db137e
Deleted: e108ae7ceb2b0c5d46ec1d206eb5b6e629bf9120572e77974c68e94077ab216c
Deleted: 032e7ae8eda85b20ab5e7778839819c727fbce2ec5fc9b39fc010b73ae42163d
Deleted: 9969fa71ca0c96b58365c45d3fa8704679dcd7a234d276c49e44881d6e7956aa
Deleted: 0a17decee4139b0de68478f149cc16346f5e711c5ae3bb969895f22dd6723751
Deleted: 3c9a9d7cc6a235eb2de58ca9ef3551c67ae42a991933ba4958d207b29142902b
Deleted: eeb7cb91b09d5de9edb2798301aeedf50848eacc2123e98538f9d014f80f243c
Deleted: f9a9f253f6105141e0f8e091a6bcdb19e3f27af949842db93acba9048ed2410b
[ec2-user@ip-172-30-1-192 ~]$ █
```

Figure 3-13. *Removing Docker Image*

Summary

In this chapter we used a Docker image to install Oracle Database 11g XE on an Amazon EC2 instance. We logged into SQL*Plus and created a database table to demonstrate the use of Oracle Database running in a Docker container. In the next chapter, we shall run the MySQL Database in a Docker container.

CHAPTER 4

Using MySQL Database

MySQL is the most commonly used open source relational database. MySQL is similar to Oracle Database in some regards such as users are kept in grant tables by the database. But MySQL is different from Oracle Database in some regards too:

1. MySQL does not have roles and privileges have to be granted individually to users.

2. Database and table names are case-insensitive in Oracle but are case sensitive if the underlying OS is case-sensitive.

3. MySQL provides a default value for columns that do not allow a NULL value and a value is not provided explicitly in the INSERT statement, if the strict mode is not enabled. Oracle database does not generate a default value for columns with the NOT NULL constraint.

4. MySQL database supports AUTO_INCREMENT for a column while a Sequence is used in Oracle Database.

5. Some of the data types in MySQL are different. For example, MySQL does not support the VARCHAR2 data type.

In this chapter we shall run MySQL database in a Docker container. This chapter has the following sections.

Setting the Environment

Starting MySQL CLI Shell

Setting the Database to Use

Creating a Database Table

Adding Table Data

Querying a Table

Listing Databases and Tables

Exiting TTY Terminal

Starting Another MySQL Server Instance

Listing Docker Container Log

Setting the Environment

The following software is required for this chapter.

-Docker Engine (version 1.8 used)

-Docker image for MySQL Database

Login to an Amazon EC2 instance using the public IP address of the instance.

```
ssh -i "docker.pem" ec2-user@52.91.169.69
```

Start the Docker service.

```
sudo service docker start
```

Verify that the Docker service is running.

```
sudo service docker status
```

The output from the docker start command should be OK and the output from the docker status command should be **active (running)** for the Active field as shown in Figure 4-1.

```
[ec2-user@ip-172-30-1-192 ~]$ sudo service docker start
Starting docker (via systemctl):                        [  OK  ]
[ec2-user@ip-172-30-1-192 ~]$ sudo service docker status
docker.service - Docker Application Container Engine
   Loaded: loaded (/usr/lib/systemd/system/docker.service; disabled)
   Active: active (running) since Sat 2015-10-17 12:17:26 EDT; 11s ago
     Docs: https://docs.docker.com
 Main PID: 1988 (docker)
   CGroup: /system.slice/docker.service
           └─1988 /usr/bin/docker daemon -H fd://

Oct 17 12:17:26 ip-172-30-1-192.ec2.internal docker[1988]: time="2015-10-17T1...
Oct 17 12:17:26 ip-172-30-1-192.ec2.internal docker[1988]: time="2015-10-17T1...
Oct 17 12:17:26 ip-172-30-1-192.ec2.internal docker[1988]: time="2015-10-17T1...
Oct 17 12:17:26 ip-172-30-1-192.ec2.internal docker[1988]: time="2015-10-17T1...
Oct 17 12:17:26 ip-172-30-1-192.ec2.internal docker[1988]: ..........
Oct 17 12:17:26 ip-172-30-1-192.ec2.internal docker[1988]: time="2015-10-17T1...
Oct 17 12:17:26 ip-172-30-1-192.ec2.internal docker[1988]: time="2015-10-17T1...
Oct 17 12:17:26 ip-172-30-1-192.ec2.internal docker[1988]: time="2015-10-17T1...
Oct 17 12:17:26 ip-172-30-1-192.ec2.internal docker[1988]: time="2015-10-17T1...
Oct 17 12:17:26 ip-172-30-1-192.ec2.internal systemd[1]: Started Docker Appli...
Hint: Some lines were ellipsized, use -l to show in full.
[ec2-user@ip-172-30-1-192 ~]$
```

Figure 4-1. Starting Docker Service and verifying Status

Docker Hub provides an official Docker image. Download the Docker image with the following command.

```
sudo docker pull mysql
```

The latest Docker image mysql:latest gets downloaded as shown in Figure 4-2.

```
[ec2-user@ip-172-30-1-192 ~]$ sudo docker pull mysql
Using default tag: latest
latest: Pulling from library/mysql
6c7f15b7a5fd: Pull complete
8b62f738ecbc: Pull complete
70b841ef7298: Pull complete
6936ac5989ac: Pull complete
5314f0b093b4: Pull complete
6e55870e00e6: Pull complete
85d818292063: Pull complete
65223b102c95: Pull complete
3039d061bb1c: Pull complete
5b8a0c2103d4: Pull complete
87ef1ec188f2: Pull complete
efa6d8a4aa0d: Pull complete
066b96453e3e: Pull complete
d7da97aedce5: Pull complete
7a42f1433a16: Already exists
3d88cbf54477: Already exists
Digest: sha256:bd9f21d22da65e47878b1562c6c5de9457b016efdd2f085d755980626e7476d7
Status: Downloaded newer image for mysql:latest
[ec2-user@ip-172-30-1-192 ~]$
```

Figure 4-2. *Downloading Docker Image for MySQL Database*

List the Docker images with the following command.

```
sudo docker images
```

The mysql image gets listed as shown in Figure 4-3.

```
[ec2-user@ip-172-30-1-192 ~]$ sudo docker images
REPOSITORY              TAG             IMAGE ID          CREATED
VIRTUAL SIZE
mongo                   latest          910678a338ed      2 days ago
261.6 MB
couchbase               latest          bace3bc64d06      3 days ago
371.2 MB
cassandra               latest          b87e7f05a105      3 days ago
362.6 MB
mysql                   latest          d7da97aedce5      3 days ago
324.3 MB
oraclelinux             6.6             e87e65fe4000      4 weeks ago
157.7 MB
oraclelinux             7.0             707f44423637      4 weeks ago
197.2 MB
[ec2-user@ip-172-30-1-192 ~]$
```

Figure 4-3. *Listing Docker Image for MySQL Database*

Starting MySQL Server

In this section we shall run MySQL database in a Docker container. MySQL database uses the /var/lib/mysql directory by default for storing data, but another directory may also be used. We shall use the /mysql/data directory for storing MySQL data. Create the /mysql/data directory and set its permissions to global (777).

```
sudo mkdir -p /mysql/data
sudo chmod -R 777 /mysql/data
```

The /mysql/data directory gets created as shown in Figure 4-4.

```
[ec2-user@ip-172-30-1-192 ~]$ sudo mkdir -p /mysql/data
[ec2-user@ip-172-30-1-192 ~]$ sudo chmod -R 777 /mysql/data
```

Figure 4-4. *Creating the Data Directory*

When the docker run command is run to start MySQL in a Docker container, certain environment variables may be specified as discussed in the following table.

Env Variable	Description	Required
MYSQL_ROOT_PASSWORD	Password for the "root" user.	Yes
MYSQL_DATABASE	Creates a database	No
MYSQL_USER, MYSQL_PASSWORD	Specify the username and password to create a new user. The user is granted superuser privileges on the database specified in the MYSQL_DATABASE variable. Both the user name and password must be set if either is set.	No
MYSQL_ALLOW_EMPTY_PASSWORD	Specifies whether the "root" user is permitted to have an empty password.	No

Other than the MYSQL_ROOT_PASSWORD environment variable, all the other variables are optional, but we shall run a MySQL instance container using all the environment variables. We shall run the docker run command using the following command parameters.

Command Parameter	Value
MYSQL_ROOT_PASSWORD	''
MYSQL_DATABASE	mysqldb
MYSQL_USER, MYSQL_PASSWORD	mysql, mysql
MYSQL_ALLOW_EMPTY_PASSWORD	yes
-v	/mysql/data:/var/lib/mysql
--name	mysqldb
-d	

The environment variables are specified with –e. Run the following docker run command to start a MySQL instance in a Docker container.

```
sudo docker run -v /mysql/data:/var/lib/mysql --name mysqldb -e MYSQL_DATABASE='mysqldb'
-e MYSQL_USER='mysql' -e MYSQL_PASSWORD='mysql' -e MYSQL_ALLOW_EMPTY_PASSWORD='yes'
-e MYSQL_ROOT_PASSWORD='' -d mysql
```

The output from the docker run command is shown in Figure 4-5.

```
me mysqldb -e MYSQL_DATABASE='mysqldb' -e MYSQL_USER='mysql' -e MYSQL_PASSWORD='
mysql' -e MYSQL_ALLOW_EMPTY_PASSWORD='yes' -e MYSQL_ROOT_PASSWORD='' -d mysql
969088c84a4fc9a4d3ebb4e6d133797c2bf73e25d910bf89c9037043b9325d3f
```

Figure 4-5. *Running MySQL Database in a Docker Container*

Run the following command to list the Docker containers that are running.

```
sudo docker ps
```

The Docker container mysqldb that is running the MySQL database instance gets listed as shown in Figure 4-6.

```
[ec2-user@ip-172-30-1-192 ~]$ sudo docker ps
CONTAINER ID        IMAGE               COMMAND                 CREATED
    STATUS              PORTS               NAMES
969088c84a4f        mysql               "/entrypoint.sh mysql"  26 seconds ago
    Up 25 seconds       3306/tcp            mysqldb
```

Figure 4-6. *Listing Docker Containers*

45

Starting MySQL CLI Shell

Next, we shall log into the MySQL CLI shell. But first we need to start an interactive terminal to run the `mysql` command to start the MySQL CLI. Start the interactive terminal or shell with the following command.

```
sudo docker exec -it mysqldb bash
```

In the interactive terminal run the following command.

```
mysql
```

The MySQL CLI gets started as shown in Figure 4-7.

```
[ec2-user@ip-172-30-1-192 ~]$ sudo docker exec -it mysqldb bash
root@969088c84a4f:/# mysql
Welcome to the MySQL monitor.  Commands end with ; or \g.
Your MySQL connection id is 1
Server version: 5.6.27 MySQL Community Server (GPL)

Copyright (c) 2000, 2015, Oracle and/or its affiliates. All rights reserved.

Oracle is a registered trademark of Oracle Corporation and/or its
affiliates. Other names may be trademarks of their respective
owners.

Type 'help;' or '\h' for help. Type '\c' to clear the current input statement.

mysql>
```

Figure 4-7. Starting MySQL CLI

The interactive terminal may also be started using the container id instead of the container name.

```
sudo docker exec -it 969088c84a4f bash
```

Setting the Database to Use

Set the database with the "use" command. The "test" database is not provided by the MySQL database started in a Docker container by default. If the "use test" command is run, the following error message is output.

```
mysql> use test
ERROR 1049 (42000): Unknown database 'test'
```

We created a database called "mysqldb" when we started the Docker container for MySQL database with the `docker run` command. Set the database to "mysqldb" with the following command.

```
mysql> use mysqldb
```

The output from the preceding commands is as follows. The database gets set to "mysqldb" as shown in Figure 4-8.

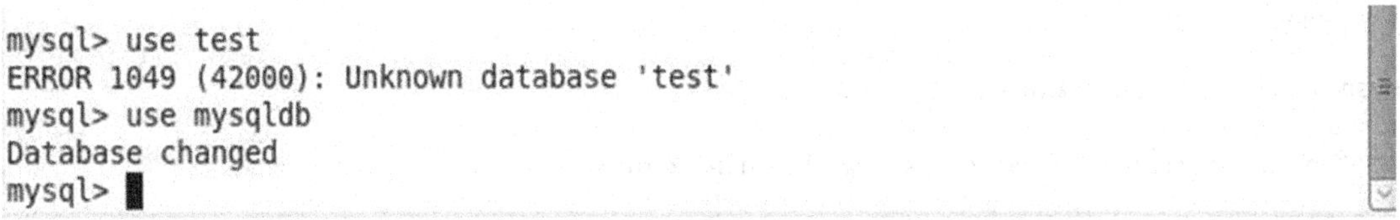

```
mysql> use test
ERROR 1049 (42000): Unknown database 'test'
mysql> use mysqldb
Database changed
mysql>
```

Figure 4-8. *Setting Database to mysqldb*

Creating a Database Table

Next, create a database table called "Catalog" with columns CatalogId, Journal, Publisher, Edition, Title and Author. Run the following SQL statement.

```
mysql> CREATE TABLE Catalog(CatalogId INTEGER PRIMARY KEY,Journal VARCHAR(25),Publisher
VARCHAR(25),Edition VARCHAR(25),Title VARCHAR(45),Author VARCHAR(25));
```

The Catalog table gets created as shown in Figure 4-9.

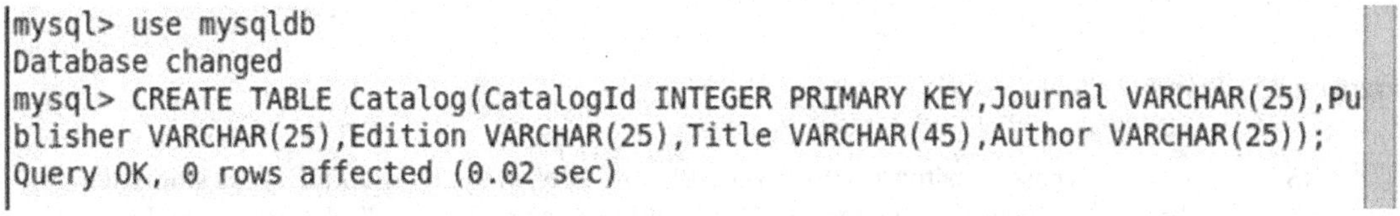

```
mysql> use mysqldb
Database changed
mysql> CREATE TABLE Catalog(CatalogId INTEGER PRIMARY KEY,Journal VARCHAR(25),Pu
blisher VARCHAR(25),Edition VARCHAR(25),Title VARCHAR(45),Author VARCHAR(25));
Query OK, 0 rows affected (0.02 sec)
```

Figure 4-9. *Creating a MySQL Database Table*

Adding Table Data

Add data to the Catalog table with the following INSERT statement.

```
mysql> INSERT INTO Catalog VALUES('1','Oracle Magazine','Oracle Publishing','November
December 2013','Engineering as a Service','David A. Kelly');
```

A row of data gets added to the Catalog table as shown in Figure 4-10.

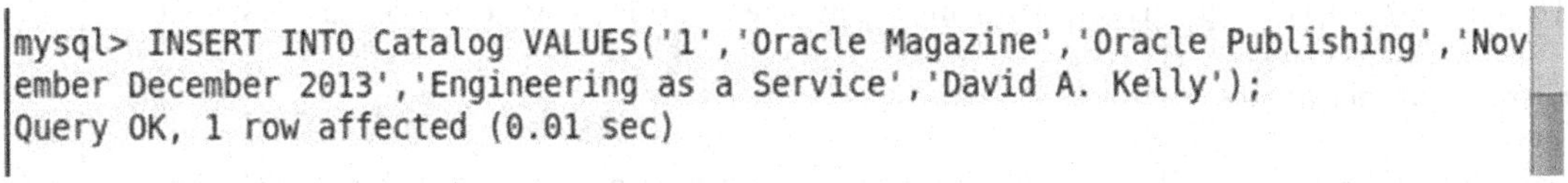

```
mysql> INSERT INTO Catalog VALUES('1','Oracle Magazine','Oracle Publishing','Nov
ember December 2013','Engineering as a Service','David A. Kelly');
Query OK, 1 row affected (0.01 sec)
```

Figure 4-10. *Adding a Row of Data to MySQL Table*

47

Querying a Table

Next, query the Catalog table with a SQL query. The following SELECT statement selects all the data in the Catalog table.

```
mysql> SELECT * FROM Catalog;
```

The one row of data added gets listed as shown in Figure 4-11.

```
mysql> SELECT * FROM Catalog;
+-----------+-----------------+--------------------+-----------------------+-----
------------------------+----------------+
| CatalogId | Journal         | Publisher          | Edition               | Tit
le                       | Author         |
+-----------+-----------------+--------------------+-----------------------+-----
------------------------+----------------+
|         1 | Oracle Magazine | Oracle Publishing  | November December 2013 | Eng
ineering as a Service | David A. Kelly  |
+-----------+-----------------+--------------------+-----------------------+-----
------------------------+----------------+
1 row in set (0.00 sec)

mysql>
```

Figure 4-11. *Running a SQL Query*

MySQL table name is case sensitive on the OS (RHEL 7.1 OS) used in this chapter. If a variation of the table name Catalog is used, an error is generated. For example, use table name CATALOG in the SQL query and the following error gets generated as shown in Figure 4-12.

```
mysql> SELECT * FROM CATALOG;
ERROR 1146 (42S02): Table 'mysqldb.CATALOG' doesn't exist
mysql>
```

Figure 4-12. *The table name is Case-sensitive in MySQL*

Listing Databases and Tables

The databases in a MySQL server instance may be listed with the following command in MySQL CLI.

```
mysql> show databases;
```

The databases get listed, including the newly created database "mysqldb" as shown in Figure 4-13.

```
mysql> show databases;
+--------------------+
| Database           |
+--------------------+
| information_schema |
| mysql              |
| mysqldb            |
| performance_schema |
+--------------------+
4 rows in set (0.00 sec)

mysql> █
```

Figure 4-13. *Listing MySQL Databases*

Exiting TTY Terminal

Exit the MySQL CLI with the "exit" command.

```
mysql> exit
Bye
```

Exit the interactive shell or tty with the "exit" command.

```
root@969088c84a4f:/# exit
exit
```

The output from the preceding commands is shown in Figure 4-14.

```
mysql> exit
Bye
root@969088c84a4f:/# exit
exit
[ec2-user@ip-172-30-1-192 ~]$ █
```

Figure 4-14. *Exiting MySQL CLI*

Stopping a Docker Container

Stop the Docker container with the docker stop command.

```
[ec2-user@ip-172-30-1-192 ~]$ sudo docker stop 969088c84a4f
969088c84a4f
```

Subsequently, list the running Docker containers with the docker ps command. The mysqldb container does not get listed.

```
sudo docker ps
[ec2-user@ip-172-30-1-192 ~]$ sudo docker ps
CONTAINER ID     IMAGE       COMMAND       CREATED       STATUS      PORTS       NAMES
```

In the next section we shall create another MySQL Server instance just as we created the MySQL server instance earlier in this chapter. But we cannot use the same container name as an existing container. Another Docker container running a MySQL database, or any other software, may be started if the Docker container name is different. If we created a Docker container to run another MySQL server with the same name "mysqldb", an error gets generated. For example, run the following docker run command to create another container called "mysqldb".

```
sudo docker run --name mysqldb -e MYSQL_ROOT_PASSWORD=mysql -d mysql
```

The following error gets output.

```
Error response from daemon: Conflict. The name "mysqldb" is already in use by container
969088c84a4f. You have to delete (or rename) that container to be able to reuse that name.
```

To create a new Docker container called "mysqldb" first remove the "mysqldb" container already created with the docker rm command. Either the container id or the container name may be used in docker commands for a container such as stop, start, and rm.

```
sudo docker rm 969088c84a4f
```

Starting Another MySQL Server Instance

Having removed the "mysqldb" container, create the container again with the docker run command. We shall create the new "mysqldb" container differently. Specify different environment variables for the second run of the docker run command. Specify only the required environment variable MYSQL_ROOT_PASSWORD and set its value to "mysql".

```
sudo docker run --name mysqldb -e MYSQL_ROOT_PASSWORD=mysql -d mysql
```

Subsequently, start the interactive shell with the following command.

```
sudo docker exec -it 113458c31ce5 bash
```

Login to the MySQL CLI with the following command in the interactive shell.

```
mysql -u root -p mysql
```

Specify the password for the "root" user, which is mysql. MySQL CLI gets started as shown in Figure 4-15.

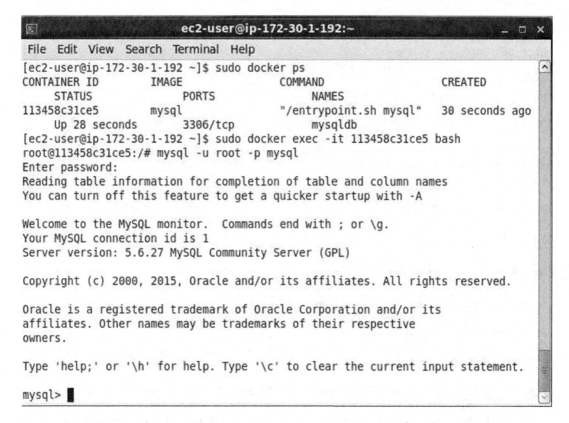

Figure 4-15. *Using a Password to Start MySQL CLI*

The mysql command may also be issued as follows.

```
mysql -u root -p
```

Specify the password for the "mysql" user. MySQL CLI gets started as shown in Figure 4-16.

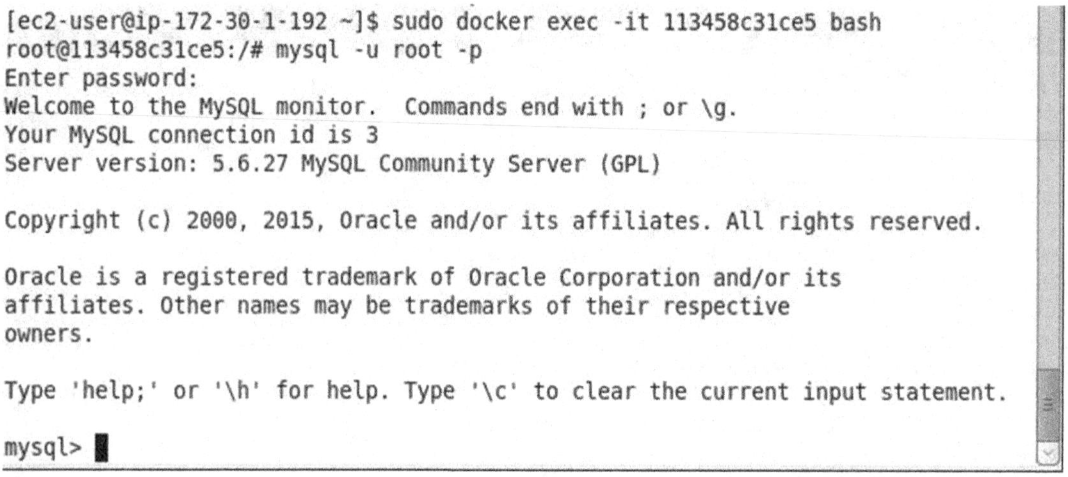

```
[ec2-user@ip-172-30-1-192 ~]$ sudo docker exec -it 113458c31ce5 bash
root@113458c31ce5:/# mysql -u root -p
Enter password:
Welcome to the MySQL monitor.  Commands end with ; or \g.
Your MySQL connection id is 3
Server version: 5.6.27 MySQL Community Server (GPL)

Copyright (c) 2000, 2015, Oracle and/or its affiliates. All rights reserved.

Oracle is a registered trademark of Oracle Corporation and/or its
affiliates. Other names may be trademarks of their respective
owners.

Type 'help;' or '\h' for help. Type '\c' to clear the current input statement.

mysql>
```

Figure 4-16. *Alternative mysql Login command*

The following mysql command does not start a MySQL CLI.

root@113458c31ce5:/# mysql -u root

The following error is generated.

ERROR 1045 (28000): Access denied for user 'root'@'localhost' (using password: NO)

List the databases with the show databases command. The default databases include the "mysql" database as shown in Figure 4-17. Previously, the "mysqldb" database also got listed with the show databases command because the "mysqldb" database was created when the docker run command was run.

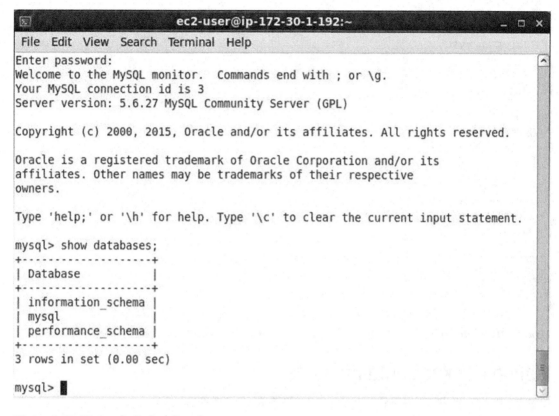

Figure 4-17. *Listing the Default Databases*

Set the database as the "mysql" database with the "use mysql" command as shown in Figure 4-18.

```
mysql> use mysql;
Reading table information for completion of table and column names
You can turn off this feature to get a quicker startup with -A

Database changed
mysql>
```

Figure 4-18. *Using the mysql Database*

List the database tables in the mysql database with the show tables command as shown in Figure 4-19.

```
mysql> show tables;
+--------------------------+
| Tables_in_mysql          |
+--------------------------+
| columns_priv             |
| db                       |
| event                    |
| func                     |
| general_log              |
| help_category            |
| help_keyword             |
| help_relation            |
| help_topic               |
| innodb_index_stats       |
| innodb_table_stats       |
| ndb_binlog_index         |
| plugin                   |
| proc                     |
| procs_priv               |
| proxies_priv             |
| servers                  |
```

Figure 4-19. *Listing Tables*

Listing Docker Container Logs

Next, list the logs for the mysqldb container with the docker logs command.

```
sudo docker logs -f mysqldb
```

The logs for the mysqldb container get listed as shown in Figure 4-20.

```
[ec2-user@ip-172-30-1-192 ~]$ sudo docker logs -f mysqldb
Running mysql_install_db
2015-10-17 16:30:35 0 [Note] /usr/sbin/mysqld (mysqld 5.6.27) starting as proces
s 15 ...
2015-10-17 16:30:35 15 [Note] InnoDB: Using atomics to ref count buffer pool pag
es
2015-10-17 16:30:35 15 [Note] InnoDB: The InnoDB memory heap is disabled
2015-10-17 16:30:35 15 [Note] InnoDB: Mutexes and rw_locks use GCC atomic builti
ns
2015-10-17 16:30:35 15 [Note] InnoDB: Memory barrier is not used
2015-10-17 16:30:35 15 [Note] InnoDB: Compressed tables use zlib 1.2.8
2015-10-17 16:30:35 15 [Note] InnoDB: Using Linux native AIO
2015-10-17 16:30:35 15 [Note] InnoDB: Using CPU crc32 instructions
2015-10-17 16:30:35 15 [Note] InnoDB: Initializing buffer pool, size = 128.0M
2015-10-17 16:30:35 15 [Note] InnoDB: Completed initialization of buffer pool
2015-10-17 16:30:35 15 [Note] InnoDB: The first specified data file ./ibdata1 di
d not exist: a new database to be created!
2015-10-17 16:30:35 15 [Note] InnoDB: Setting file ./ibdata1 size to 12 MB
2015-10-17 16:30:35 15 [Note] InnoDB: Database physically writes the file full:
wait...
2015-10-17 16:30:35 15 [Note] InnoDB: Setting log file ./ib_logfile101 size to 4
8 MB
```

Figure 4-20. *Listing Docker Container Log*

Summary

In this chapter we used a Docker image to run MySQL Server in a Docker container. We ran two different variations of the docker run command; one included all the environment variables that may be set for the "mysql" image and the other included only the required environment variable/s. In the next chapter we shall discuss running MongoDB on Docker.

CHAPTER 5

■ ■ ■

Using MongoDB

MongoDB is the most commonly used NoSQL database. MongoDB is based on the Document store data model and stores data as BSON (Binary JSON) documents. MongoDB provides a flexible schema-less storage format in which different records could have different fields, implying that no fixed data structure is applied. Field values have no data types associated with them and different fields could be of different data types. With the JSON format, hierarchies of data structures become feasible, and a field could store multiple values using an array. In this chapter we shall use a Docker image to run MongoDB in a Docker container. This chapter has the following sections.

Setting the Environment

The following software is required for this chapter:

>   -Docker Engine (version 1.8)

>   -Docker image for MongoDB

We have used an Amazon EC2 instance (Amazon Machine Image Red Hat Enterprise Linux 7.1 (HVM), SSD Volume Type - ami-12663b7a) to install the Docker image and run MongoDB in a Docker container. SSH login to the Amazon EC2 instance.

```
ssh -i "docker.pem" ec2-user@54.174.254.96
```

Start the Docker service.

```
sudo service docker start
```

Verify the Docker service status.

```
sudo service docker status
```

Docker service should be **active (running)** as shown in Figure 5-1.

```
[ec2-user@ip-172-30-1-61 ~]$ sudo service docker start
Starting docker (via systemctl):                          [  OK  ]
[ec2-user@ip-172-30-1-61 ~]$ sudo service docker status
docker.service - Docker Application Container Engine
   Loaded: loaded (/usr/lib/systemd/system/docker.service; disabled)
   Active: active (running) since Thu 2015-10-15 13:14:55 EDT; 50s ago
     Docs: https://docs.docker.com
 Main PID: 2149 (docker)
   CGroup: /system.slice/docker.service
           └─2149 /usr/bin/docker daemon -H fd://

Oct 15 13:14:55 ip-172-30-1-61.ec2.internal docker[2149]: time="2015-10-15T13...
Oct 15 13:14:55 ip-172-30-1-61.ec2.internal docker[2149]: time="2015-10-15T13...
Oct 15 13:14:55 ip-172-30-1-61.ec2.internal docker[2149]: time="2015-10-15T13...
Oct 15 13:14:55 ip-172-30-1-61.ec2.internal docker[2149]: time="2015-10-15T13...
Oct 15 13:14:55 ip-172-30-1-61.ec2.internal docker[2149]: time="2015-10-15T13...
Oct 15 13:14:55 ip-172-30-1-61.ec2.internal docker[2149]: time="2015-10-15T13...
Oct 15 13:14:55 ip-172-30-1-61.ec2.internal docker[2149]: time="2015-10-15T13...
Oct 15 13:14:55 ip-172-30-1-61.ec2.internal docker[2149]: time="2015-10-15T13...
Oct 15 13:14:55 ip-172-30-1-61.ec2.internal systemd[1]: Started Docker Applic...
Oct 15 13:14:55 ip-172-30-1-61.ec2.internal docker[2149]: time="2015-10-15T13...
Hint: Some lines were ellipsized, use -l to show in full.
[ec2-user@ip-172-30-1-61 ~]$ 
```

Figure 5-1. *Starting Docker Service and verifying Status*

Download the official Docker image for MongoDB database.

```
sudo docker pull mongo:latest
```

List the Docker images.

```
sudo docker images
```

The Docker image called "mongo" gets listed as shown in Figure 5-2.

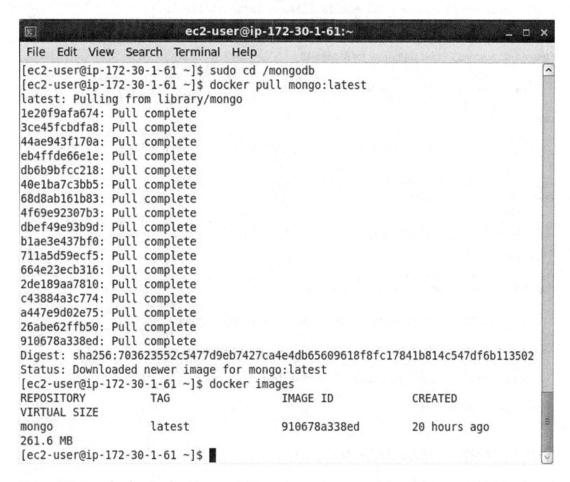

Figure 5-2. *Downloading Docker Image mongo*

Starting MongoDB

Next, start MongoDB in a Docker container. MongoDB stores data in the /data/db directory in the Docker container by default. A directory could be mounted from the underlying host system to the container running the MongoDB database. For example, create a directory /data on the host.

```
sudo mkdir -p /data
```

Start the Docker container using the docker run command on the mongo image with the /data directory in the container mounted as /data directory on the host. Specify container name as "mongodb".

```
sudo docker run -t -i -v /data:/data --name mongodb -d mongo
```

The Docker container, and the MongoDB server in the container, gets started as shown in Figure 5-3.

```
[ec2-user@ip-172-30-1-192 ~]$ sudo docker run -t -i -v /data:/data --name mongod
b -d mongo
68fe88ca79fe5c8606a8576e60aadbec5218ea314dcec49888316d11ef81c4ca
[ec2-user@ip-172-30-1-192 ~]$ █
```

Figure 5-3. *Starting Docker Container for MongoDB*

List the running Docker containers.

```
sudo docker ps
```

The mongodb container gets listed as running on port 27017 as shown in Figure 5-4.

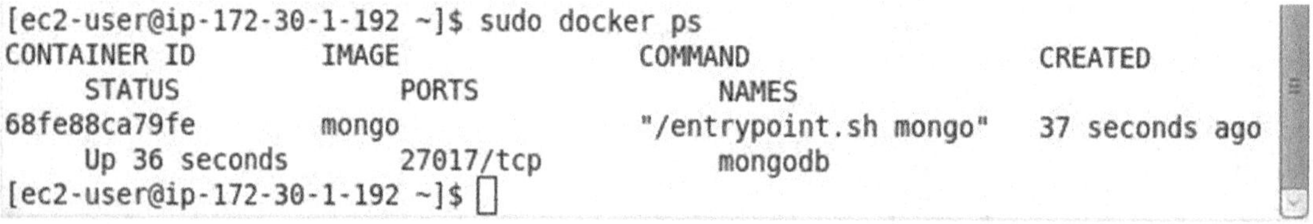

```
[ec2-user@ip-172-30-1-192 ~]$ sudo docker ps
CONTAINER ID        IMAGE            COMMAND                 CREATED
    STATUS              PORTS            NAMES
68fe88ca79fe        mongo            "/entrypoint.sh mongo"  37 seconds ago
    Up 36 seconds       27017/tcp        mongodb
[ec2-user@ip-172-30-1-192 ~]$ []
```

Figure 5-4. *Listing Docker Container for MongoDB*

The MongoDB port could also be specified explicitly using the –p option.

```
docker run -t -i -v /data:/data -p 27017:27017 --name mongodb -d mongo
```

The container logs may be listed using the docker logs command.

```
sudo docker logs mongodb
```

Starting an Interactive Terminal

Start an interactive terminal (tty) using the following command.

```
sudo docker exec -it mongodb bash
```

Starting a Mongo Shell

To start the MongoDB shell, run the following command.

```
mongo
```

The MongoDB shell gets started and the > prompt gets displayed as shown in Figure 5-5.

```
[ec2-user@ip-172-30-1-192 ~]$ sudo docker exec -it mongodb bash
root@68fe88ca79fe:/# mongo
MongoDB shell version: 3.0.7
connecting to: test
Welcome to the MongoDB shell.
For interactive help, type "help".
For more comprehensive documentation, see
        http://docs.mongodb.org/
Questions? Try the support group
        http://groups.google.com/group/mongodb-user
Server has startup warnings:
2015-10-15T18:19:07.312+0000 I CONTROL  [initandlisten]
2015-10-15T18:19:07.312+0000 I CONTROL  [initandlisten] ** WARNING: /sys/kernel/
mm/transparent_hugepage/enabled is 'always'.
2015-10-15T18:19:07.312+0000 I CONTROL  [initandlisten] **        We suggest set
ting it to 'never'
2015-10-15T18:19:07.312+0000 I CONTROL  [initandlisten]
2015-10-15T18:19:07.312+0000 I CONTROL  [initandlisten] ** WARNING: /sys/kernel/
mm/transparent_hugepage/defrag is 'always'.
2015-10-15T18:19:07.312+0000 I CONTROL  [initandlisten] **        We suggest set
ting it to 'never'
2015-10-15T18:19:07.312+0000 I CONTROL  [initandlisten]
> █
```

Figure 5-5. *Starting MongoDB Shell from TTY*

The MongoDB shell may also be started on a specific host and port as follows.

```
mongo -host localhost -port 27017
```

MongoDB shell gets started on host localhost, port 27017 as shown in Figure 5-6. The "test" database instance gets connected to.

```
root@68fe88ca79fe:/# mongo --host localhost --port 27017
MongoDB shell version: 3.0.7
connecting to: localhost:27017/test
Server has startup warnings:
2015-10-15T18:19:07.312+0000 I CONTROL  [initandlisten]
2015-10-15T18:19:07.312+0000 I CONTROL  [initandlisten] ** WARNING: /sys/kernel/
mm/transparent_hugepage/enabled is 'always'.
2015-10-15T18:19:07.312+0000 I CONTROL  [initandlisten] **        We suggest set
ting it to 'never'
2015-10-15T18:19:07.312+0000 I CONTROL  [initandlisten]
2015-10-15T18:19:07.312+0000 I CONTROL  [initandlisten] ** WARNING: /sys/kernel/
mm/transparent_hugepage/defrag is 'always'.
2015-10-15T18:19:07.312+0000 I CONTROL  [initandlisten] **        We suggest set
ting it to 'never'
2015-10-15T18:19:07.312+0000 I CONTROL  [initandlisten]
↘ █
```

Figure 5-6. *Starting MongoDB Shell using Host and Port*

Alternatively, only one of the host or the port may be specified to start the MongoDB shell.

```
mongo -port 27017
```

MongoDB shell gets started and gets connected to MongoDB server on 127.0.0.1:27071/test as shown in Figure 5-7.

```
root@68fe88ca79fe:/# mongo --port 27017
MongoDB shell version: 3.0.7
connecting to: 127.0.0.1:27017/test
Server has startup warnings:
2015-10-15T18:19:07.312+0000 I CONTROL  [initandlisten]
2015-10-15T18:19:07.312+0000 I CONTROL  [initandlisten] ** WARNING: /sys/kernel/
mm/transparent_hugepage/enabled is 'always'.
2015-10-15T18:19:07.312+0000 I CONTROL  [initandlisten] **       We suggest set
ting it to 'never'
2015-10-15T18:19:07.312+0000 I CONTROL  [initandlisten]
2015-10-15T18:19:07.312+0000 I CONTROL  [initandlisten] ** WARNING: /sys/kernel/
mm/transparent_hugepage/defrag is 'always'.
2015-10-15T18:19:07.312+0000 I CONTROL  [initandlisten] **       We suggest set
ting it to 'never'
2015-10-15T18:19:07.312+0000 I CONTROL  [initandlisten]
>
```

Figure 5-7. *Starting MongoDB Shell using only the Port*

Another form of specifying the host and port is host:port. For example, start the MongoDB shell and connect to localhost:27017 with the following command.

```
mongo localhost:27017
```

MongoDB Shell gets connected to localhost:27017/test database as shown in Figure 5-8.

```
root@68fe88ca79fe:/# mongo localhost:27017
MongoDB shell version: 3.0.7
connecting to: localhost:27017/test
Server has startup warnings:
2015-10-15T18:19:07.312+0000 I CONTROL  [initandlisten]
2015-10-15T18:19:07.312+0000 I CONTROL  [initandlisten] ** WARNING: /sys/kernel/
mm/transparent_hugepage/enabled is 'always'.
2015-10-15T18:19:07.312+0000 I CONTROL  [initandlisten] **       We suggest set
ting it to 'never'
2015-10-15T18:19:07.312+0000 I CONTROL  [initandlisten]
2015-10-15T18:19:07.312+0000 I CONTROL  [initandlisten] ** WARNING: /sys/kernel/
mm/transparent_hugepage/defrag is 'always'.
2015-10-15T18:19:07.312+0000 I CONTROL  [initandlisten] **       We suggest set
ting it to 'never'
2015-10-15T18:19:07.312+0000 I CONTROL  [initandlisten]
>
```

Figure 5-8. *Starting MongoDB Shell using host:port Format*

Creating a Database

List the databases from the MongoDB shell with the following command help method (also called command helper).

```
show dbs
```

A new database is created implicitly when the database name is set to the database to be created. For example, set the database to "mongodb" with the following command.

```
use mongodb
```

The show dbs command help method does not list the mongodb database till the database is used. Use the db.createCollection() method to create a collection called "catalog". Subsequently, run the show dbs command again.

```
show dbs
db.createCollection("catalog")
show dbs
```

The show dbs command does not list the "mongodb" database before the "catalog" collection is created, but lists the "mongodb" database after the collection has been created as shown in Figure 5-9.

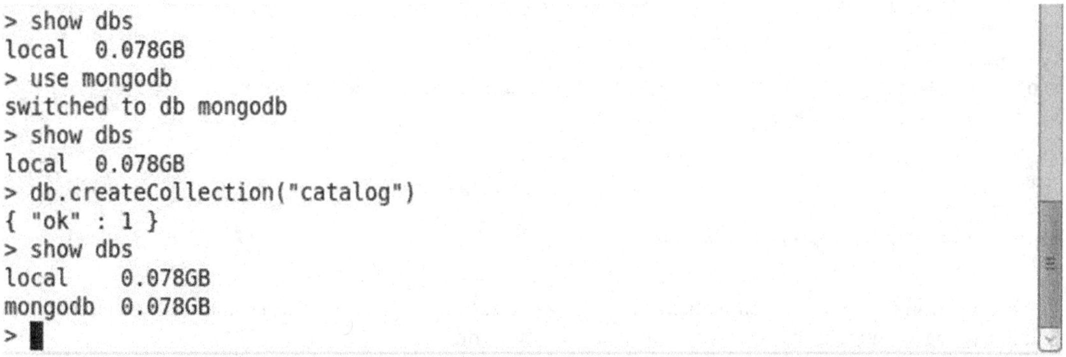

```
> show dbs
local   0.078GB
> use mongodb
switched to db mongodb
> show dbs
local   0.078GB
> db.createCollection("catalog")
{ "ok" : 1 }
> show dbs
local      0.078GB
mongodb    0.078GB
>
```

Figure 5-9. *Creating a Database*

List the collections in the mongodb database with the following command.

```
show collections
```

The "catalog" collection gets listed in addition to the system collection system.indexes as shown in Figure 5-10.

```
> show dbs
local     0.078GB
mongodb   0.078GB
> show collections
catalog
system.indexes
> █
```

Figure 5-10. *Listing Collections*

Creating a Collection

In the previous section we created a collection called "catalog" using the db.createCollection command. Next, create a capped collection "catalog_capped" by setting the capped option field to true. A capped collection is a fixed size collection that keeps track of the insertion order while adding and getting a document, and as a result provides high throughput.

```
db.createCollection("catalog_capped", {capped: true, autoIndexId: true, size: 64 * 1024,
max: 1000} )
```

A capped collection called "catalog_capped" gets created as shown in Figure 5-11.

```
> show collections
catalog
system.indexes
> db.createCollection("catalog_capped", {capped: true, autoIndexId: true, size:
64 * 1024, max: 1000} )
{ "ok" : 1 }
> █
```

Figure 5-11. *Creating a Capped Collection*

A collection may also be created using the db.runCommand command. Create another capped collection called "catalog_capped_2" using the db.runCommand command.

```
db.runCommand( { create: "catalog_capped_2", capped: true, size: 64 * 1024, max: 1000 } )
```

Capped collection catalog_capped_2 gets created as shown in Figure 5-12.

```
> db.createCollection("catalog_capped", {capped: true, autoIndexId: true, size:
64 * 1024, max: 1000} )
{ "ok" : 1 }
> db.runCommand( { create: "catalog_capped_2", capped: true, size: 64 * 1024, ma
x: 1000 } )
{ "ok" : 1 }
> show collections
catalog
catalog_capped
catalog_capped_2
system.indexes
>
```

Figure 5-12. *Creating a Capped Collection using db.runCommand()*

Creating a Document

Next, we shall add documents to a MongoDB collection. Initially the catalog collection is empty. Run
the mongo shell method db.<collection>.count() to count the documents in the catalog collection.
Substitute <collection> with the collection name "catalog".

```
db.catalog.count()
```

The number of documents in the catalog collection gets listed as 0 as shown in Figure 5-13.

```
> db.catalog.count()
0
```

Figure 5-13. *Finding Document Count*

Next, we shall add a document to the catalog collection. Create a JSON document structure with fields
catalogId, journal, publisher, edition, title and author.

```
doc1 = {"catalogId" : "catalog1", "journal" : 'Oracle Magazine', "publisher" :
'Oracle Publishing', "edition" : 'November December 2013',"title" : 'Engineering as a
Service',"author" : 'David A. Kelly'}
```

Add the document to the catalog collection using the db.<collection>.insert() method.

```
db.catalog.insert(doc1)
```

Subsequently output the document count again.

```
db.catalog.count()
```

The output from the db.catalog.insert() method, shown in Figure 5-14, is an object of type
WriteResult with nInserted as 1, which implies that one document got added. The document count is
listed as 1.

```
> doc1 = {"catalogId" : "catalog1", "journal" : 'Oracle Magazine', "publisher" :
 'Oracle Publishing', "edition" : 'November December 2013',"title" : 'Engineerin
g as a Service',"author" : 'David A. Kelly'}
{
        "catalogId" : "catalog1",
        "journal" : "Oracle Magazine",
        "publisher" : "Oracle Publishing",
        "edition" : "November December 2013",
        "title" : "Engineering as a Service",
        "author" : "David A. Kelly"
}
>
> db.catalog.insert(doc1)
WriteResult({ "nInserted" : 1 })
> db.catalog.count()
1
> ▋
```

Figure 5-14. *Adding a Document*

Finding Documents

The db.collection.find(query, projection) method is used to find document/s. The query parameter of type document specifies selection criteria using query operators. The projection parameter also of type document specifies the fields to return. Both the parameters are optional. To select all documents do not specify any args or specify an empty document {}. For example, find all documents in the catalog collection.

```
db.catalog.find()
```

The one document added previously gets listed as a JSON document as shown in Figure 5-15. The _id field is added to the documented automatically if not specified explicitly.

```
> db.catalog.find()
{ "_id" : ObjectId("561fefa7380a18f6587b0aa4"), "catalogId" : "catalog1", "journ
al" : "Oracle Magazine", "publisher" : "Oracle Publishing", "edition" : "Novembe
r December 2013", "title" : "Engineering as a Service", "author" : "David A. Kel
ly" }
> ▋
```

Figure 5-15. *Running a Query using find() Method*

Adding Another Document

Similarly, create the JSON structure for another document. The same document may be added again if the _id is unique. In the JSON include the _id field as an explicit field/attribute. The _id field value must be an object of type ObjectId and not a string literal.

```
doc2 = {"_id": ObjectId("507f191e810c19729de860ea"), "catalogId" : "catalog1", "journal"
: 'Oracle Magazine', "publisher" : 'Oracle Publishing', "edition" : 'November December
2013',"title" : 'Engineering as a Service',"author" : 'David A. Kelly'};
```

Add the document using the db.<collection>.insert() method.

```
db.catalog.insert(doc2)
```

Another document gets added to the catalog collection as indicated by the nInserted value of 1 shown in Figure 5-16.

```
> doc2 = {"_id": ObjectId("507f191e810c19729de860ea"), "catalogId" : "catalog1",
 "journal" : 'Oracle Magazine', "publisher" : 'Oracle Publishing', "edition" : '
November December 2013',"title" : 'Engineering as a Service',"author" : 'David A
. Kelly'};
{
        "_id" : ObjectId("507f191e810c19729de860ea"),
        "catalogId" : "catalog1",
        "journal" : "Oracle Magazine",
        "publisher" : "Oracle Publishing",
        "edition" : "November December 2013",
        "title" : "Engineering as a Service",
        "author" : "David A. Kelly"
}
>
> db.catalog.insert(doc2)
WriteResult({ "nInserted" : 1 })
>
```

Figure 5-16. *Adding Another Document*

Subsequently query the catalog collection using db.<collection>.find() method.

```
db.catalog.find()
```

The two documents added to the catalog collection get listed as shown in Figure 5-17. The two documents have all the same name/value pairs in the JSON except the _id field, which has a unique value.

```
> db.catalog.find()
{ "_id" : ObjectId("561fefa7380a18f6587b0aa4"), "catalogId" : "catalog1", "journ
al" : "Oracle Magazine", "publisher" : "Oracle Publishing", "edition" : "Novembe
r December 2013", "title" : "Engineering as a Service", "author" : "David A. Kel
ly" }
{ "_id" : ObjectId("507f191e810c19729de860ea"), "catalogId" : "catalog1", "journ
al" : "Oracle Magazine", "publisher" : "Oracle Publishing", "edition" : "Novembe
r December 2013", "title" : "Engineering as a Service", "author" : "David A. Kel
ly" }
>
```

Figure 5-17. *Running the find() Method*

Querying a Single Document

The db.<collection>.findOne() method is used to find a single document. Find a single document from the catalog collection.

```
db.catalog.findOne()
```

One of the documents gets output by the query as shown in Figure 5-18.

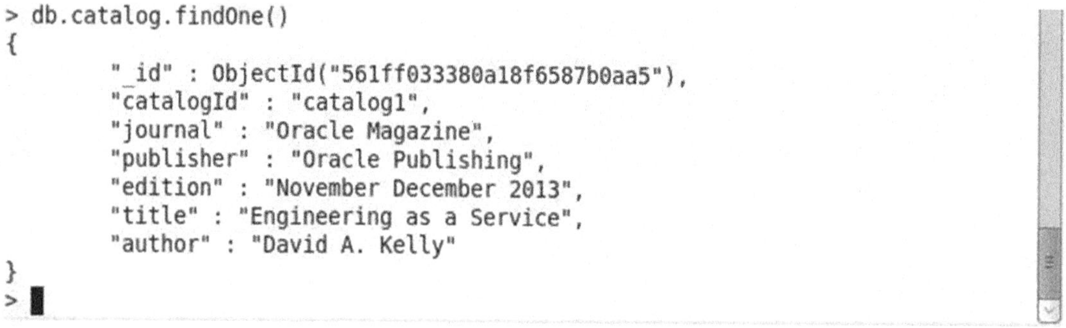

```
> db.catalog.findOne()
{
        "_id" : ObjectId("561ff033380a18f6587b0aa5"),
        "catalogId" : "catalog1",
        "journal" : "Oracle Magazine",
        "publisher" : "Oracle Publishing",
        "edition" : "November December 2013",
        "title" : "Engineering as a Service",
        "author" : "David A. Kelly"
}
>
```

Figure 5-18. *Using the findOne() Method*

The db.collection.findOne(query, projection) method also takes two args both of type document and both optional. The query parameter specifies the query selection criteria and the projection parameter specifies the fields to select. For example, select the edition, title and author fields and specify the query document as {}.

```
db.catalog.findOne(
    { },
{ edition: 1, title: 1, author: 1 }
)
```

The edition, title and author fields get listed. The _id field is always output by a query as shown in Figure 5-19.

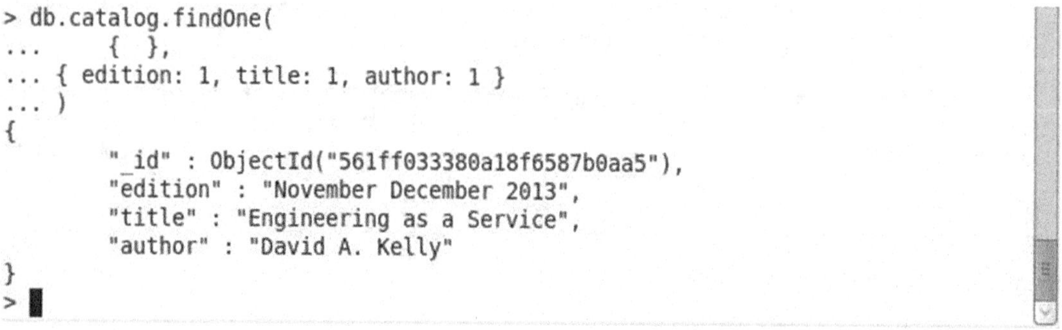

```
> db.catalog.findOne(
...     { },
... { edition: 1, title: 1, author: 1 }
... )
{
        "_id" : ObjectId("561ff033380a18f6587b0aa5"),
        "edition" : "November December 2013",
        "title" : "Engineering as a Service",
        "author" : "David A. Kelly"
}
>
```

Figure 5-19. *Using a Query Projection*

Dropping a Collection

The db.collection.drop() method drops or removes a collection. For example, remove the catalog collection.

```
db.catalog.drop()
```

Subsequently, the show collections method does not list the catalog collection as shown in Figure 5-20.

```
> db.catalog.drop()
true
> show collections
catalog_capped
catalog_capped_2
system.indexes
>
```

Figure 5-20. *Dropping a Collection*

Adding a Batch of Documents

Previously, we added a single document at a time. Next, we shall add a batch of documents. Drop the catalog collection if not already dropped in the previous section.

```
db.catalog.drop()
```

Add an array of documents using the db.catalog.insert() method invocation with the doc1 and doc2 being the same as earlier. The writeConcern option specifies the guarantee MongoDB provides and a value of "majority" implies that the insert() method does not return till the write has been propagated to the majority of the nodes. Setting the ordered option to true adds the documents in the order specified.

```
db.catalog.insert([doc1, doc2], { writeConcern: { w: "majority", wtimeout: 5000 },
ordered:true })
```

The full syntax of the insert method is made use of in the preceding method invocation and is as follows.

```
db.collection.insert(
   <document or array of documents>,
   {
     writeConcern: <document>,
     ordered: <boolean>
   }
)
```

The first parameter is a single document or an array of documents. The second parameter is a document with fields writeConcern and ordered. The writeConcern specifies the write concern or the guarantee that MongoDB provides on the success of an insert. The ordered parameter is set to true, which implies that the documents are added in the order specified and if an error occurs with one of the documents none of the documents are added. The nInserted in the output is 2 for the two documents added as shown in Figure 5-21.

```
> db.catalog.insert([doc1, doc2],  { writeConcern: { w: "majority", wtimeout: 50
00 }, ordered:true })
BulkWriteResult({
        "writeErrors" : [ ],
        "writeConcernErrors" : [ ],
        "nInserted" : 2,
        "nUpserted" : 0,
        "nMatched" : 0,
        "nModified" : 0,
        "nRemoved" : 0,
        "upserted" : [ ]
})
>
```

Figure 5-21. *Adding a Batch of Documents*

Run the db.catalog.find() method to query the documents in the catalog collection as shown in Figure 5-22.

```
> db.catalog.insert([doc1, doc2],  { writeConcern: { w: "majority", wtimeout: 50
00 }, ordered:true })
BulkWriteResult({
        "writeErrors" : [ ],
        "writeConcernErrors" : [ ],
        "nInserted" : 2,
        "nUpserted" : 0,
        "nMatched" : 0,
        "nModified" : 0,
        "nRemoved" : 0,
        "upserted" : [ ]
})
> db.catalog.find()
{ "_id" : ObjectId("561ff033380a18f6587b0aa5"), "catalogId" : "catalog1", "journ
al" : "Oracle Magazine", "publisher" : "Oracle Publishing", "edition" : "Novembe
r December 2013", "title" : "Engineering as a Service", "author" : "David A. Kel
ly" }
{ "_id" : ObjectId("507f191e810c19729de860ea"), "catalogId" : "catalog1", "journ
al" : "Oracle Magazine", "publisher" : "Oracle Publishing", "edition" : "Novembe
r December 2013", "title" : "Engineering as a Service", "author" : "David A. Kel
ly" }
>
```

Figure 5-22. *Running the find() Method to list Documents added in a Batch*

Updating a Document

The db.collection.save() method has the following syntax and updates a document if the document already exists, and ads a new document if the document does not exist.

```
db.collection.save(
   <document>,
   {
      writeConcern: <document>
   }
)
```

A document is identified by the unique _id of type ObjectId. Next, we shall update document with _id as ObjectId("507f191e810c19729de860ea"). Create an updated JSON document with some of the field values modified.

```
doc1 = {"_id": ObjectId("507f191e810c19729de860ea"), "catalogId" : 'catalog1', "journal" :
'Oracle Magazine', "publisher" : 'Oracle Publishing', "edition" : '11-12-2013',"title" :
'Engineering as a Service',"author" : 'Kelly, David A.'}
```

Save the document using the db.collection.save() method in the catalog collection.

```
db.catalog.save(doc1,{ writeConcern: { w: "majority", wtimeout: 5000 } })
```

The document gets saved by updating an existing document. The nMatched is 1 and nUpserted is 0, and nModified is 1 in the WriteResult object returned as shown in Figure 5-23. The nUpserted field refers to the number of new documents added in contrast to modifying an existing document.

```
> doc1 = {"_id": ObjectId("507f191e810c19729de860ea"), "catalogId" : 'catalog1',
 "journal" : 'Oracle Magazine', "publisher" : 'Oracle Publishing', "edition" : '
11-12-2013',"title" : 'Engineering as a Service',"author" : 'Kelly, David A.'}
{
        "_id" : ObjectId("507f191e810c19729de860ea"),
        "catalogId" : "catalog1",
        "journal" : "Oracle Magazine",
        "publisher" : "Oracle Publishing",
        "edition" : "11-12-2013",
        "title" : "Engineering as a Service",
        "author" : "Kelly, David A."
}
> db.catalog.save(doc1,{ writeConcern: { w: "majority", wtimeout: 5000 } })
WriteResult({ "nMatched" : 1, "nUpserted" : 0, "nModified" : 1 })
>
```

Figure 5-23. *Using the save() Method to Update a Document*

Query the catalog collection using the find() method.

```
db.catalog.find()
```

The updated document gets listed as one of the documents as shown in Figure 5-24.

```
> db.catalog.save(doc1,{ writeConcern: { w: "majority", wtimeout: 5000 } })
WriteResult({ "nMatched" : 1, "nUpserted" : 0, "nModified" : 1 })
> db.catalog.find()
{ "_id" : ObjectId("561ff033380a18f6587b0aa5"), "catalogId" : "catalog1", "journ
al" : "Oracle Magazine", "publisher" : "Oracle Publishing", "edition" : "Novembe
r December 2013", "title" : "Engineering as a Service", "author" : "David A. Kel
ly" }
{ "_id" : ObjectId("507f191e810c19729de860ea"), "catalogId" : "catalog1", "journ
al" : "Oracle Magazine", "publisher" : "Oracle Publishing", "edition" : "11-12-2
013", "title" : "Engineering as a Service", "author" : "Kelly, David A." }
> ▮
```

Figure 5-24. *Querying Updated Document*

Outputting Documents as JSON

The db.collection.find(query, projection) method returns a cursor over the documents that are selected by the query. Invoke the forEach(printjson) method on the cursor to output the documents as formatted JSON.

```
db.catalog.find().forEach(printjson)
```

The documents get output as JSON as shown in Figure 5-25.

```
> db.catalog.find().forEach(printjson)
{
        "_id" : ObjectId("561ff033380a18f6587b0aa5"),
        "catalogId" : "catalog1",
        "journal" : "Oracle Magazine",
        "publisher" : "Oracle Publishing",
        "edition" : "November December 2013",
        "title" : "Engineering as a Service",
        "author" : "David A. Kelly"
}
{
        "_id" : ObjectId("507f191e810c19729de860ea"),
        "catalogId" : "catalog1",
        "journal" : "Oracle Magazine",
        "publisher" : "Oracle Publishing",
        "edition" : "11-12-2013",
        "title" : "Engineering as a Service",
        "author" : "Kelly, David A."
}
> ▮
```

Figure 5-25. *Outputting JSON*

Making a Backup of the Data

The mongodump utility is used for creating a binary export of the data in a database. The mongorestore utility is used in conjunction with mongodump to restore a database from backup. The mongorestore utility either creates a new database instance or adds to an existing database.

Run the following mongodump command to export the test database to the /data/backup directory.

```
mongodump --db test --out /data/backup
```

The test database gets exported to the /data/backup directory as shown in Figure 5-26.

```
root@68fe88ca79fe:/# mongodump --db test --out /data/backup
root@68fe88ca79fe:/# █
```

Figure 5-26. *Exporting the test Database*

List the directories in the /data/backup directory. The test database directory gets listed as shown in Figure 5-27.

```
[ec2-user@ip-172-30-1-192 ~]$ ls -la /data/backup
total 0
drwxr-xr-x. 3 root root 17 Oct 15 14:41 .
drwxr-xr-x. 4 root root 28 Oct 15 14:41 ..
drwxr-xr-x. 2 root root  6 Oct 15 14:41 test
[ec2-user@ip-172-30-1-192 ~]$ █
```

Figure 5-27. *Listing the test Database*

Run the following mongorestore command to restore the exported data from /data/backup/test to the testrestore database.

```
mongorestore --db testrestore /data/backup/test
```

The /data/backup/test directory data gets restored in the testrestore database as shown in Figure 5-28.

```
root@68fe88ca79fe:/# mongodump --db test --out /data/backup
root@68fe88ca79fe:/# mongorestore --db testrestore /data/backup/test
2015-10-15T18:43:18.829+0000    building a list of collections to restore from /
data/backup/test dir
2015-10-15T18:43:18.829+0000    done
root@68fe88ca79fe:/# █
```

Figure 5-28. *Restoring a Database*

Connect to the MongoDB shell with the following command.

```
mongo localhost:27017/testrestore
```

The MongoDB shell gets started as shown in Figure 5-29.

```
root@68fe88ca79fe:/# mongo localhost:27017/testrestore
MongoDB shell version: 3.0.7
connecting to: localhost:27017/testrestore
Server has startup warnings:
2015-10-15T18:19:07.312+0000 I CONTROL  [initandlisten]
2015-10-15T18:19:07.312+0000 I CONTROL  [initandlisten] ** WARNING: /sys/kernel/
mm/transparent_hugepage/enabled is 'always'.
2015-10-15T18:19:07.312+0000 I CONTROL  [initandlisten] **       We suggest set
ting it to 'never'
2015-10-15T18:19:07.312+0000 I CONTROL  [initandlisten]
2015-10-15T18:19:07.312+0000 I CONTROL  [initandlisten] ** WARNING: /sys/kernel/
mm/transparent_hugepage/defrag is 'always'.
2015-10-15T18:19:07.312+0000 I CONTROL  [initandlisten] **       We suggest set
ting it to 'never'
2015-10-15T18:19:07.312+0000 I CONTROL  [initandlisten]
>
```

Figure 5-29. *Connecting to the Restored Database*

List the databases with the following command.

```
show dbs
```

As we restored the backup to the testrestore database the mongodb database, which was previously exported, gets listed as shown in Figure 5-30.

```
root@68fe88ca79fe:/# mongo localhost:27017/testrestore
MongoDB shell version: 3.0.7
connecting to: localhost:27017/testrestore
Server has startup warnings:
2015-10-15T18:19:07.312+0000 I CONTROL  [initandlisten]
2015-10-15T18:19:07.312+0000 I CONTROL  [initandlisten] ** WARNING: /sys/kernel/
mm/transparent_hugepage/enabled is 'always'.
2015-10-15T18:19:07.312+0000 I CONTROL  [initandlisten] **       We suggest set
ting it to 'never'
2015-10-15T18:19:07.312+0000 I CONTROL  [initandlisten]
2015-10-15T18:19:07.312+0000 I CONTROL  [initandlisten] ** WARNING: /sys/kernel/
mm/transparent_hugepage/defrag is 'always'.
2015-10-15T18:19:07.312+0000 I CONTROL  [initandlisten] **       We suggest set
ting it to 'never'
2015-10-15T18:19:07.312+0000 I CONTROL  [initandlisten]
> show dbs
local      0.078GB
mongodb    0.078GB
>
```

Figure 5-30. *Listing the Restored Database*

Set the database name as mongodb.

```
use mongodb
```

List the collections.

```
show collections
```

Query the documents in the catalog collection.

```
db.catalog.find()
```

Output from the preceding commands is shown in Figure 5-31.

```
> show dbs
local      0.078GB
mongodb  0.078GB
> use mongodb
switched to db mongodb
> show collections
catalog
catalog_capped
catalog_capped_2
system.indexes
> db.catalog.find()
{ "_id" : ObjectId("561ff033380a18f6587b0aa5"), "catalogId" : "catalog1", "journ
al" : "Oracle Magazine", "publisher" : "Oracle Publishing", "edition" : "Novembe
r December 2013", "title" : "Engineering as a Service", "author" : "David A. Kel
ly" }
{ "_id" : ObjectId("507f191e810c19729de860ea"), "catalogId" : "catalog1", "journ
al" : "Oracle Magazine", "publisher" : "Oracle Publishing", "edition" : "11-12-2
013", "title" : "Engineering as a Service", "author" : "Kelly, David A." }
>
```

Figure 5-31. *Listing and Querying the Restored Collection*

Removing Documents

The db.collection.remove method is used to remove document/s and has the following syntax.

```
db.collection.remove(
    <query>,
    <justOne>
)
```

For example, remove the document with ObjectId("561ff033380a18f6587b0aa5").

```
db.catalog.remove({ _id: ObjectId("561ff033380a18f6587b0aa5") })
```

The nRemoved in the WriteResult is 1 indicating that one document got removed. Run the db.catalog.find() method before and after the db.catalog.remove() method invocation. Before the db.catalog.remove() method is invoked, two documents get listed, and afterward only one document gets listed as shown in Figure 5-32.

```
> db.catalog.find()
{ "_id" : ObjectId("561ff033380a18f6587b0aa5"), "catalogId" : "catalog1", "journ
al" : "Oracle Magazine", "publisher" : "Oracle Publishing", "edition" : "Novembe
r December 2013", "title" : "Engineering as a Service", "author" : "David A. Kel
ly" }
{ "_id" : ObjectId("507f191e810c19729de860ea"), "catalogId" : "catalog1", "journ
al" : "Oracle Magazine", "publisher" : "Oracle Publishing", "edition" : "11-12-2
013", "title" : "Engineering as a Service", "author" : "Kelly, David A." }
> db.catalog.remove({ _id: ObjectId("561ff033380a18f6587b0aa5")})
WriteResult({ "nRemoved" : 1 })
> db.catalog.find()
{ "_id" : ObjectId("507f191e810c19729de860ea"), "catalogId" : "catalog1", "journ
al" : "Oracle Magazine", "publisher" : "Oracle Publishing", "edition" : "11-12-2
013", "title" : "Engineering as a Service", "author" : "Kelly, David A." }
>
```

Figure 5-32. *Removing a Single Document*

To remove all documents, provide an empty document {} to the db.catalog.remove() method invocation.

```
db.catalog.remove({})
```

Multiple documents get removed as indicated by nRemoved value of 2 as shown in Figure 5-33.

```
ec2-user@ip-172-30-1-192:~
File Edit View Search Terminal Help
        "edition" : "November December 2013",
        "title" : "Engineering as a Service",
        "author" : "David A. Kelly"
}
>
> db.catalog.insert(doc1)
WriteResult({ "nInserted" : 1 })
> doc2 = {"_id": ObjectId("507f191e810c19729de860ea"), "catalogId" : "catalog1",
 "journal" : 'Oracle Magazine', "publisher" : 'Oracle Publishing', "edition" : '
November December 2013',"title" : 'Engineering as a Service',"author" : 'David A
. Kelly'};
{
        "_id" : ObjectId("507f191e810c19729de860ea"),
        "catalogId" : "catalog1",
        "journal" : "Oracle Magazine",
        "publisher" : "Oracle Publishing",
        "edition" : "November December 2013",
        "title" : "Engineering as a Service",
        "author" : "David A. Kelly"
}
>
> db.catalog.insert(doc2)
WriteResult({ "nInserted" : 1 })
> db.catalog.remove({})
WriteResult({ "nRemoved" : 2 })
> 
```

Figure 5-33. *Removing All Documents*

An empty query document must be supplied to the `db.catalog.remove()` method invocation. If an empty document {} is not supplied, an error is generated indicating that a query is needed as shown in Figure 5-34.

```
> db.catalog.remove()
2015-10-15T19:06:49.774+0000 E QUERY    Error: remove needs a query
    at Error (<anonymous>)
    at DBCollection._parseRemove (src/mongo/shell/collection.js:305:32)
    at DBCollection.remove (src/mongo/shell/collection.js:328:23)
    at (shell):1:12 at src/mongo/shell/collection.js:305
> db.catalog.remove({})
WriteResult({ "nRemoved" : 1 })
> 
```

Figure 5-34. *An empty document must be provided to the remove() method to remove all documents*

Stopping and Restarting the MongoDB Database

The Docker container running the MongoDB instance may be stopped with the docker stop command.

```
sudo docker stop mongo
```

List the running Docker containers with the following command.

```
sudo docker ps
```

Start the Docker container again with the docker start command.

```
sudo docker start mongo
```

Run the following command again to list the running containers.

```
sudo docker ps
```

The output from the preceding commands is shown in Figure 5-35. The Docker container mongodb is again listed as running.

```
[ec2-user@ip-172-30-1-192 ~]$ sudo docker stop mongodb
mongodb
[ec2-user@ip-172-30-1-192 ~]$ sudo docker ps
CONTAINER ID        IMAGE               COMMAND             CREATED
STATUS              PORTS               NAMES
[ec2-user@ip-172-30-1-192 ~]$ sudo docker start mongodb
mongodb
[ec2-user@ip-172-30-1-192 ~]$ sudo docker ps
CONTAINER ID        IMAGE               COMMAND             CREATED
    STATUS              PORTS               NAMES
68fe88ca79fe        mongo               "/entrypoint.sh mongo"   51 minutes ago
    Up 5 seconds        27017/tcp              mongodb
[ec2-user@ip-172-30-1-192 ~]$ ▊
```

Figure 5-35. *Listing a Docker Container after Restarting the Container*

Start the interactive terminal with the following command in which the container ID is used instead of the container name.

```
sudo docker exec -it 68fe88ca79fe bash
```

Start the MongoDB shell with the mongo command in the interactive shell as shown in Figure 5-36.

```
[ec2-user@ip-172-30-1-192 ~]$ sudo docker ps
CONTAINER ID          IMAGE              COMMAND                   CREATED
     STATUS              PORTS                  NAMES
68fe88ca79fe          mongo              "/entrypoint.sh mongo"    51 minutes ago
     Up 5 seconds        27017/tcp              mongodb
[ec2-user@ip-172-30-1-192 ~]$ sudo docker exec -it 68fe88ca79fe bash
root@68fe88ca79fe:/# mongo
MongoDB shell version: 3.0.7
connecting to: test
Server has startup warnings:
2015-10-15T19:10:31.640+0000 I CONTROL  [initandlisten]
2015-10-15T19:10:31.640+0000 I CONTROL  [initandlisten] ** WARNING: /sys/kernel/
mm/transparent_hugepage/enabled is 'always'.
2015-10-15T19:10:31.640+0000 I CONTROL  [initandlisten] **        We suggest set
ting it to 'never'
2015-10-15T19:10:31.640+0000 I CONTROL  [initandlisten]
2015-10-15T19:10:31.640+0000 I CONTROL  [initandlisten] ** WARNING: /sys/kernel/
mm/transparent_hugepage/defrag is 'always'.
2015-10-15T19:10:31.640+0000 I CONTROL  [initandlisten] **        We suggest set
ting it to 'never'
2015-10-15T19:10:31.640+0000 I CONTROL  [initandlisten]
>
```

Figure 5-36. *Starting the MongoDB Shell*

Set the database to local and list the collections with the show collections command. Subsequently set the database to mongodb and list the collections. The db.catalog.find() method does not list any documents as shown in Figure 5-37.

```
> use local
switched to db local
> show collections
startup_log
system.indexes
> use mongodb
switched to db mongodb
> show collections
catalog
catalog_capped
catalog_capped_2
system.indexes
> db.catalog.find()
>
```

Figure 5-37. *Listing Documents in the catalog Collection in local Database*

Exiting the Mongo Shell

To exit the interactive terminal use the "exit" command and exit the MongoDB shell with the "exit" command also as shown in Figure 5-38.

```
> db.catalog.insert(doc2)
WriteResult({ "nInserted" : 1 })
> db.catalog.remove({})
WriteResult({ "nRemoved" : 2 })
> ^C
bye
root@68fe88ca79fe:/# ^C
root@68fe88ca79fe:/# exit
exit
[ec2-user@ip-172-30-1-192 ~]$ █
```

Figure 5-38. Exiting MongoDB Shell and TTY

Summary

In this chapter we used a Docker image for MongoDB to run a MongoDB instance in a Docker container. We created a database, added collections to the database, and added documents to the collections. We also queried the documents in MongoDB. We demonstrated stopping and starting the Docker container. We also made a backup of a MongoDB database and subsequently restored the database from the backup. In the next chapter we shall discuss running another NoSQL database, Apache Cassandra, in a Docker container.

■ ■ ■

CHAPTER 6

Using Apache Cassandra

Apache Cassandra is a wide-column, open source NoSQL database and the most commonly used NoSQL database in its category. The container of data, equivalent to a database schema in a relational database, in Apache Cassandra is a *Keyspace*. The basic unit of storage is a *column family* (also called *table*), and each record in a table is stored in a row with the data being stored in columns. A column has a name, a value, and a timestamp associated with it. A column is not required to store a value and the column could be empty. Apache Cassandra is based on a flexible schema (or schema-free or dynamic schema) data model in which different rows could have different columns and the columns are not required to be pre-specified in a table definition. Apache Cassandra supports data types for column names (called *comparators*) and column values (called *validators*), but does not require the data types (validators and comparators) to be specified. The validators and comparators may be added or modified after a table (column family) has been defined. Apache Cassandra provides a Cassandra Query Language (CQL) for CRUD (add, get, update, delete) operations on a table. Apache Cassandra installation includes a cqlsh utility, which is an interactive shell, from which CQL commands may be run. An official Docker image for Apache Cassandra is available and in this chapter we shall run Apache Cassandra in a Docker container.

Setting the Environment

Starting Apache Cassandra

Starting the TTY

Connecting to CQL Shell

Creating a Keyspace

Altering A Keyspace

Using A Keyspace

Creating a Table

Adding Table Data

Querying a Table

Deleting from a Table

Truncating a Table

Dropping A Table

Dropping a Keyspace

Exiting CQLSh

Stopping Apache Cassandra

Starting Multiple Instances of Apache Cassandra

Setting the Environment

The following software is required for this chapter.

-Docker (version 1.8)

-Docker image for Apache Cassandra

We have used an Amazon EC2 AMI as in other chapters to install Docker and the Docker image. First, SSH to the Amazon EC2 instance.

```
ssh -i "docker.pem" ec2-user@54.86.243.122
```

Installing Docker is discussed in Chapter 1. Start the Docker service. The following command should output an OK message.

```
sudo service docker start
```

Verify that the Docker service has been started. The following command should output active (running) in the Active field.

```
sudo service docker status
```

Output from the preceding commands is shown in Figure 6-1.

```
[ec2-user@ip-172-30-1-192 ~]$ sudo service docker start
Starting docker (via systemctl):                          [  OK  ]
[ec2-user@ip-172-30-1-192 ~]$ sudo service docker status
docker.service - Docker Application Container Engine
   Loaded: loaded (/usr/lib/systemd/system/docker.service; disabled)
   Active: active (running) since Thu 2015-10-15 18:02:38 EDT; 9s ago
     Docs: https://docs.docker.com
 Main PID: 2405 (docker)
   CGroup: /system.slice/docker.service
           └─2405 /usr/bin/docker daemon -H fd://

Oct 15 18:02:38 ip-172-30-1-192.ec2.internal docker[2405]: time="2015-10-15T1...
Oct 15 18:02:38 ip-172-30-1-192.ec2.internal docker[2405]: time="2015-10-15T1...
Oct 15 18:02:38 ip-172-30-1-192.ec2.internal docker[2405]: time="2015-10-15T1...
Oct 15 18:02:38 ip-172-30-1-192.ec2.internal docker[2405]: time="2015-10-15T1...
Oct 15 18:02:38 ip-172-30-1-192.ec2.internal docker[2405]: ..
Oct 15 18:02:38 ip-172-30-1-192.ec2.internal docker[2405]: time="2015-10-15T1...
Oct 15 18:02:38 ip-172-30-1-192.ec2.internal docker[2405]: time="2015-10-15T1...
Oct 15 18:02:38 ip-172-30-1-192.ec2.internal docker[2405]: time="2015-10-15T1...
Oct 15 18:02:38 ip-172-30-1-192.ec2.internal systemd[1]: Started Docker Appli...
Hint: Some lines were ellipsized, use -l to show in full.
[ec2-user@ip-172-30-1-192 ~]$
```

Figure 6-1. *Starting Docker Service and verifying Status*

Next, download the latest cassandra Docker image.

```
sudo docker pull cassandra:latest
```

List the Docker images downloaded.

```
sudo docker images
```

The cassandra image should get listed as shown in Figure 6-2.

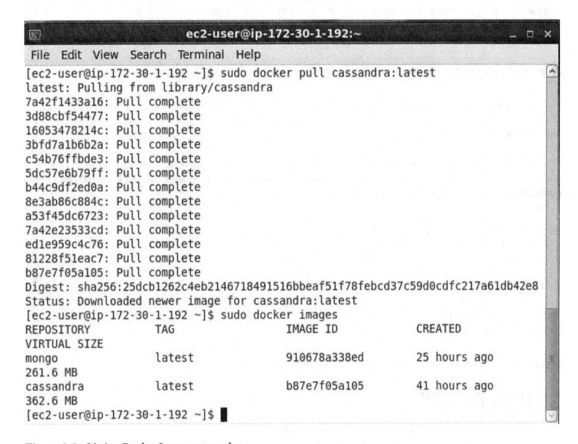

Figure 6-2. *Listing Docker Image cassandra*

Starting Apache Cassandra

Start the Apache Cassandra server process in a Docker container with the following command in which the inter-node Apache Cassandra cluster communication port is specified as 7000 and the directory in which Apache Cassandra stores data is /cassandra/data. The container name is specified with the –name option as cassandradb. The syntax to start a Cassandra instance in detached mode is as follows.

```
docker run --name some-cassandra -d cassandra:tag
```

The –d parameter starts the container in a detached mode, implying that an interactive shell is not connected to with the docker run command even if the –t –i options are specified.

```
sudo docker run -t -i -v /cassandra/data:/var/lib/cassandra/data --name cassandradb -d -p
7000:7000  cassandra
```

A Docker container running an Apache Cassandra server process gets started as shown in Figure 6-3.

```
[ec2-user@ip-172-30-1-192 ~]$ sudo docker run -t -i -v /cassandra/data:/var/lib/
cassandra/data --name cassandradb -d -p 7000:7000  cassandra
dfade563f871691d834f019c38c964a4413d8cb6a5bacb3451c4cdf26264d8c1
[ec2-user@ip-172-30-1-192 ~]$ █
```

Figure 6-3. *Starting Docker Container for Apache Cassandra*

List the running Docker containers with the following command.

```
sudo docker ps
```

The cassandradb container, which is running an Apache Cassandra server instance, gets listed. The container id is also listed. By default, port 9042 is the client port on which Apache Cassandra listens for client connections. Port 9160 is Thrift API as shown in Figure 6-4.

```
[ec2-user@ip-172-30-1-192 ~]$ sudo docker ps
CONTAINER ID          IMAGE              COMMAND                  CREATED
      STATUS              PORTS
            NAMES
dfade563f871          cassandra               "/docker-entrypoint.s"    48 seconds ago
      Up 47 seconds        7001/tcp, 7199/tcp, 9042/tcp, 0.0.0.0:7000->7000/tcp, 9
160/tcp    cassandradb
[ec2-user@ip-172-30-1-192 ~]$ █
```

Figure 6-4. *Listing Docker Containers that are Running*

Starting the TTY

Start the interactive terminal (tty) with the following command.

```
sudo docker exec -it cassandradb bash
```

The tty gets connected to and the command prompt gets set to user@containerid. If the user is root and the container id is dfade56f871, the command prompt becomes root@dfade56f871 as shown in Figure 6-5.

```
[ec2-user@ip-172-30-1-192 ~]$ sudo docker exec -it cassandradb bash
root@dfade563f871:/# █
```

Figure 6-5. *Starting the TTY*

Connecting to CQL Shell

The cqlsh terminal is used to connect to an Apache Cassandra instance and run CQL commands. Start the cqlsh terminal with the following command.

```
cqlsh
```

A connection gets established to the Test Cluster at 127.0.0.1:9042. The Apache Cassandra version gets output as 2.2.2 and the CQL spec version as 3.3.1. The cqlsh> command prompt gets displayed as shown in Figure 6-6.

```
[ec2-user@ip-172-30-1-192 ~]$ sudo docker exec -it cassandradb bash
root@dfade563f871:/# cqlsh
Connected to Test Cluster at 127.0.0.1:9042.
[cqlsh 5.0.1 | Cassandra 2.2.2 | CQL spec 3.3.1 | Native protocol v4]
Use HELP for help.
cqlsh>
```

Figure 6-6. Connecting the CQL Shell

We started the interactive terminal using the container name, but the tty may also be started using the container id. The cqlsh shell is started with the cqlsh command regardless of how the tty is started.

```
sudo docker exec -it dfade56f871 bash
cqlsh
```

The cqlsh> command prompt gets displayed as before as shown in Figure 6-7.

```
[ec2-user@ip-172-30-1-192 ~]$ sudo docker exec -it dfade563f871 bash
root@dfade563f871:/# cqlsh
Connected to Test Cluster at 127.0.0.1:9042.
[cqlsh 5.0.1 | Cassandra 2.2.2 | CQL spec 3.3.1 | Native protocol v4]
Use HELP for help.
cqlsh>
```

Figure 6-7. Connecting to CQL Shell using the Container ID

Creating a Keyspace

A Keyspace is the container of application data and is used to group column families. Replication is set at a per-keyspace basis. The DDL command for creating a Keyspace is as follows.

```
CREATE KEYSPACE (IF NOT EXISTS)? <identifier> WITH <properties>
```

By default, the keyspace name is case-insensitive and may consist exclusively of alpha-numeric characters with a maximum length of 32. To make a keyspace name case-sensitive add quotes. The supported properties by the CREATE KEYSPACE statement, which creates a top-level keyspace, are replication for specifying the replication strategy and options and durable_writes for whether a commit log is to be used for updates on the keyspace, with the replication property being mandatory. As an example, create a keyspace called CatalogKeyspace with replication strategy class as SimpleStrategy and replication factor as 3.

```
CREATE KEYSPACE CatalogKeyspace
        WITH replication = {'class': 'SimpleStrategy', 'replication_factor' : 3};
```

The CatalogKeyspace keyspace gets created as shown in Figure 6-8.

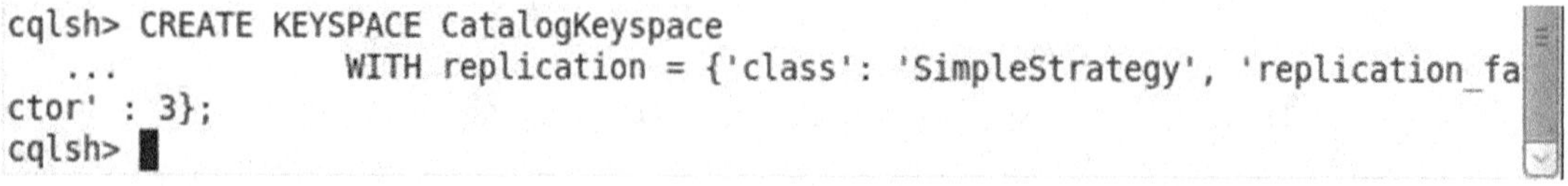

```
cqlsh> CREATE KEYSPACE CatalogKeyspace
   ...             WITH replication = {'class': 'SimpleStrategy', 'replication_fa
ctor' : 3};
cqlsh>
```

Figure 6-8. *Creating a Keyspace*

Altering A Keyspace

The ALTER KEYSPACE statement is used to alter a keyspace and has the following syntax with the supported properties being the same as for the CREATE KEYSPACE statement.

```
ALTER KEYSPACE <identifier> WITH <properties>
```

As an example, alter the CatalogKeyspace keyspace to make the replication factor 1.

```
ALTER KEYSPACE CatalogKeyspace
        WITH replication = {'class': 'SimpleStrategy', 'replication_factor' : 1};
```

The replication factor gets set to 1 as shown in Figure 6-9.

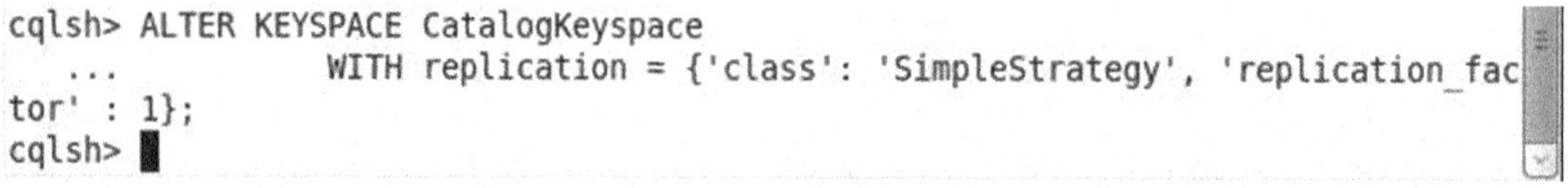

```
cqlsh> ALTER KEYSPACE CatalogKeyspace
   ...             WITH replication = {'class': 'SimpleStrategy', 'replication_fac
tor' : 1};
cqlsh>
```

Figure 6-9. *Altering a Keyspace*

Using A Keyspace

The USE statement is used to set the current keyspace and has the following syntax.

```
USE <identifier>
```

All subsequent commands are run in the context of the Keyspace set with the USE statement. As an example, set the current Keyspace as CatalogKeyspace.

```
use CatalogKeyspace;
```

The cqlsh> command prompt becomes cqlsh:catalogkeyspace> as shown in Figure 6-10.

```
cqlsh> use CatalogKeyspace;
cqlsh:catalogkeyspace> █
```

Figure 6-10. *Using a Keyspace*

Creating a Table

A TABLE is also called a COLUMN FAMILY, and the CREATE TABLE or CREATE COLUMN FAMILY statement is used to create a table (column family).

```
CREATE ( TABLE | COLUMNFAMILY ) ( IF NOT EXISTS )? <tablename>
                    '(' <column-definition> ( ',' <column-definition> )* ')'
                    ( WITH <option> ( AND <option>)* )?
```

For the complete syntax of the CREATE TABLE statement refer to https://cassandra.apache.org/doc/cql3/CQL.html#createTableStmt. As an example create a table called 'catalog' with columns catalog_id, journal, publisher, edition, title and author all of type text. Specify the primary key as catalog_id and set the compaction class as LeveledCompactionStrategy.

```
CREATE TABLE catalog(catalog_id text,journal text,publisher text,edition text,title
text,author text,PRIMARY KEY (catalog_id)) WITH  compaction = { 'class' :
'LeveledCompactionStrategy' };
```

The catalog table gets created as shown in Figure 6-11.

```
cqlsh:catalogkeyspace> CREATE TABLE catalog(catalog_id text,journal text,publish
er text,edition text,title text,author text,PRIMARY KEY (catalog_id))  WITH  com
paction = { 'class' : 'LeveledCompactionStrategy' };
```

Figure 6-11. *Creating a Table*

Adding Table Data

The INSERT DML statement is used to add data into a table and has the following syntax.

```
INSERT INTO <tablename>
                    '(' <identifier> ( ',' <identifier> )* ')'
                VALUES '(' <term-or-literal> ( ',' <term-or-literal> )* ')'
                ( IF NOT EXISTS )?
                ( USING <option> ( AND <option> )* )?
```

For complete syntax for the INSERT statement refer https://cassandra.apache.org/doc/cql3/CQL.html#insertStmt. As an example add two rows of data to the catalog table and include the IF NOT EXISTS clause to add a row if a row identified by the primary key does not exist.

```
INSERT INTO catalog (catalog_id, journal, publisher, edition,title,author) VALUES
('catalog1','Oracle Magazine', 'Oracle Publishing', 'November-December 2013', 'Engineering
as a Service','David A.  Kelly') IF NOT EXISTS;
```

```
INSERT INTO catalog (catalog_id, journal, publisher, edition,title,author) VALUES
('catalog2','Oracle Magazine', 'Oracle Publishing', 'November-December 2013',
'Quintessential and Collaborative','Tom Haunert') IF NOT EXISTS;
```

As indicated by the [applied] True output, two rows of data get added as shown in Figure 6-12.

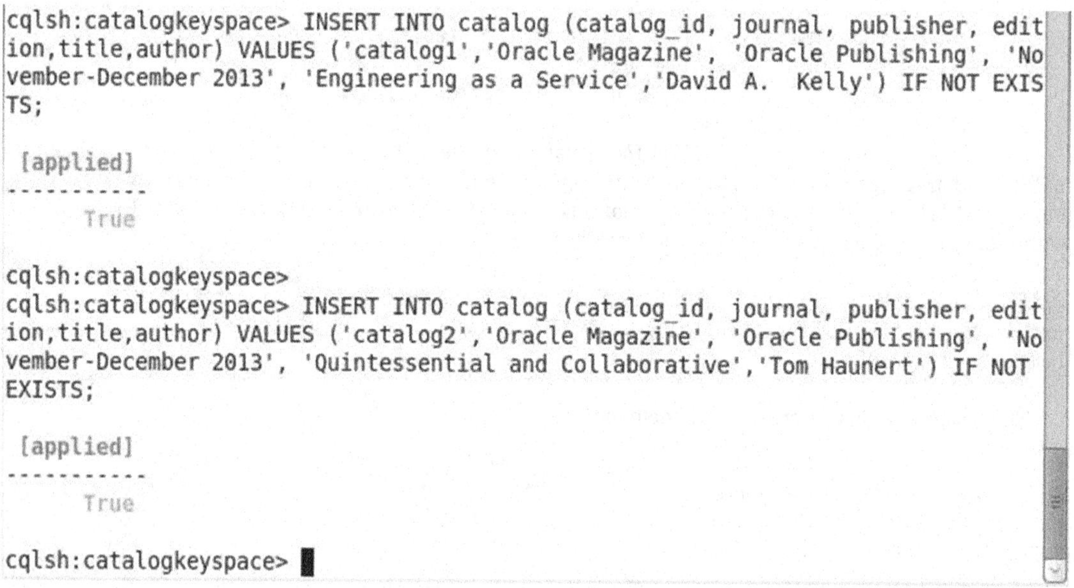

Figure 6-12. *Adding Table Data*

Querying a Table

The SELECT statement, which has the following syntax, is used to query a table.

```
SELECT <select-clause>
                FROM <tablename>
                ( WHERE <where-clause> )?
                ( ORDER BY <order-by> )?
                ( LIMIT <integer> )?
                ( ALLOW FILTERING )?
```

For the complete syntax for the SELECT statement refer to https://cassandra.apache.org/doc/cql3/ CQL.html#selectStmt. As an example select all columns from the catalog table.

```
SELECT * FROM catalog;
```

The two rows of data added previously get listed as shown in Figure 6-13.

```
cqlsh:catalogkeyspace> SELECT * FROM catalog;

 catalog_id | author          | edition               | journal         | publi
sher        | title
------------+-----------------+-----------------------+-----------------+-------
------------+----------------------------------------
   catalog1 | David A.  Kelly | November-December 2013 | Oracle Magazine | Oracl
e Publishing |          Engineering as a Service
   catalog2 |     Tom Haunert | November-December 2013 | Oracle Magazine | Oracl
e Publishing | Quintessential and Collaborative

(2 rows)
cqlsh:catalogkeyspace> █
```

Figure 6-13. *Querying Table*

Deleting from a Table

The DELETE statement is used to delete columns and rows and has the following syntax.

```
DELETE ( <selection> ( ',' <selection> )* )?
               FROM <tablename>
               ( USING TIMESTAMP <integer>)?
               WHERE <where-clause>
               ( IF ( EXISTS | ( <condition> ( AND <condition> )*) ) )?
```

For complete syntax for the DELETE statement refer to https://cassandra.apache.org/doc/cql3/ CQL.html#deleteStmt. As an example, delete all columns from the row with catalog_id as catalog1.

```
DELETE catalog_id, journal, publisher, edition, title, author from catalog WHERE catalog_
id='catalog1';
```

Subsequently, query the catalog table with the SELECT statement.

```
SELECT * FROM catalog;
```

Column values from the row with catalog_id as catalog1 get deleted, but the row itself including the primary key column value do not get deleted even though the primary key catalog_id is listed as one of the columns to delete. Subsequent query lists the primary key column value but lists the column values for the other columns as null as shown in Figure 6-14.

```
cqlsh:catalogkeyspace> DELETE  journal, publisher, edition, title, author from c
atalog WHERE catalog_id='catalog1';
cqlsh:catalogkeyspace> SELECT * FROM catalog;

 catalog_id | author      | edition            | journal         | publisher
            | title
------------+-------------+--------------------+-----------------+-----------
--------+-------------------------------------
   catalog1 |        null |               null |            null |       null |
    null |                              null
   catalog2 | Tom Nummert | November-December 2013 | Oracle Magazine | Oracle Pu
blishing | Quintessential and Collaborative

(2 rows)
```

Figure 6-14. *Deleting Table Data*

Truncating a Table

The TRUNCATE statement removes all data from a table and has the following syntax.

```
TRUNCATE <tablename>
```

As an example, truncate the catalog table. Subsequently, run a query with the SELECT statement.

```
TRUNCATE catalog;
SELECT * from catalog;
```

As the output of the query indicates, no data is listed because the TRUNCATE statement has removed all data as shown in Figure 6-15.

```
cqlsh:catalogkeyspace> TRUNCATE catalog;
cqlsh:catalogkeyspace> SELECT * FROM catalog;

 catalog_id | author | edition | journal | publisher | title
------------+--------+---------+---------+-----------+-------

(0 rows)
```

Figure 6-15. *Truncating a Table*

Dropping A Table

The DROP TABLE or DROP COLUMN FAMILY statement is used to drop a table and has the following syntax.

```
DROP TABLE ( IF EXISTS )? <tablename>
```

As an example, drop the catalog table.

```
DROP TABLE IF EXISTS catalog;
```

If the IF EXISTS clause is not specified and the table does not exist, an error is generated. But with the IF EXISTS clause, an error is not generated as indicated by two consecutively run DROP TABLE statements with the IF EXISTS clause included in Figure 6-16.

```
cqlsh:catalogkeyspace> DROP TABLE IF EXISTS catalog;
cqlsh:catalogkeyspace> DROP TABLE IF EXISTS catalog;
```

Figure 6-16. *Dropping a Table*

Dropping a Keyspace

The DROP KEYSPACE statement, which has the following syntax, removes the specified key space including the column families in the key space and the data in the column families, and the keyspace does not have to be empty before being dropped.

```
DROP KEYSPACE ( IF EXISTS )? <identifier>
```

As an example, drop the CatalogKeyspace keyspace.

```
DROP KEYSPACE IF EXISTS CatalogKeyspace;
```

If the IF EXISTS clause is not specified and the keyspace does not exist, an error is generated. But with the IF EXISTS clause, an error is not generated as indicated by two consecutively run DROP KEYSPACE statements with the IF EXISTS clause included as shown in Figure 6-17.

```
cqlsh:catalogkeyspace> DROP KEYSPACE IF EXISTS CatalogKeyspace;
cqlsh:catalogkeyspace> DROP KEYSPACE IF EXISTS CatalogKeyspace;
```

Figure 6-17. *Dropping a Keyspace*

Exiting CQL Shell

To exit the cqlsh shell specify the exit command as shown in Figure 6-18. Subsequently exit the tty with the exit command also.

```
cqlsh:catalogkeyspace> exit

root@dfade563f871:/# exit
exit
[ec2-user@ip-172-30-1-192 ~]$
```

Figure 6-18. *Exiting CQL Shell*

Stopping Apache Cassandra

To stop Apache Cassandra, stop the Docker container running the Apache Cassandra server.

```
sudo docker stop cassandradb
```

Subsequently, run the following command to list the running containers.

```
sudo docker ps
```

The cassndradb container does not get listed as running as shown in Figure 6-19.

```
[ec2-user@ip-172-30-1-192 ~]$ sudo docker stop cassandradb
cassandradb
[ec2-user@ip-172-30-1-192 ~]$  sudo docker ps
CONTAINER ID      IMAGE              COMMAND              CREATED
STATUS            PORTS              NAMES
[ec2-user@ip-172-30-1-192 ~]$ █
```

Figure 6-19. *Stopping Cassandra DB Docker Container*

Starting Multiple Instances of Apache Cassandra

Multiple Docker containers running Apache Cassandra instances may be started, but the container name has to be unique. As an example, start a new Docker container also called cassandradb to run another instance of Apache Cassandra database.

```
sudo docker run -t -i -v /cassandra/data:/var/lib/cassandra/data --name cassandradb -d -p
7000:7000  cassandra
```

Because a Docker container with the same name (cassandradb) was already created earlier, an error is generated even though the container has been stopped as shown in Figure 6-20. A container has to be removed with the docker rm command to be able to create a new container with the same name.

```
[ec2-user@ip-172-30-1-192 ~]$ sudo docker run -t -i --name cassandradb -d cassan
dra
Error response from daemon: Conflict. The name "cassandradb" is already in use b
y container dfade563f871. You have to delete (or rename) that container to be ab
le to reuse that name.
```

Figure 6-20. *Duplicate Docker Container name error*

Another container with a different name, cassandradb2 for example, may be started.

```
sudo docker run -t -i -v /cassandra/data:/var/lib/cassandra/data --name cassandradb2 -d -p
7000:7000  cassandra
```

Start a third container and specify the CASSANDRA_SEEDS environment variable for the IP address/es to be used to run multiple nodes in the cluster if required.

```
sudo docker run -t -i -v /cassandra/data:/var/lib/cassandra/data --name cassandradb3 -d -p
7000:7000 -e CASSANDRA_SEEDS=52.91.214.50,54.86.243.122,54.86.205.95 cassandra
```

Subsequently, run the following command to list the running containers.

```
sudo docker ps
```

The cassandradb2 and cassandradb3 containers get listed as running as shown in Figure 6-21.

```
[ec2-user@ip-172-30-1-192 ~]$ sudo docker run -t -i --name cassandradb2 -d cassa
ndra
3629909b411b927ccde3d5a42fcfbe1754e6f8c7f3acf90cea2505827c29eac8
[ec2-user@ip-172-30-1-192 ~]$ sudo docker run -t -i -v /cassandra/data:/var/lib/
cassandra/data --name cassandradb3 -d -p 7000:7000 -e CASSANDRA_SEEDS=52.91.214.
50,54.86.243.122,54.86.205.95 cassandra
d965cbf2ad18931d84f4df32dc2832704c92523f9f5e5199f5cd5ae1326dd308
[ec2-user@ip-172-30-1-192 ~]$ sudo docker ps
CONTAINER ID        IMAGE             COMMAND               CREATED
      STATUS          PORTS
            NAMES
d965cbf2ad18          cassandra            "/docker-entrypoint.s"    27 seconds ago
      Up 26 seconds       7001/tcp, 7199/tcp, 9042/tcp, 0.0.0.0:7000->7000/tcp, 9
160/tcp    cassandradb3
3629909b411b          cassandra            "/docker-entrypoint.s"    51 seconds ago
      Up 50 seconds       7000-7001/tcp, 7199/tcp, 9042/tcp, 9160/tcp
            cassandradb2
[ec2-user@ip-172-30-1-192 ~]$ █
```

Figure 6-21. *Running Multiple Docker Containers for Instances of Apache Cassandra*

Summary

In this chapter we use the Docker image for Apache Cassandra to run Apache Cassandra in a Docker container. We used the different CQL statements in a cqlsh shell to create a Keyspace, create a table in the Keyspace and add data to the table. We also ran CQL statements to query a table, delete data from the table, truncate a table, drop a table, and drop a keyspace. We also demonstrated creating multiple Docker containers to run multiple instances of Apache Cassandra. In the next chapter we shall run Couchbase Server in Docker.

CHAPTER 7

■ ■ ■

Using Couchbase Server

Couchbase Server is a distributed NoSQL database. Couchbase is a JSON (JavaScript Object Notation) based document store. Couchbase, like other NoSQL datastores, does not have a fixed schema for data storage. Couchbase differs from MongoDB in that MongoDB is based on the BSON (binary JSON) document data model. Couchbase provides a Web Console for accessing the Couchbase server from a graphical user interface (GUI). Couchbase also provides a command-line interface (CLI) including several tools to run in the CLI. In this chapter we shall run Couchbase server in a Docker container.

Setting the Environment

Starting Couchbase

Accessing Couchbase Web Console

Configuring Couchbase Server

Adding Documents

Starting Interactive Terminal

Running Couchbase CLI Tools

Stopping Couchbase Server

Setting the Environment

The following software is required for this chapter.

-Docker (version 1.8)

-Docker image for Couchbase (version latest)

We have used the Ubuntu Server AMI shown in Figure 7-1 for running software in this chapter. Installing and configuring an Amazon EC2 instance is discussed in Appendix A.

Figure 7-1. *Ubuntu Server AMI*

SSH Login to the Ubuntu Amazon EC2 instance using user as "ubuntu" and the public IP address of the Amazon EC2 instance. The public IP address would be different for different users (multiple public IP addresses are also used in this chapter based on multiple runs of the sample discussed).

```
ssh -i "docker.pem" ubuntu@54.152.90.139
```

We need to modify the IP address setting for localhost in the hosts IP addresses file /etc/hosts. Set the IP address to the public IP address of the Amazon EC2 instance. Obtaining the public IP address of an Amazon EC2 instance is discussed in Appendix A. Open the /etc/hosts file in a vi editor.

```
sudo vi /etc/hosts
```

Replace "127.0.0.1" with the public IP address; replace the following line:

```
127.0.0.1 localhost
```

with:

```
54.152.90.139 localhost
```

Install Docker on Ubuntu as discussed in Chapter 1. Run the hello-world Docker image to test the Docker installation.

```
sudo docker run hello-world
```

The output from the hello-world application is shown in Figure 7-2.

Figure 7-2. *Output from hello-world*

Download the official Couchbase Docker image called "couchbase".

```
sudo docker pull couchbase
```

The latest Docker image gets downloaded as shown in Figure 7-3.

```
ubuntu@ip-172-30-1-190:~$ sudo docker pull couchbase
sudo: unable to resolve host ip-172-30-1-190
Using default tag: latest
latest: Pulling from library/couchbase
c0de77b824d9: Pull complete
7f183271ade4: Pull complete
02cc7e934fcc: Pull complete
fd97fd3cdea7: Pull complete
d28869c6aca6: Pull complete
63bf59e0c713: Pull complete
b33db0ff9d8b: Pull complete
6aa99012b457: Pull complete
8828e29d95f0: Pull complete
28087ef36a81: Pull complete
618bca76e9ce: Pull complete
1e040ef5e848: Pull complete
da7f5c40fc89: Pull complete
541fbf32b9aa: Pull complete
ff61ecf3bacb: Pull complete
Digest: sha256:261cab57c6e40f1eb414abece1a70ea4ecce01d4640414b40868a1bdaee79a88
Status: Downloaded newer image for couchbase:latest
ubuntu@ip-172-30-1-190:~$ ▮
```

Figure 7-3. *Downloading Docker Image couchbase*

Starting Couchbase

Next, run a Docker container for Docker image "couchbase", which would start a Couchbase server process in the Docker container. Run the following docker command in which the port for the Couchbase Web Console to connect to Couchbase Server is specified as 8091. The container name is specified as "couchbasedb".

```
sudo docker run --name couchbasedb -d -p 8091:8091 couchbase
```

Couchbase server could require non-default ulimit settings.

Ulimit Setting	Value	Description
ulimit -n	40960	nofile: max number of open files
ulimit -c	100000000	core: max core file size. The 100000000 setting is equivalent to "unlimited", which is not directly supported.
ulimit -l	100000000	memlock: maximum locked-in-memory address space. The 100000000 setting is equivalent to "unlimited", which is not directly supported.

A Docker container stores all persistent data in the /opt/couchbase/var directory, which could be mounted from the host using the -v command parameter. The -ulimit command parameter is used to set the docker run command. Run the following command to run a Docker container to run a Couchbase server as shown in Figure 7-4.

```
sudo docker run --name couchbasedb -v ~/couchbase/data:/opt/couchbase/var -d --ulimit
nofile=40960:40960 --ulimit core=100000000:100000000 --ulimit memlock=100000000:100000000 -p
8091:8091 couchbase
```

Subsequently, list the running Docker containers.

```
sudo docker ps
```

The couchbasedb container gets listed as shown in Figure 7-4.

```
ubuntu@ip-172-30-1-251:~$ sudo docker run --name couchbasedb -v ~/couchbase/data
:/opt/couchbase/var -d --ulimit nofile=40960:40960 --ulimit core=100000000:10000
0000 --ulimit memlock=100000000:100000000 -p 8091:8091 couchbase
bff916e55a52395a65baf06e9cda5586ccfe7fd70dfed5396fc035d63686d00d
ubuntu@ip-172-30-1-251:~$ sudo docker ps
CONTAINER ID        IMAGE              COMMAND                CREATED
    STATUS          PORTS
                    NAMES
bff916e55a52        couchbase          "/entrypoint.sh couch"  6 seconds ago
    Up 5 seconds        8092-8093/tcp, 11207/tcp, 11210-11211/tcp, 0.0.0.0:8091
->8091/tcp, 18091-18092/tcp    couchbasedb
ubuntu@ip-172-30-1-251:~$ █
```

Figure 7-4. *Running Docker Container for Couchbase*

Output the logs for the container with the docker logs command.

```
sudo docker logs couchbasedb
```

The message shown in Figure 7-5 gets displayed.

```
ubuntu@ip-172-30-1-251:~$ sudo docker logs couchbasedb
Starting Couchbase Server -- Web UI available at http://<ip>:8091
```

Figure 7-5. *Listing Docker Container Log*

Accessing Couchbase Web Console

Next, we shall access the Couchbase Web Console from the URL indicated in the logs: http://<ip>:8091. The <ip> address to use would vary from which host system the Web Console is accessed. If on the same host as on which the Docker container is running, use the public IP address of the host Amazon EC2 instance. If on a remote host system as we have accessed, use the public DNS for the Amazon EC2 instance. Obtaining the public IP address and the public DNS are discussed in Appendix A. If the public DNS is ec2-54-152-90-139.compute-1.amazonaws.com, the URL to access the Couchbase WebConsole becomes the following.

```
http://ec2-54-152-90-139.compute-1.amazonaws.com:8091
```

Open a browser at the preceding URL. The Couchbase Console gets displayed as shown in Figure 7-6. In the next section we shall setup a Couchbase server cluster.

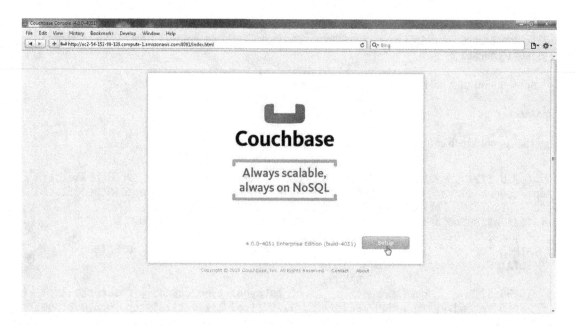

Figure 7-6. *Accessing Couchbase Admin Console*

If a Couchbase cluster has already been configured, the Couchbase Console URL would display the login page as shown in Figure 7-7.

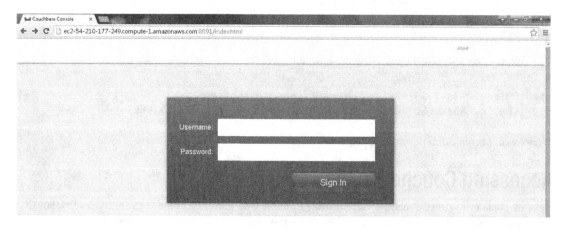

Figure 7-7. *Login Page*

Specify the Username (Administrator) and the Password and click on Sign In as shown in Figure 7-8.

Figure 7-8. *Specifying Username and Password*

Configuring Couchbase Server Cluster

In this section we shall configure the Couchbase Server cluster. Access the Couchbase Web Console as discussed in previous section and shown in Figure 7-6, with URL http://ec2-54-152-90-139.compute-1. amazonaws.com:8091. Click on Setup in the Web Console; the "Setup" page is displayed only the first time the Web Console is accessed. Subsequently, after a cluster has been configured the Login page is displayed as discussed in the previous section.

Use the default settings for the Configure Disk Storage section. In Configure Server Hostname specify the Hostname as the Public IP Address of the Amazon EC2 instance, which would be different for different users, as shown in Figure 7-9. Short names are not acceptable for the Hostname field and at least one dot is required in the host name.

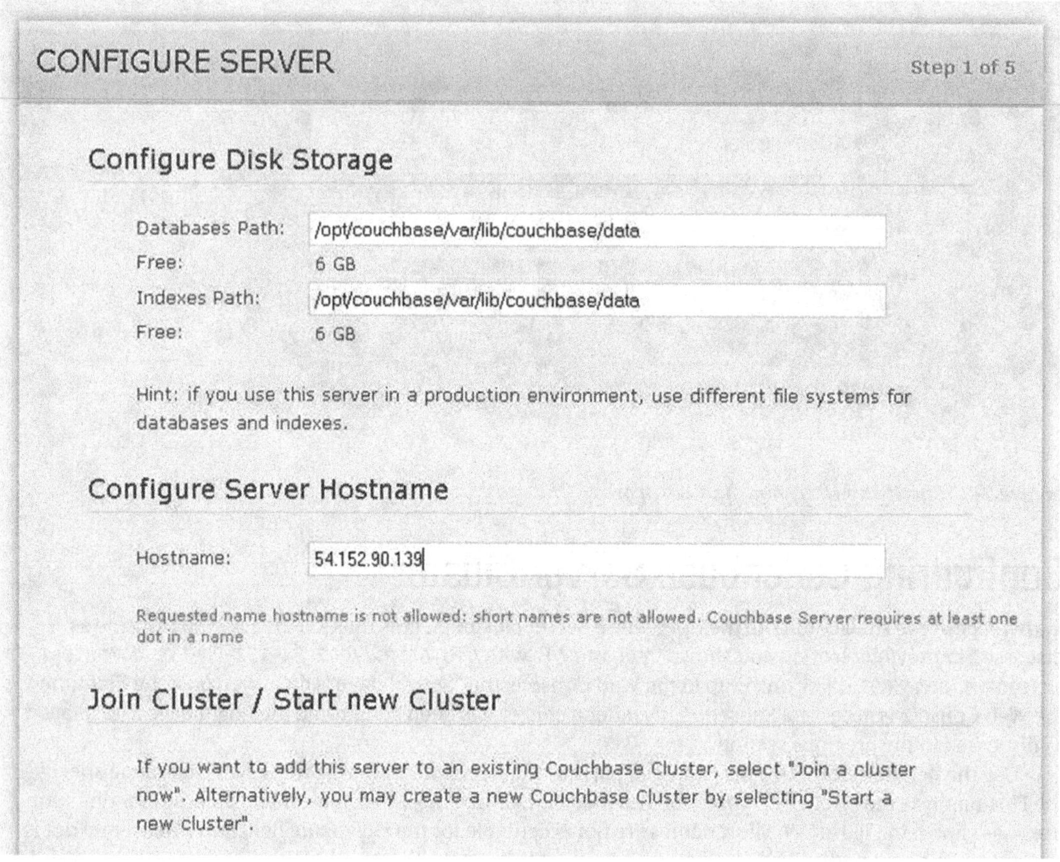

CONFIGURE SERVER

Step 1 of 5

Configure Disk Storage

Databases Path: /opt/couchbase/var/lib/couchbase/data

Free: 6 GB

Indexes Path: /opt/couchbase/var/lib/couchbase/data

Free: 6 GB

Hint: if you use this server in a production environment, use different file systems for databases and indexes.

Configure Server Hostname

Hostname: 54.152.90.139

Requested name hostname is not allowed: short names are not allowed. Couchbase Server requires at least one dot in a name

Join Cluster / Start new Cluster

If you want to add this server to an existing Couchbase Cluster, select "Join a cluster now". Alternatively, you may create a new Couchbase Cluster by selecting "Start a new cluster".

Figure 7-9. *Configuring Server*

Two options are provided in the Join Cluster/ Start new cluster section. As we are configuring a new cluster, select Start a new cluster as shown in Figure 7-10. Select the default settings or modify the settings keeping in consideration the total RAM configurable per server. Click on Next.

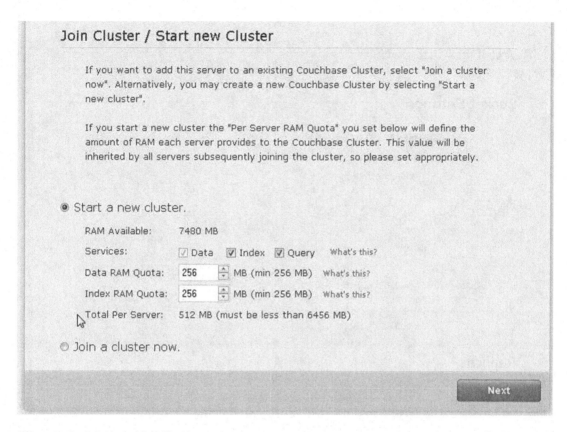

Figure 7-10. *Starting a New Cluster*

Couchbase server stores data in data buckets. In the Sample Buckets section the sample buckets are listed. A sample bucket is not required to be selected. Click on Next. In the Create Default Bucket screen the Bucket Name is pre-specified as "default". Select Bucket Type as "Couchbase". Select the default Memory Size & Replicas settings. Also select the default Disk I/O Optimization setting.

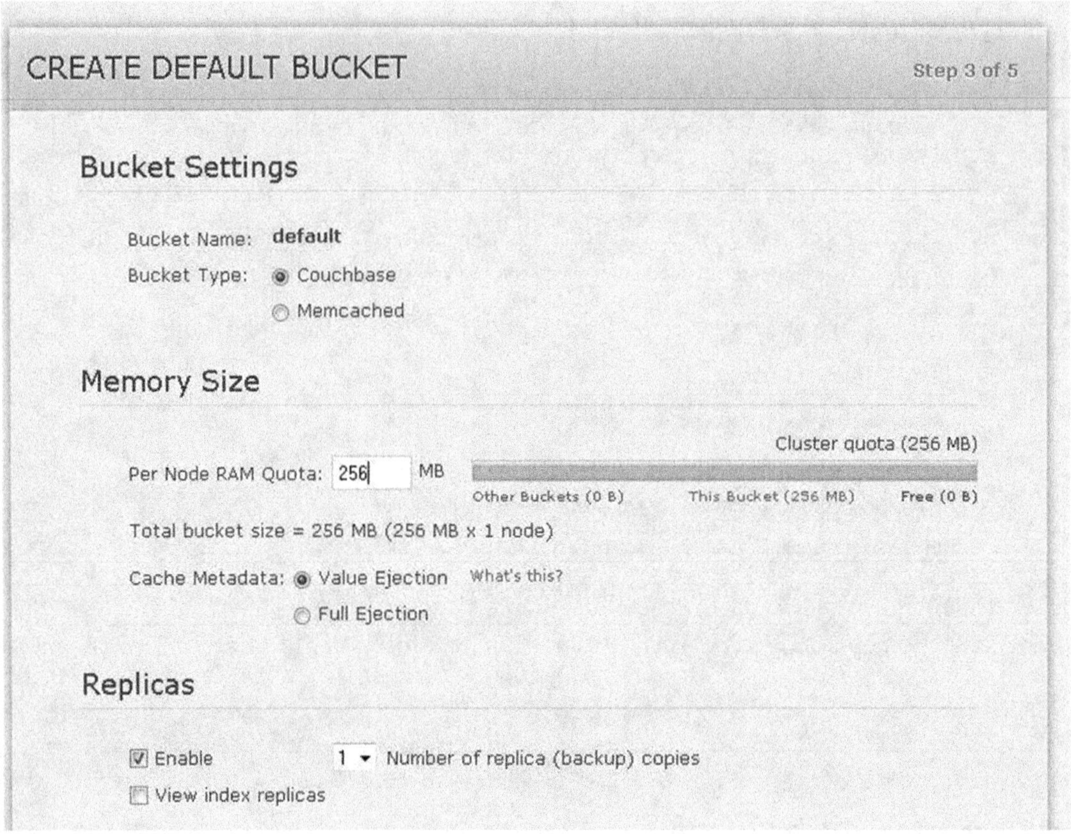

CREATE DEFAULT BUCKET   Step 3 of 5

Bucket Settings

Bucket Name: **default**

Bucket Type: ◉ Couchbase

              ○ Memcached

Memory Size

                                              Cluster quota (256 MB)

Per Node RAM Quota: 256 MB

Other Buckets (0 B)   This Bucket (256 MB)   Free (0 B)

Total bucket size = 256 MB (256 MB x 1 node)

Cache Metadata: ◉ Value Ejection   What's this?

               ○ Full Ejection

Replicas

☑ Enable   1 ▾ Number of replica (backup) copies

☐ View index replicas

Figure 7-11. *Configuring the Default Cluster*

In Flush select Enable and click on Next as shown in Figure 7-12. To be able to flush (delete) data from a bucket, 'Flush' must be enabled.

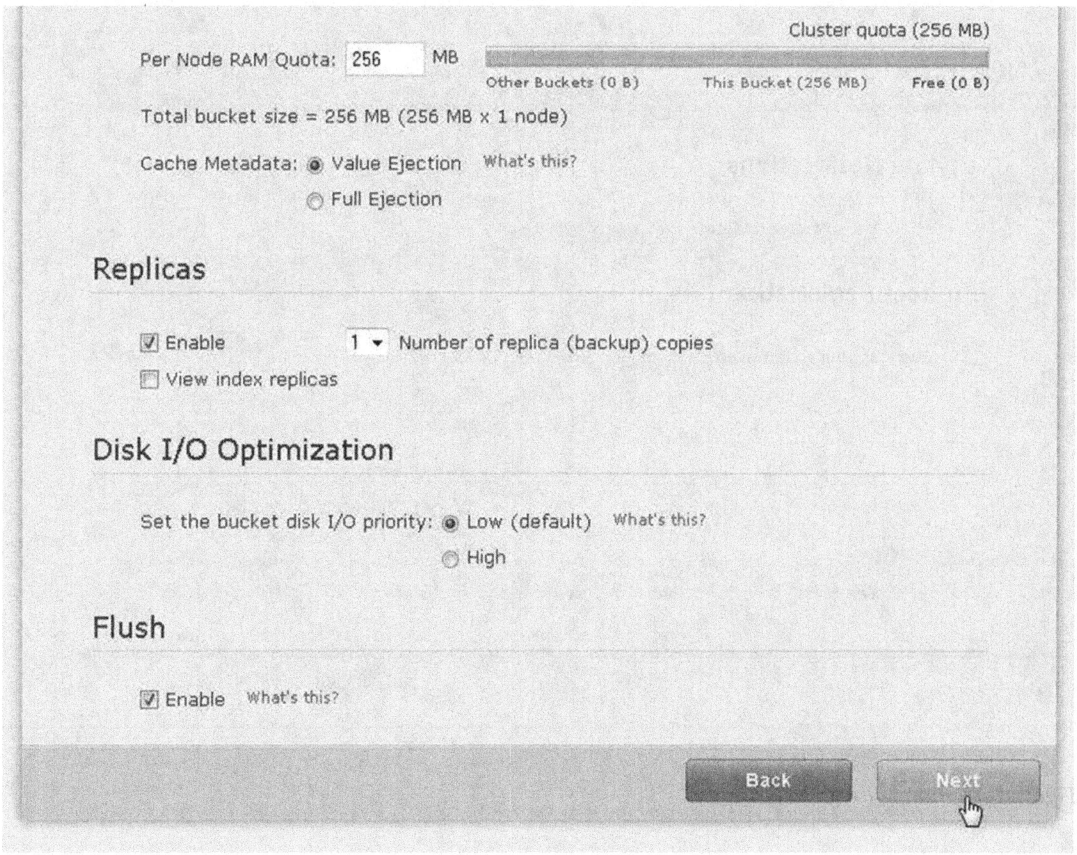

Figure 7-12. *Enabling Flush*

In Notifications, select the default settings and the "I agree..." checkbox and click on Next as shown in Figure 7-13.

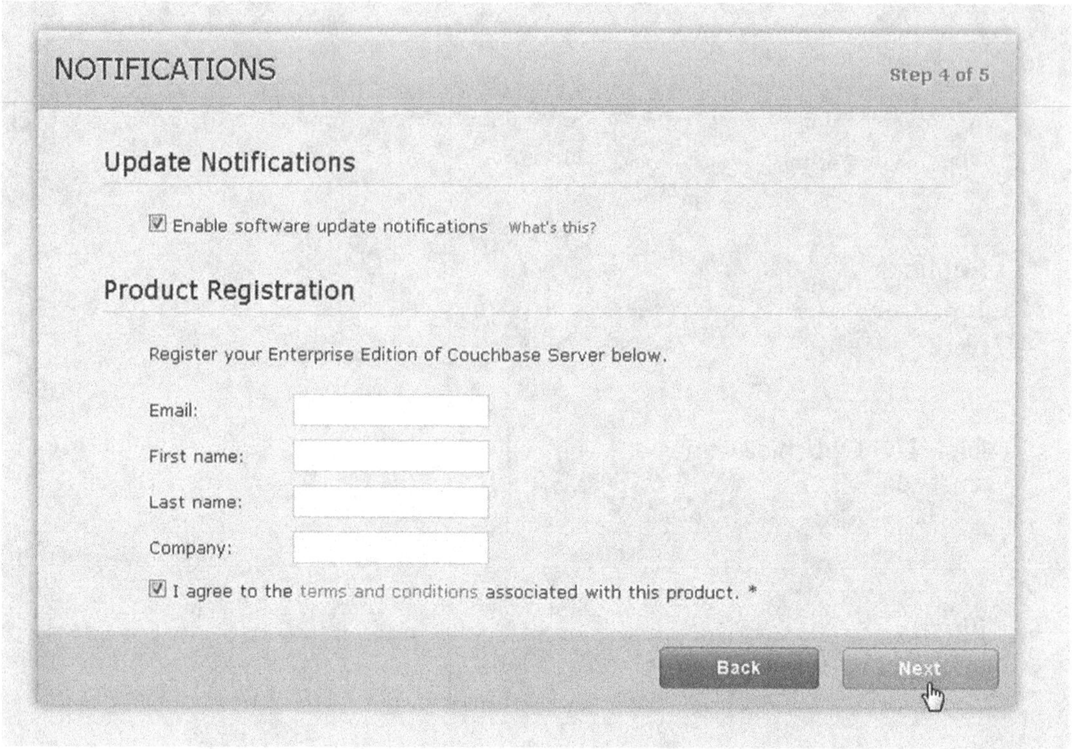

Figure 7-13. *Configuring Notifications*

In Secure this Server screen specify the Username as Administrator (default setting) as shown in Figure 7-14. Specify a password in the Password field and specify the same password in Verify Password field. Click on Next.

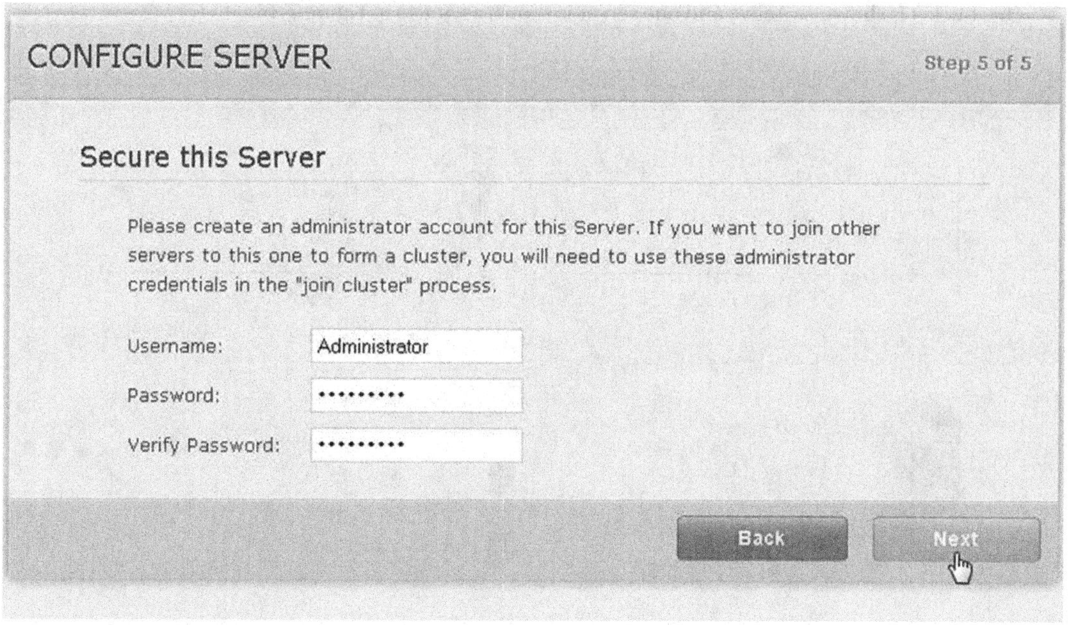

Figure 7-14. *Specifying Username and Password*

Click on the Cluster Overview tab to display the Cluster summary including the RAM allocated and in use, and the Disk storage allocated and in use as shown in Figure 7-15.

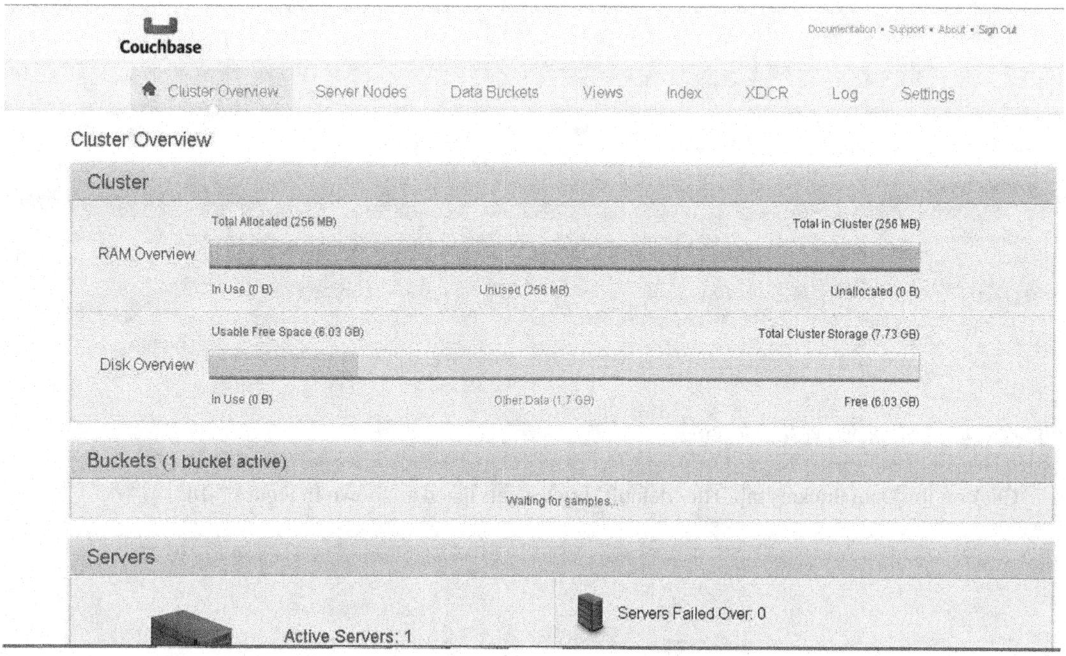

Figure 7-15. *Displaying Cluster Summary*

One bucket is shown as Active and one server is shown as Active in Figure 7-16.

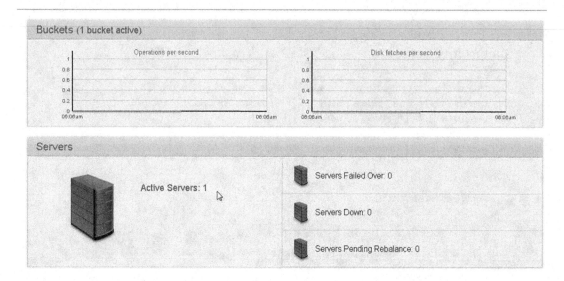

Figure 7-16. *Displaying Servers Summary*

Click on Server Nodes to list the server nodes. The server running at IP address 172.17.0.1 gets listed as shown in Figure 7-17.

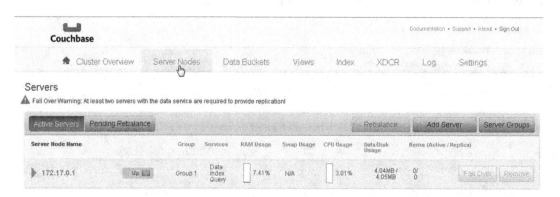

Figure 7-17. *Listing Server IP Address*

Click on the Data Buckets tab. The "default" bucket gets listed as shown in Figure 7-18.

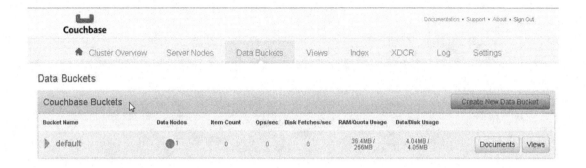

Figure 7-18. *Listing the Default Buckets*

Adding Documents

In this section we shall add documents to the Couchbase server from the Couchbase Console. Click on the Documents button for the default bucket as shown in Figure 7-19.

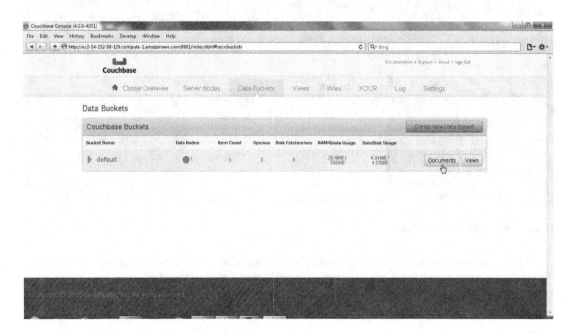

Figure 7-19. *Clicking on the Documents button*

In the default ➤ Documents no document is listed to start with. Click on Create Document button as shown in Figure 7-20.

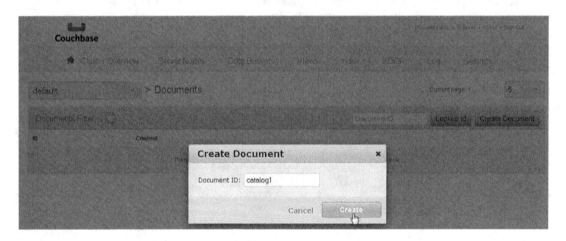

Figure 7-20. *Clicking on 'Create Document'*

In the Create Document dialog specify a Document ID, catalog1 for example and click on Create as shown in Figure 7-21.

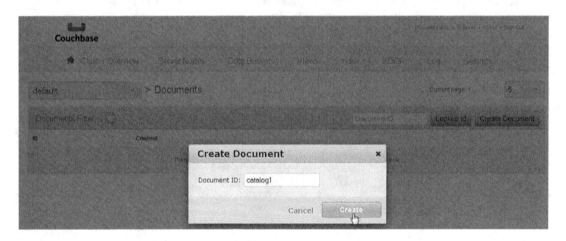

Figure 7-21. *Creating a Document*

A JSON document with Id catalog1 gets added to the default bucket as shown in Figure 7-22. The new document has some default fields, which would probably be required to be modified.

Figure 7-22. *New Document with ID as catalog1*

Replace the sample JSON document with the following JSON document.

```
{
  "journal": "Oracle Magazine",
  "publisher": "Oracle Publishing",
  "edition": "November-December 2013",
  "title": "Quintessential and Collaborative",
  "author": "Tom Haunert"
}
```

Click on Save to save the modified JSON document as shown in Figure 7-23.

Figure 7-23. *Saving a Couchbase Document*

The catalog1 JSON document gets saved and also formatted in the Couchbase Console as shown in Figure 7-24.

111

Figure 7-24. *Formatted JSON Document*

In Couchbase Buckets, the Item Count for the "default" bucket gets listed as 1 as shown in Figure 7-25. Click on the Documents button to display the documents in the default bucket.

Figure 7-25. *Item Count for default Bucket*

The catalog1 document gets listed as shown in Figure 7-26. Click on the Edit Document button to display the document JSON if required.

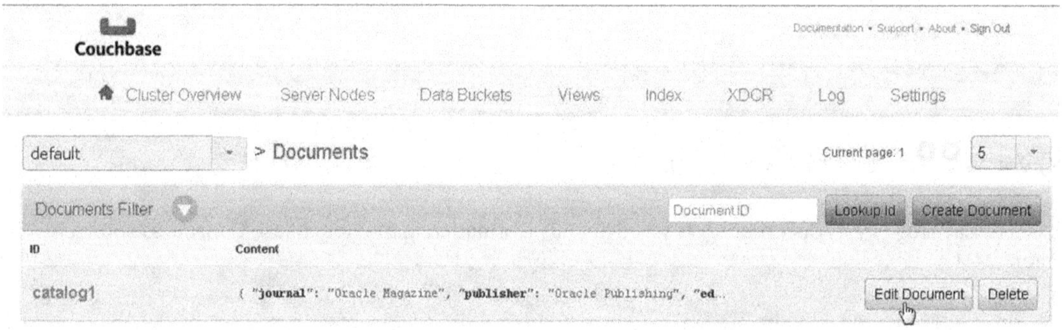

Figure 7-26. *Listing Documents in the default Bucket*

Similarly add another document with document id as catalog2. The JSON for `catalog2` document is as follows.

```
{
"journal": "Oracle Magazine",
"publisher": "Oracle Publishing",
"edition": "November December 2013",
"title": "Engineering as a Service",
"author": "David A. Kelly",
}
```

Add the JSON the sample document for `catalog2` as we did for the catalog1 document and click on Save as shown in Figure 7-27.

Figure 7-27. *Adding another JSON Document*

The two documents `catalog1` and `catalog2` get listed as shown in Figure 7-28.

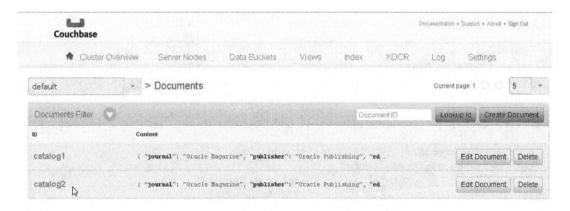

Figure 7-28. *Listing the Two Documents Added*

Starting Interactive Terminal

To access the Couchbase server from a command line, start the interactive terminal (tty).

```
sudo docker exec -it couchbasedb bash
```

The interactive shell gets started as shown in Figure 7-29.

```
ubuntu@ip-172-30-1-251:~$ sudo docker exec -it couchbasedb bash
root@bff916e55a52:/#
```

Figure 7-29. *Starting the Interactive Shell*

The interactive terminal may also be started using the container id instead of the container name.

```
sudo docker exec -it bff916e55a52 bash
```

Running Couchbase CLI Tools

Couchbase Server provides several command-line interface tools (CLI) to monitor and manage Couchbase server buckets, nodes and cluster.

Some of these CLI tools are the couchbase-cli tool for operations on the entire cluster, the cbbackup tool to create a backup, the cbdocloader tool to load JSON documents, and the cbtransfer tool to transfer data between clusters and data files on the host.

As an example, run the cbtransfer tool to transfer data from the Couchbase server to the stdout with the following command run from the tty.

```
cbtransfer http://ec2-54-152-90-139.compute-1.amazonaws.com:8091/ stdout:
```

The two JSON documents previously added to the Couchbase cluster from the Couchbase Console get output the stdout as shown in Figure 7-30.

```
ubuntu@ip-172-30-1-251:~$ sudo docker exec -it couchbasedb bash
<sfer http://ec2-54-152-90-139.compute-1.amazonaws.com:8091/ stdout:
set catalog2 0 0 157
{"journal":"Oracle Magazine","publisher":"Oracle Publishing","edition":"November
 December 2013","title":"Engineering as a Service","author":"David A. Kelly"}
set catalog1 0 0 162
{"journal":"Oracle Magazine","publisher":"Oracle Publishing","edition":"November
-December 2013","title":"Quintessential and Collaborative","author":"Tom Haunert
"}
  [###################] 100.0% (2/estimated 2 msgs)
bucket: default, msgs transferred...
          :              total |     last |    per sec
 byte    :                319 |      319 |      643.1
done
root@bff916e55a52:/#
```

Figure 7-30. *Running cbtransfer*

Stopping Couchbase Server and Container

To stop the Couchbase Server and container, exit the interactive terminal with exit command as shown in Figure 7-31.

```
root@bff916e55a52:/# exit
exit
ubuntu@ip-172-30-1-251:~$
```

Figure 7-31. *Stopping Couchbase Server*

In the host system, run the docker stop command to stop the Docker container.

```
sudo docker stop couchbasedb
```

Subsequently, list the running Docker containers.

```
sudo docker ps
```

The couchbasedb container does not get listed as shown in Figure 7-32.

```
ubuntu@ip-172-30-1-251:~$ sudo docker stop couchbasedb
couchbasedb
ubuntu@ip-172-30-1-251:~$ sudo docker ps
CONTAINER ID        IMAGE               COMMAND             CREATED
STATUS              PORTS               NAMES
ubuntu@ip-172-30-1-251:~$
```

Figure 7-32. *The Docker Container for couchbasedb does not get listed*

Summary

In this chapter we used the official Docker image for Couchbase Server to run a Couchbase Server instance in a Docker container. We accessed the Couchbase Sever from the Couchbase Console and added some JSON documents. Subsequently, we used the cbtransfer CLI tool to output the documents stored to the stdout. In the next chapter we shall discuss using Apache Hadoop.

■ ■ ■

Using Apache Hadoop

Apache Hadoop is the de facto framework for processing large data sets. Apache Hadoop is a distributed software application that runs across several (up to hundreds and thousands) of nodes across a cluster. Apache Hadoop comprises of two main components: Hadoop Distributed File System (HDFS) and MapReduce. The HDFS is used for storing large data sets and MapReduce is used for processing the large data sets. Hadoop is linearly scalable without degradation in performance and makes use of commodity hardware rather than any specialized hardware. Hadoop is designed to be fault tolerant and makes use of data locality by moving the computation to the data rather than data to the computation. MapReduce framework has two versions MapReduce1 (MR1) and MapReduce2 (MR2) (also called YARN). MR1 is the default MapReduce framework in earlier versions of Hadoop (Hadoop 1.x) and YARN is the default in latter versions of Hadoop (Hadoop 2.x).

> Setting the Environment
>
> Starting Hadoop
>
> Starting the Interactive Shell
>
> Creating Input Files for a MapReduce Word Count Application
>
> Running a MapReduce Word Count Application
>
> Stopping the Hadoop Docker Container
>
> Using a CDH Docker Image

Setting the Environment

The following software is used in this chapter.

> -Docker (version 1.8)
>
> -Apache Hadoop Docker Image
>
> -Cloudera Hadoop (CDH) Docker Image

As in other chapters we have used an Amazon EC2 instance based on Red Hat Enterprise Linux 7.1 (HVM), SSD Volume Type - ami-12663b7a for installing the software. SSH login to the Amazon EC2 instance.

```
ssh -i "docker.pem" ec2-user@52.23.207.240
```

Install Docker as discussed in Chapter 1. Start the Docker service.

```
sudo service docker start
```

An OK message indicates that the Docker service has been started as shown in Figure 8-1.

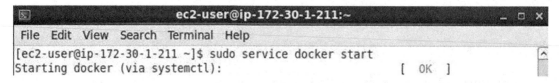

Figure 8-1. *Starting the Docker Service*

Add a group called "hadoop" and a user called "hadoop".

```
groupadd hadoop
useradd -g hadoop hadoop
```

Several Docker images are available for Apache Hadoop. We have used the sequenceiq/hadoop-docker
Docker image available from the Docker Hub. Download the Docker image with label 2.7.0 or the latest tag
image if different.
   sudo docker pull sequenceiq/hadoop-docker:2.7.0
   The docker pull command is shown in Figure 8-2.

```
[ec2-user@ip-172-30-1-211 ~]$ sudo docker pull sequenceiq/hadoop-docker:2.7.0
2.7.0: Pulling from sequenceiq/hadoop-docker
bf8622e5890e: Pulling fs layer
f378deb69e60: Pulling fs layer
e72ac57a5ca4: Pulling fs layer
5d32476d095f: Pulling fs layer
e8ef4721ce78: Pulling fs layer
4ba1516b7324: Pulling fs layer
9e15cf33fd16: Pulling fs layer
3c19d23c1a9a: Pulling fs layer
75161165b85c: Pulling fs layer
590c0e5d7008: Pulling fs layer
dbdb1b52f3da: Pulling fs layer
0c031babb191: Pulling fs layer
54ed83ba6569: Pulling fs layer
e1c1f4a38c78: Pulling fs layer
01c749264ddc: Pulling fs layer
368c32f0e407: Pulling fs layer
936e391b7ce3: Pulling fs layer
590e41abc605: Pulling fs layer
647ab508657a: Pulling fs layer
22a3743806b7: Pulling fs layer
d3b3ecea18e7: Pulling fs layer
bd6b151ceb45: Pulling fs layer
124bac6063a3: Pulling fs layer
6bec6cb9c97d: Pulling fs layer
a228dc98c941: Pulling fs layer
cf392acc6304: Pulling fs layer
8f59e3ab71c7: Pulling fs layer
a36807fd30e6: Pulling fs layer
```

Figure 8-2. *Running the docker pull Command*

The Docker image `sequenceiq/hadoop-docker` gets downloaded as shown in Figure 8-3.

```
┌────────────────────────────────────────────────────────────────────────────┐
│  ▣              ec2-user@ip-172-30-1-86:~                        _  □  ✕      │
├────────────────────────────────────────────────────────────────────────────┤
│  File  Edit  View  Search  Terminal  Help                                    │
│ a67dbdaa3483: Pull complete                                                  │
│ 7738d90ca912: Pull complete                                                  │
│ 999867c8eb92: Pull complete                                                  │
│ b25731f9c681: Pull complete                                                  │
│ d3758b55e6eb: Pull complete                                                  │
│ 13718e471b2d: Pull complete                                                  │
│ b08aadcc5362: Pull complete                                                  │
│ 316acd54632c: Pull complete                                                  │
│ 7acef3eb3f48: Pull complete                                                  │
│ 8be9869b36a0: Pull complete                                                  │
│ 8ac20a7a614b: Pull complete                                                  │
│ 446af44e8851: Pull complete                                                  │
│ de40cb5733bd: Pull complete                                                  │
│ d70a4c5c7d80: Pull complete                                                  │
│ d87ea7766237: Pull complete                                                  │
│ 7711f4bfbd4d: Pull complete                                                  │
│ 2d5ae4dfb209: Pull complete                                                  │
│ 1c48867840a2: Pull complete                                                  │
│ 7e7e85248613: Pull complete                                                  │
│ a6f24ed3591a: Pull complete                                                  │
│ 679730efaea5: Pull complete                                                  │
│ Digest: sha256:a40761746eca036fee6aafdf9fdbd6878ac3dd9a7cd83c0f3f5d8a0e6350c76a│
│ Status: Downloaded newer image for sequenceiq/hadoop-docker:2.7.0            │
│ [ec2-user@ip-172-30-1-86 ~]$ ▯                                               │
└────────────────────────────────────────────────────────────────────────────┘
```

Figure 8-3. *Downloading Docker Image sequenceiq/hadoop-docker*

Starting Hadoop

Next, start the Hadoop components HDFS and MapReduce. The Docker image `sequenceiq/hadoop-docker` is configured by default to start the YARN or MR2 framework. Run the following docker run command, which starts a Docker container in detached mode, to start the HDFS (NameNode and DataNode) and YARN (ResourceManager and NodeManager).

```
sudo docker  run -d --name hadoop sequenceiq/hadoop-docker:2.7.0
```

Subsequently, list the running Docker containers.

```
sudo docker ps
```

The output from the preceding two commands is shown in Figure 8-4 including the running Docker container for Apache Hadoop based on the `sequenceiq/hadoop-docker` image. The Docker container name is "hadoop" and container id is "27436aa7c645".

```
[ec2-user@ip-172-30-1-211 ~]$ sudo docker run -d --name hadoop sequenceiq/hadoop
-docker:2.7.0
27436aa7c645c0053dd5729ae73bb09bb988dc0341c496f55f30b3e708bfb92a
[ec2-user@ip-172-30-1-211 ~]$ sudo docker ps
CONTAINER ID        IMAGE                              COMMAND                 CR
EATED               STATUS              PORTS

            NAMES
27436aa7c645          sequenceiq/hadoop-docker:2.7.0   "/etc/bootstrap.sh -d"   9
seconds ago         Up 8 seconds           2122/tcp, 8030-8033/tcp, 8040/tcp, 8042/tc
p, 8088/tcp, 19888/tcp, 49707/tcp, 50010/tcp, 50020/tcp, 50070/tcp, 50075/tcp, 5
0090/tcp    hadoop
[ec2-user@ip-172-30-1-211 ~]$ ▮
```

Figure 8-4. *Running Docker Container for Apache Hadoop*

Starting the Interactive Shell

Start the interactive shell or terminal (tty) with the following command.

```
sudo docker exec -it hadoop bash
```

The interactive terminal prompt gets displayed as shown in Figure 8-5.

```
[ec2-user@ip-172-30-1-86 ~]$ sudo docker exec -it hadoop bash
bash-4.1# ▮
```

Figure 8-5. *Starting Interactive Terminal*

The interactive shell may also be started using the container id instead of the container name.

```
sudo docker exec -it  27436aa7c645 bash
```

If the –d command parameter is omitted from the docker run command and the –it parameters (which is –i and –t supplied together) are supplied using the following command, the Docker container starts in foreground mode.

```
sudo docker run -it --name hadoop sequenceiq/hadoop-docker:2.7.0 /etc/bootstrap.sh –bash
```

The Hadoop components start and attach a console to the Hadoop stdin, stdout and stderr streams as shown in Figure 8-6. A message gets output to the console for each Hadoop component started. The –it parameter starts an interactive terminal (tty).

```
[ec2-user@ip-172-30-1-211 ~]$ sudo docker run -it --name hadoop sequenceiq/hadoo
p-docker:2.7.0 /etc/bootstrap.sh -bash
/
Starting sshd:                                               [  OK  ]
Starting namenodes on [ebb125a12e13]
ebb125a12e13: starting namenode, logging to /usr/local/hadoop/logs/hadoop-root-n
amenode-ebb125a12e13.out
localhost: starting datanode, logging to /usr/local/hadoop/logs/hadoop-root-data
node-ebb125a12e13.out
Starting secondary namenodes [0.0.0.0]
0.0.0.0: starting secondarynamenode, logging to /usr/local/hadoop/logs/hadoop-ro
ot-secondarynamenode-ebb125a12e13.out
starting yarn daemons
starting resourcemanager, logging to /usr/local/hadoop/logs/yarn--resourcemanage
r-ebb125a12e13.out
localhost: starting nodemanager, logging to /usr/local/hadoop/logs/yarn-root-nod
emanager-ebb125a12e13.out
bash-4.1# ▮
```

Figure 8-6. *Starting Docker Container in Foreground*

Creating Input Files for a MapReduce Word Count Application

In this section we shall create input files for a MapReduce Word Count application, which is included in the examples packaged with the Hadoop distribution. To create the input files, change the directory (cd) to the $HADOOP_PREFIX directory.

```
bash-4.1# cd $HADOOP_PREFIX
```

The preceding command is to be run from the interactive terminal (tty) as shown in Figure 8-7.

```
[ec2-user@ip-172-30-1-86 ~]$ sudo docker exec -it hadoop bash
bash-4.1# cd $HADOOP_PREFIX
```

Figure 8-7. *Setting Current Directory to $HADOOP_PREFIX Directory*

Create a directory called /input in the HDFS for the input files. Subsequently, set the directory permissions to global (777).

```
bash-4.1# bin/hdfs dfs -mkdir  /input
bash-4.1# bin/hdfs dfs -chmod -R 777 /input
```

The preceding commands are also run from the interactive terminal as shown in Figure 8-8.

```
bash-4.1# bin/hdfs dfs -mkdir  /input
bash-4.1# bin/hdfs dfs -chmod -R 777 /input
bash-4.1# █
```

Figure 8-8. *Creating Input Directory*

Add two text files (input1.txt and input2.txt) with some sample text to the /input directory. To create a text file input1.txt run the following vi editor command in the tty.

```
vi input1.txt
```

Add the following two lines of text in the input1.txt.

```
Hello World Application for Apache Hadoop
Hello World and Hello Apache Hadoop
```

Save the input1.txt file with the :wq command as shown in Figure 8-9.

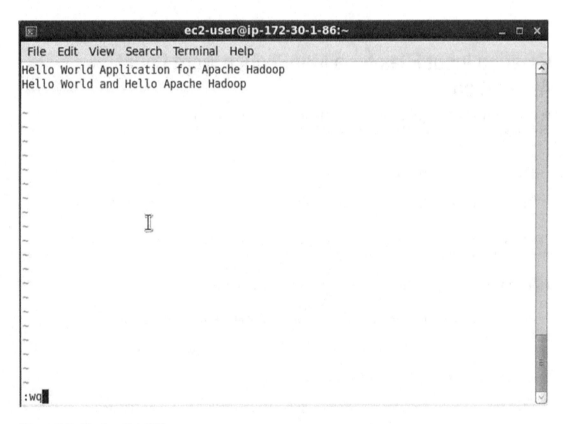

Figure 8-9. *The input1.txt File*

Put the input1.txt file in the HDFS directory /input with the following command, also shown in Figure 8-10.

```
bin/hdfs dfs -put input1.txt /input
```

```
"input1.txt" [New] 3L, 79C written
bash-4.1# bin/hdfs dfs -put input1.txt /input
bash-4.1# █
```

Figure 8-10. *Putting the input1.txt in the HDFS*

The input1.txt file gets added to the /input directory in the HDFS.
Similarly, open another new text file input2.txt with the following vi command.

```
vi input2.txt
```

Add the following two lines of text in the input2.txt file.

```
Hello World
Hello Apache Hadoop
```

Save the input2.txt file with the :wq command as shown in Figure 8-11.

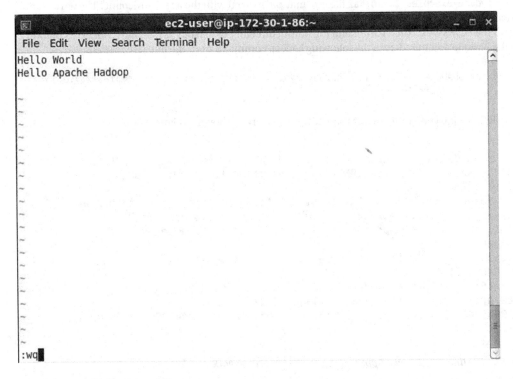

Figure 8-11. *The input2.txt File*

Put the input2.txt file in the HDFS directory /input.

```
bin/hdfs dfs -put input2.txt /input
```

Subsequently, run the following command to run the files in the /input directory.

```
bin/hdfs -ls /input
```

The two files added to the HDFS get listed as shown in Figure 8-12.

```
"input2.txt" [New] 3L, 33C written
bash-4.1# bin/hdfs dfs -put input2.txt /input
bash-4.1# bin/hdfs dfs -ls /input
Found 2 items
-rw-r--r--   1 root supergroup          79 2015-10-18 15:43 /input/input1.txt
-rw-r--r--   1 root supergroup          33 2015-10-18 15:45 /input/input2.txt
bash-4.1# 
```

Figure 8-12. *Listing the Input Files in the HDFS*

Running a MapReduce Word Count Application

In this section we shall run a MapReduce application for word count; the application is packaged in the hadoop-mapreduce-examples-2.7.0.jar file and may be invoked with the arg "wordcount". The wordcount application requires the input and output directories to be supplied. The input directory is the /input directory in the HDFS we created earlier and the output directory is /output, which must not exists before running the hadoop command. Run the following hadoop command from the interactive shell.

```
bin/hadoop jar $HADOOP_PREFIX/share/hadoop/mapreduce/hadoop-mapreduce-examples-2.7.0.jar
wordcount  /input /output
```

A MapReduce job gets started using the YARN framework as shown in Figure 8-13.

```
<mapreduce/hadoop-mapreduce-examples-2.7.0.jar wordcount  /input /output
15/10/18 15:46:17 INFO client.RMProxy: Connecting to ResourceManager at /0.0.0.0
:8032
15/10/18 15:46:19 INFO input.FileInputFormat: Total input paths to process : 2
15/10/18 15:46:19 INFO mapreduce.JobSubmitter: number of splits:2
15/10/18 15:46:20 INFO mapreduce.JobSubmitter: Submitting tokens for job: job_14
45197241840_0001
15/10/18 15:46:21 INFO impl.YarnClientImpl: Submitted application application_14
45197241840_0001
15/10/18 15:46:21 INFO mapreduce.Job: The url to track the job: http://fb25c4cab
c55:8088/proxy/application_1445197241840_0001/
15/10/18 15:46:21 INFO mapreduce.Job: Running job: job_1445197241840_0001
```

Figure 8-13. *Starting MapReduce Application with YARN Framework*

The YARN job completes as shown in Figure 8-14, and the word count application gets output to the /output directory in the HDFS.

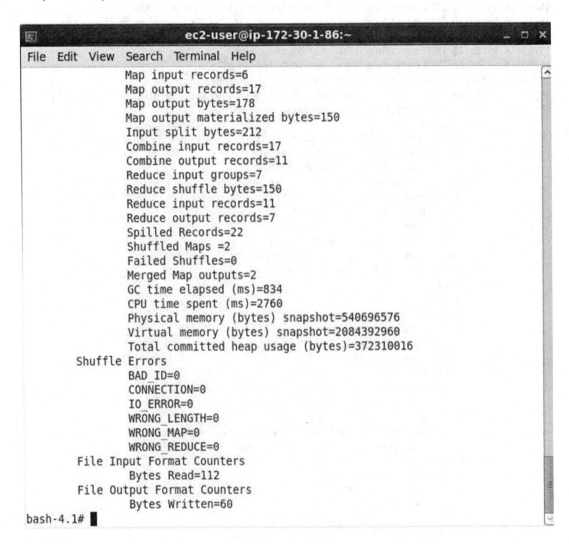

Figure 8-14. *Output from the MapReduce Application*

The complete output from the hadoop command is as follows.

```
<mapreduce/hadoop-mapreduce-examples-2.7.0.jar wordcount  /input /output
15/10/18 15:46:17 INFO client.RMProxy: Connecting to ResourceManager at /0.0.0.0:8032
15/10/18 15:46:19 INFO input.FileInputFormat: Total input paths to process : 2
15/10/18 15:46:19 INFO mapreduce.JobSubmitter: number of splits:2
15/10/18 15:46:20 INFO mapreduce.JobSubmitter: Submitting tokens for job:
job_1445197241840_0001
15/10/18 15:46:21 INFO impl.YarnClientImpl: Submitted application
application_1445197241840_0001
```

```
15/10/18 15:46:21 INFO mapreduce.Job: The url to track the job: http://fb25c4cabc55:8088/
proxy/application_1445197241840_0001/
15/10/18 15:46:21 INFO mapreduce.Job: Running job: job_1445197241840_0001
15/10/18 15:46:40 INFO mapreduce.Job: Job job_1445197241840_0001 running in uber mode :
false
15/10/18 15:46:40 INFO mapreduce.Job:  map 0% reduce 0%
15/10/18 15:47:03 INFO mapreduce.Job:  map 100% reduce 0%
15/10/18 15:47:17 INFO mapreduce.Job:  map 100% reduce 100%
15/10/18 15:47:18 INFO mapreduce.Job: Job job_1445197241840_0001 completed successfully
15/10/18 15:47:18 INFO mapreduce.Job: Counters: 49
        File System Counters
                FILE: Number of bytes read=144
                FILE: Number of bytes written=345668
                FILE: Number of read operations=0
                FILE: Number of large read operations=0
                FILE: Number of write operations=0
                HDFS: Number of bytes read=324
                HDFS: Number of bytes written=60
                HDFS: Number of read operations=9
                HDFS: Number of large read operations=0
                HDFS: Number of write operations=2
        Job Counters
                Launched map tasks=2
                Launched reduce tasks=1
                Data-local map tasks=2
                Total time spent by all maps in occupied slots (ms)=41338
                Total time spent by all reduces in occupied slots (ms)=11578
                Total time spent by all map tasks (ms)=41338
                Total time spent by all reduce tasks (ms)=11578
                Total vcore-seconds taken by all map tasks=41338
                Total vcore-seconds taken by all reduce tasks=11578
                Total megabyte-seconds taken by all map tasks=42330112
                Total megabyte-seconds taken by all reduce tasks=11855872
        Map-Reduce Framework
                Map input records=6
                Map output records=17
                Map output bytes=178
                Map output materialized bytes=150
                Input split bytes=212
                Combine input records=17
                Combine output records=11
                Reduce input groups=7
                Reduce shuffle bytes=150
                Reduce input records=11
                Reduce output records=7
                Spilled Records=22
                Shuffled Maps =2
                Failed Shuffles=0
                Merged Map outputs=2
                GC time elapsed (ms)=834
                CPU time spent (ms)=2760
                Physical memory (bytes) snapshot=540696576
```

```
            Virtual memory (bytes) snapshot=2084392960
            Total committed heap usage (bytes)=372310016
    Shuffle Errors
            BAD_ID=0
            CONNECTION=0
            IO_ERROR=0
            WRONG_LENGTH=0
            WRONG_MAP=0
            WRONG_REDUCE=0
    File Input Format Counters
            Bytes Read=112
    File Output Format Counters
            Bytes Written=60
bash-4.1#
```

List the output files in the /output directory in HDFS with the following command.

```
bin/hdfs dfs -ls  /output
```

Two files get listed: _SUCCESS, which indicates that the YARN job completed successfully, and part-r-00000, which is the output from the wordcount application as shown in Figure 8-15.

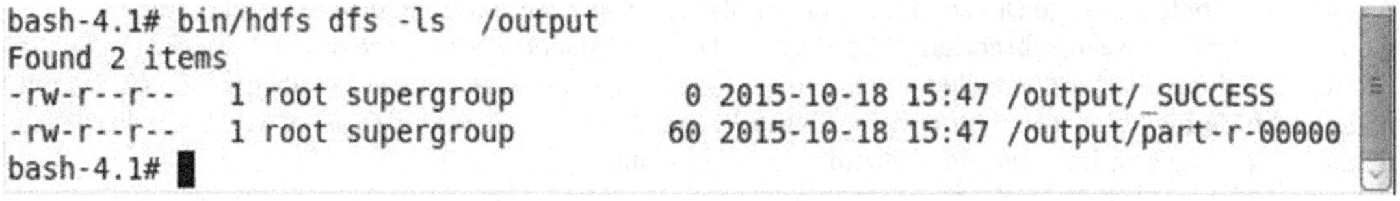

```
bash-4.1# bin/hdfs dfs -ls  /output
Found 2 items
-rw-r--r--   1 root supergroup          0 2015-10-18 15:47 /output/_SUCCESS
-rw-r--r--   1 root supergroup         60 2015-10-18 15:47 /output/part-r-00000
bash-4.1#
```

Figure 8-15. *Files Output by the YARN Application*

List the output from the wordcount application using the following command.

```
hdfs dfs -cat /output/part-r-00000
```

The word count for each distinct word in the input files input1.txt and input2.txt gets output as shown in Figure 8-16.

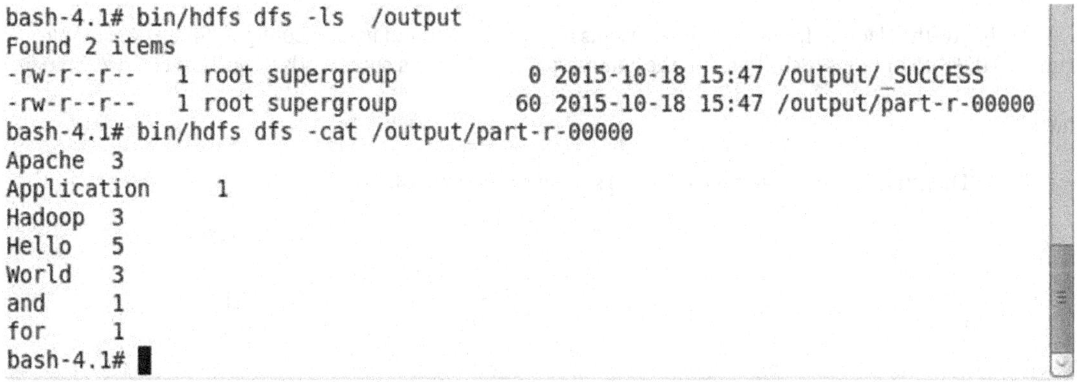

```
bash-4.1# bin/hdfs dfs -ls  /output
Found 2 items
-rw-r--r--   1 root supergroup          0 2015-10-18 15:47 /output/_SUCCESS
-rw-r--r--   1 root supergroup         60 2015-10-18 15:47 /output/part-r-00000
bash-4.1# bin/hdfs dfs -cat /output/part-r-00000
Apache   3
Application    1
Hadoop   3
Hello    5
World    3
and      1
for      1
bash-4.1#
```

Figure 8-16. *Listing the Word Count*

Stopping the Hadoop Docker Container

The Docker container running the Hadoop processes may be stopped with the docker stop command.

```
sudo docker stop hadoop
```

Subsequently run the docker ps command and no container gets listed as running as shown in Figure 8-17.

```
bash-4.1# exit[ec2-user@ip-172-30-1-86 ~]$ sudo docker stop hadoop
hadoop
[ec2-user@ip-172-30-1-86 ~]$ sudo docker ps
CONTAINER ID        IMAGE               COMMAND             CREATED
STATUS              PORTS               NAMES
[ec2-user@ip-172-30-1-86 ~]$ █
```

Figure 8-17. *Listing Running Docker Containers after stopping Apache Hadoop Container*

Using a CDH Docker Image

As mentioned before several Docker images are available for Apache Hadoop. Another Docker image, which we shall also use in subsequent chapters based on the Apache Hadoop Ecosystem as packaged by the Cloudera Hadoop distribution called CDH, is the svds/cdh Docker image. The svds/cdh image includes not just Apache Hadoop but several frameworks in the Apache Hadoop ecosystem, some of which are discussed in later chapters. Download the svds/cdh image with the following command.

```
sudo docker pull svds/cdh
```

Start a Docker container running the CDH frameworks.

```
sudo docker run  -d --name cdh svds/cdh
```

Start an interactive terminal to run commands for the CDH frameworks.

```
sudo docker exec -it cdh bash
```

In the tty, the Hadoop framework applications may be run without further configuration. For example, run the HDFS commands with "hdfs" on the command line. The hdfs commands usage is as listed as follows.

```
hdfs
```

The HDFS commands usage gets output as shown in Figure 8-18.

```
                                 root@86f0cf0a5c8d: /                    _  □  ×

File  Edit  View  Search  Terminal  Help

root@86f0cf0a5c8d:/# hdfs
Usage: hdfs [--config confdir] COMMAND
       where COMMAND is one of:
  dfs                   run a filesystem command on the file systems supported in
Hadoop.
  namenode -format      format the DFS filesystem
  secondarynamenode     run the DFS secondary namenode
  namenode              run the DFS namenode
  journalnode           run the DFS journalnode
  zkfc                  run the ZK Failover Controller daemon
  datanode              run a DFS datanode
  dfsadmin              run a DFS admin client
  haadmin               run a DFS HA admin client
  fsck                  run a DFS filesystem checking utility
  balancer              run a cluster balancing utility
  jmxget                get JMX exported values from NameNode or DataNode.
  mover                 run a utility to move block replicas across
                        storage types
  oiv                   apply the offline fsimage viewer to an fsimage
  oiv_legacy            apply the offline fsimage viewer to a legacy fsimage
  oev                   apply the offline edits viewer to an edits file
  fetchdt               fetch a delegation token from the NameNode
  getconf               get config values from configuration
  groups                get the groups which users belong to
  snapshotDiff          diff two snapshots of a directory or diff the
                        current directory contents with a snapshot
  lsSnapshottableDir    list all snapshottable dirs owned by the current user
                                          Use -help to see options
  portmap               run a portmap service
  nfs3                  run an NFS version 3 gateway
  cacheadmin            configure the HDFS cache
```

Figure 8-18. *hdfs Command Usage*

The configuration files are available in the /etc/hadoop/conf symlink as shown in Figure 8-19.

```
root@86f0cf0a5c8d:/etc# cd hadoop
root@86f0cf0a5c8d:/etc/hadoop# ls -l
total 12
lrwxrwxrwx. 1 root root     29 Jul  5 13:34 conf -> /etc/alternatives/hadoop-con
f
drwxr-xr-x. 2 root hadoop 4096 Jul  5 13:34 conf.empty
drwxr-xr-x. 2 root hadoop 4096 Jul  5 13:34 conf.impala
drwxr-xr-x. 2 root hadoop 4096 Jul  5 13:34 conf.pseudo
root@86f0cf0a5c8d:/etc/hadoop# █
```

Figure 8-19. *Listing the Symlink for the Configuration Directory*

The configuration files in the /etc/alternatives/hadoop-conf directory to which the conf symlink points are listed as follows as shown in Figure 8-20.

```
root@86f0cf0a5c8d:/etc/hadoop# cd /etc/alternatives/hadoop-conf
root@86f0cf0a5c8d:/etc/alternatives/hadoop-conf# ls -l
total 40
-rw-r--r--. 1 root hadoop  1104 Jun 25 02:18 README
-rw-r--r--. 1 root hadoop  2133 Jun 25 02:18 core-site.xml
-rw-r--r--. 1 root hadoop  1366 Jun 25 02:18 hadoop-env.sh
-rw-r--r--. 1 root hadoop  2890 Jun 25 02:18 hadoop-metrics.properties
-rw-r--r--. 1 root hadoop  2324 Jun 25 02:56 hdfs-site.xml
-rw-r--r--. 1 root hadoop 11291 Jun 25 02:56 log4j.properties
-rw-r--r--. 1 root hadoop  1549 Jun 25 02:18 mapred-site.xml
-rw-r--r--. 1 root hadoop  2375 Jun 25 02:18 yarn-site.xml
root@86f0cf0a5c8d:/etc/alternatives/hadoop-conf#
```

Figure 8-20. Listing the Configuration Files

The cdh container may be stopped with the docker stop command.

```
sudo docker stop cdh
```

Summary

In this chapter we ran Apache Hadoop components in a Docker container. We created some files and put the files in the HDFS. Subsequently, we ran a MapReduce wordcount application packaged with the examples in the Hadoop distribution. We also introduced a Cloudera Hadoop distribution (CDH) based Docker image, which we shall also use in some of the subsequent chapters based on frameworks in the Apache Hadoop ecosystem.

CHAPTER 9

■ ■ ■

Using Apache Hive

Apache Hive is data warehouse framework for storing, managing and querying large data sets. The Hive query language HiveQL is a SQL-like language. Hive stores data in HDFS by default, and a Hive table may be used to define structure on the data. Hive supports two kinds of tables: managed tables and external tables. A managed table is managed by the Hive framework while an external table is not. When a managed table is deleted, the metadata and the table data are deleted. When a Hive external table is deleted, only the metadata is deleted, and the table data is not since the table data is not managed by the Hive framework. Hive makes use of a metastore to store metadata about Hive tables. A Hive metastore database is used for the metastore and is the Derby database by default. The metastore database may be run in *embedded mode* or *remote mode*; the default being embedded mode. In this chapter we shall use a Docker image to run Apache Hive in a Docker container.

> Setting the Environment
>
> Starting Apache Hive
>
> Connecting to Beeline CLI Shell
>
> Connecting to HiveServer2
>
> Creating a Hive Table
>
> Loading Data into Hive Table
>
> Querying Hive Table
>
> Stopping Apache Hive

Setting the Environment

The following software is required for this chapter.

> -Docker (version 1.8 used)
>
> -Docker image for Apache Hive

We have used an Amazon EC2 instance to install the software. Install Docker as discussed in Chapter 1. SSH connect to the Amazon EC2 instance.

```
ssh -i "docker.pem" ec2-user@52.23.241.186
```

Start the Docker service and verify status of the Docker service.

```
sudo service docker start
sudo service docker status
```

Download the svds/cdh Docker image, which is the same as used in some the other Apache Hadoop Ecosystem chapters on Apache HBase, Apache Sqoop and Apache Spark.

```
sudo docker pull svds/cdh
```

Starting Apache Hive

To start Apache Hive, start a Docker container running the cdh processes or components. Run the following docker run command, which starts a Docker container in detached mode and assigns the name "cdh" to the container.

```
sudo docker run  -d --name cdh svds/cdh
```

List the running Docker containers; the "cdh" container should be listed.

```
sudo docker ps
```

Start an interactive terminal to run Apache Hive shell commands.

```
sudo docker exec -it cdh bash
```

Connecting to Beeline CLI Shell

Apache Hive provides the Hive CLI to access HiveServer1 from a command line interface. In latter versions of Hive, HiveServer1 has been deprecated and replaced with HiveServer2, and Hive CLI has been deprecated and replaced with Beeline CLI. While Hive CLI is an Apache Thrift based client, Beeline is a JDBC client based on the SQLLine CLI. With Beeline, the Thrift API is still used but not directly from the client; the Thrift API is used by the JDBC driver to communicate with HiveServer2.

Before using the Hive CLI or the Beeline CLI, we need to modify the permissions for the directory in HDFS in which Hive stores its data, the /user/hive/warehouse directory. Set global permissions (777) on the /user/hive/warehouse directory.

```
hdfs dfs –chmod -R 777 /user/hive/warehouse
```

The preceding command is run in the interactive terminal as shown in Figure 9-1.

```
root@86f0cf0a5c8d:/# hdfs dfs -chmod -R 777 /user/hive/warehouse
root@86f0cf0a5c8d:/# ▮
```

Figure 9-1. *Setting Permissions on the Hive Warehouse Directory*

If the Hive CLI is to be used, run the following command in the interactive terminal.

```
hive
```

The Hive CLI is started. A WARNING message is also output indicating that Hive CLI is deprecated and migration to Beeline is recommended as shown in Figure 9-2.

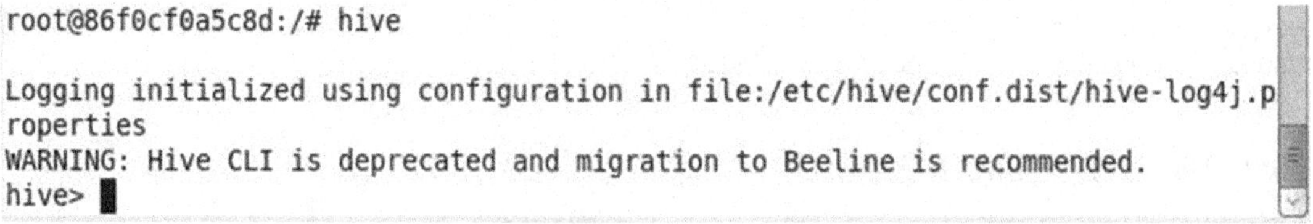

```
root@86f0cf0a5c8d:/# hive

Logging initialized using configuration in file:/etc/hive/conf.dist/hive-log4j.p
roperties
WARNING: Hive CLI is deprecated and migration to Beeline is recommended.
hive> 
```

Figure 9-2. *Message about Migration to Beeline*

We shall use the Beeline CLI in this chapter. Exit from the Hive CLI with the exit or quit command. Start the Beeline CLI with the following command.

```
beeline
```

Beeline version 1.1.0 CDH 5.4.3 gets started as shown in Figure 9-3.

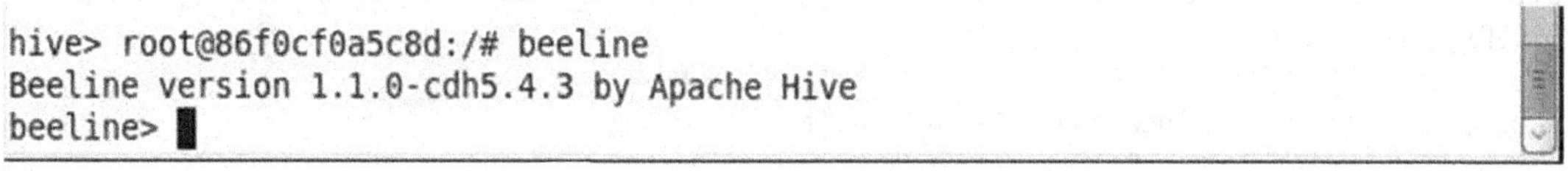

```
hive> root@86f0cf0a5c8d:/# beeline
Beeline version 1.1.0-cdh5.4.3 by Apache Hive
beeline> 
```

Figure 9-3. *Starting Beeline*

Connecting to HiveServer2

We started the Beeline CLI in the previous section, but we are not connected to the HiveServer2 yet. To demonstrate run the following commands.

```
use default;
show tables;
```

A "No current connection" message gets output as shown in Figure 9-4.

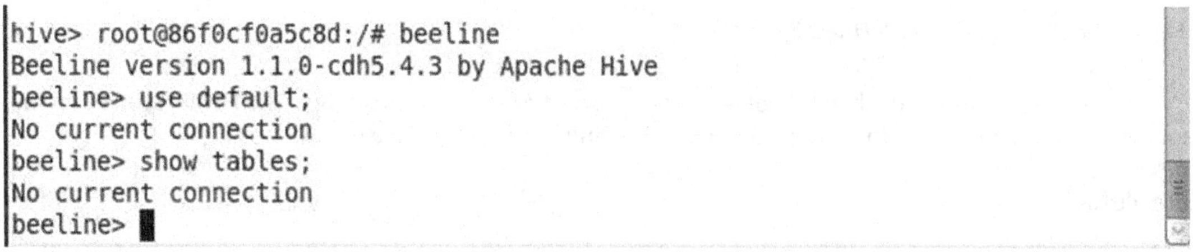

```
hive> root@86f0cf0a5c8d:/# beeline
Beeline version 1.1.0-cdh5.4.3 by Apache Hive
beeline> use default;
No current connection
beeline> show tables;
No current connection
beeline> 
```

Figure 9-4. *Message "No Current Connection"*

133

To connect to the HiveServer2, we need to run the !connect command. The !connect commanded usage may be output with the following command.

```
!connect
```

The !connect command usage gets output as shown in Figure 9-5.

```
beeline> !connect
Usage: connect <url> <username> <password> [driver]
```

Figure 9-5. *Command Usage for !connect*

HiveServer2 may be connected to in one of two modes: embedded or remote. The embedded mode may be used if the Beeline CLI is run on the same machine on which Hive is installed. The remote mode has to be used if the Beeline CLI is on a remote machine from the Hive. We shall use the embedded mode. The syntax for the connection url is the following in which the dbName is the Hive database and <host> and <port> are the hostname and port number for the HiveServer2.

```
jdbc:hive2://<host>:<port>/dbName
```

Run the following Beeline command !connect in which the connection url to HiveServer2 is specified first, followed by the username, password and the Hive JDBC driver. For the default username, password, and Hive JDBC driver specify and empty string "". The default Hive JDBS driver is org.apache.hive.jdbc.HiveDriver.

```
!connect jdbc:hive2://localhost:10000/default "" "" ""
```

A connection to Apache Hive 1.1.0 gets established as shown in Figure 9-6. Apache Hive 1.1.0 version is the renamed Hive 0.15.0 version.

```
root@86f0cf0a5c8d:/# beeline
Beeline version 1.1.0-cdh5.4.3 by Apache Hive
beeline> !connect jdbc:hive2://localhost:10000/default "" "" ""
scan complete in 16ms
Connecting to jdbc:hive2://localhost:10000/default
Connected to: Apache Hive (version 1.1.0-cdh5.4.3)
Driver: Hive JDBC (version 1.1.0-cdh5.4.3)
Transaction isolation: TRANSACTION_REPEATABLE_READ
0: jdbc:hive2://localhost:10000/default> █
```

Figure 9-6. *Connecting with Hive2 Server*

The Beeline commands that did not run previously get run after connecting to the HiveServer2. Run the following commands again to set the database as "default" and list the Hive tables.

```
use default
show tables
```

The database gets set to default and the Hive tables get listed. The database is already the "default" database as specified in the connection url and the use default command is run to demonstrate that the command gets run. No tables get listed as none have been created yet as shown in Figure 9-7. We shall create a table in the next section.

```
0: jdbc:hive2://localhost:10000/default> use default;
No rows affected (1.658 seconds)
0: jdbc:hive2://localhost:10000/default> show tables;
+-----------+--+
| tab_name  |
+-----------+--+
+-----------+--+
No rows selected (0.57 seconds)
0: jdbc:hive2://localhost:10000/default> ▮
```

Figure 9-7. *Listing Tables*

Creating a Hive Table

In this section we shall create a Hive table called "wlslog" with columns time_stamp, category, type, servername, code and msg, all of type string. Hive makes use of serializers/deserializers also called a *Serde*. A custom Serde may be used or the native Serde may be used. If a ROW FORMAT is not specified, the native Serde is used. If the ROW FORMAT DELIMITED is specified for delimited data files, the native Serde is used too. To separate fields with a ',' specify FIELDS TERMINATED BY ',' and to terminate a line of data with a newline, specify LINES TERMINATED BY '\n'.

Run the following CREATE TABLE command to create a Hive managed table; the command for a Hive external table is CREATE EXTERNAL TABLE.

```
CREATE TABLE wlslog(time_stamp STRING,category STRING,type STRING,servername STRING,code
STRING,msg STRING) ROW FORMAT DELIMITED FIELDS TERMINATED BY ',' LINES TERMINATED BY '\n';
```

A Hive table called wlslog gets created as shown in Figure 9-8. We have not used a PRIMARY KEY field in the wlslog table.

```
0: jdbc:hive2://localhost:10000/default> CREATE  TABLE  wlslog(time_stamp STRING
,category STRING, type STRING,servername STRING,code STRING,msg STRING) ROW FORM
AT DELIMITED FIELDS TERMINATED BY ',' LINES TERMINATED BY '\n';
No rows affected (0.831 seconds)
0: jdbc:hive2://localhost:10000/default> ▮
```

Figure 9-8. *Creating Hive Table*

Run the following command to describe the wlslog table.

```
desc wlslog;
```

The table structure consisting of the column names and data types gets listed as shown in Figure 9-9.

```
0: jdbc:hive2://localhost:10000/default> desc wlslog;
+-------------+-------------+----------+--+
|  col_name   |  data_type  | comment  |
+-------------+-------------+----------+--+
| time_stamp  | string      |          |
| category    | string      |          |
| type        | string      |          |
| servername  | string      |          |
| code        | string      |          |
| msg         | string      |          |
+-------------+-------------+----------+--+
6 rows selected (0.389 seconds)
0: jdbc:hive2://localhost:10000/default>
```

Figure 9-9. *Describing Table Structure*

Loading Data into the Hive Table

Next, we shall load data into the Hive table. Run the following INSERT HiveQL statement to add a row of data to the wlslog table.

```
INSERT INTO TABLE wlslog VALUES ('Apr-8-2014-7:06:16-PM-PDT','Notice','WebLogicServer',
'AdminServer','BEA-000365','Server state changed to STANDBY');
```

A MapReduce job gets started to load data into the Hive table as shown in Figure 9-10.

```
root@86f0cf0a5c8d: /                                    _ □ ✗
File  Edit  View  Search  Terminal  Help
0: jdbc:hive2://localhost:10000/default>
0: jdbc:hive2://localhost:10000/default> INSERT INTO TABLE wlslog VALUES('Apr-8-
2014-7:06:22-PM-PDT','Notice','WebLogicServer','AdminServer','BEA-000360','Serve
r started in RUNNING mode');
INFO  : Number of reduce tasks is set to 0 since there's no reduce operator
```

Figure 9-10. *Running the INSERT Command*

The MapReduce job consists of 1 mapper and 0 reducers. Data gets loaded into the default.wlslog table as shown in Figure 9-11.

```
INFO   : Hadoop job information for Stage-1: number of mappers: 1; number of redu
cers: 0
INFO   : 2015-10-20 20:17:07,076 Stage-1 map = 0%,   reduce = 0%
INFO   : 2015-10-20 20:17:20,929 Stage-1 map = 100%,   reduce = 0%, Cumulative CPU
 2.35 sec
INFO   : MapReduce Total cumulative CPU time: 2 seconds 350 msec
INFO   : Ended Job = job_1445367575035_0008
INFO   : Stage-4 is selected by condition resolver.
INFO   : Stage-3 is filtered out by condition resolver.
INFO   : Stage-5 is filtered out by condition resolver.
INFO   : Moving data to: hdfs://localhost:8020/user/hive/warehouse/wlslog/.hive-s
taging_hive_2015-10-20_20-16-49_585_3493713017925614717-2/-ext-10000 from hdfs:/
/localhost:8020/user/hive/warehouse/wlslog/.hive-staging_hive_2015-10-20_20-16-4
9_585_3493713017925614717-2/-ext-10002
INFO   : Loading data to table default.wlslog from hdfs://localhost:8020/user/hiv
e/warehouse/wlslog/.hive-staging_hive_2015-10-20_20-16-49_585_3493713017925614717
7-2/-ext-10000
INFO   : Table default.wlslog stats: [numFiles=8, numRows=8, totalSize=820, rawDa
taSize=812]
No rows affected (34.055 seconds)
0: jdbc:hive2://localhost:10000/default> █
```

Figure 9-11. *Loading Data into Hive Table*

The data in a Hive table is not constrained to have unique column values if a PRIMARY KEY is not specified, which we did not. A row with the same data may be added without a PRIMARY KEY in the table definition. Run the following INSERT statements to add 7 more rows of data including a row of data with duplicate column data.

```
INSERT INTO TABLE wlslog VALUES ('Apr-8-2014-7:06:16-PM-PDT','Notice','WebLogicServer','Admi
nServer,BEA-000365','Server state changed to STANDBY');

INSERT INTO TABLE wlslog VALUES ('Apr-8-2014-7:06:17-PM-PDT','Notice','WebLogicServer',
'AdminServer','BEA-000365','Server state changed to STARTING');
INSERT INTO TABLE wlslog VALUES ('Apr-8-2014-7:06:18-PM-PDT','Notice','WebLogicServer',
'AdminServer','BEA-000365','Server state changed to ADMIN');
INSERT INTO TABLE wlslog VALUES ('Apr-8-2014-7:06:19-PM-PDT','Notice','WebLogicServer',
'AdminServer','BEA-000365','Server state changed to RESUMING');
INSERT INTO TABLE wlslog VALUES ('Apr-8-2014-7:06:20-PM-PDT','Notice','WebLogicServer',
'AdminServer','BEA-000331','Started WebLogic AdminServer');
INSERT INTO TABLE wlslog VALUES ('Apr-8-2014-7:06:21-PM-PDT','Notice','WebLogicServer',
'AdminServer','BEA-000365','Server state changed to RUNNING');
INSERT INTO TABLE wlslog VALUES ('Apr-8-2014-7:06:22-PM-PDT','Notice','WebLogicServer',
'AdminServer','BEA-000360','Server started in RUNNING mode');
```

Querying Hive Table

Having created a Hive table and loaded data into the table, we shall query the table using a SELECT HiveQL statement. Run the following query in the Beeline CLI.

```
select * from wlslog;
```

The 8 rows of data get listed as shown in Figure 9-12.

```
0: jdbc:hive2://localhost:10000/default> select * from wlslog;
+--------------------------+-----------------+------------------+----------------
-------+-------------+--------------------------------------+--+
|      wlslog.time_stamp      |  wlslog.category  |   wlslog.type    | wlslog.serve
rname  |  wlslog.code  |              wlslog.msg               |
+--------------------------+-----------------+------------------+----------------
-------+-------------+--------------------------------------+--+
| Apr-8-2014-7:06:16-PM-PDT  | Notice          | WebLogicServer   | AdminServer
        | BEA-000365  | Server state changed to STANDBY  |
| Apr-8-2014-7:06:16-PM-PDT  | Notice          | WebLogicServer   | AdminServer
        | BEA-000365  | Server state changed to STANDBY  |
| Apr-8-2014-7:06:17-PM-PDT  | Notice          | WebLogicServer   | AdminServer
        | BEA-000365  | Server state changed to STARTING |
| Apr-8-2014-7:06:18-PM-PDT  | Notice          | WebLogicServer   | AdminServer
        | BEA-000365  | Server state changed to ADMIN    |
| Apr-8-2014-7:06:19-PM-PDT  | Notice          | WebLogicServer   | AdminServer
        | BEA-000365  | Server state changed to RESUMING |
| Apr-8-2014-7:06:20-PM-PDT  | Notice          | WebLogicServer   | AdminServer
        | BEA-000331  | Started WebLogic AdminServer     |
| Apr-8-2014-7:06:21-PM-PDT  | Notice          | WebLogicServer   | AdminServer
        | BEA-000365  | Server state changed to RUNNING  |
| Apr-8-2014-7:06:22-PM-PDT  | Notice          | WebLogicServer   | AdminServer
        | BEA-000360  | Server started in RUNNING mode   |
+--------------------------+-----------------+------------------+----------------
-------+-------------+--------------------------------------+--+
8 rows selected (0.477 seconds)
0: jdbc:hive2://localhost:10000/default>
```

Figure 9-12. *Running a SELECT HiveQL Statement*

Stopping Apache Hive

To stop the Apache Hive processes, run the docker stop command to stop the Docker container running the cdh frameworks.

```
sudo docker stop cdh
```

Summary

In this chapter we used a Docker image to run CDH frameworks including the Apache Hive framework in a Docker container. We started a Beeline CLI, which has replaced the Hive CLI and connected to the HiveServer2 from the Beeline CLI. We created a Hive managed table and loaded data into the Hive table. Subsequently, we queried the Hive table from the Beeline CLI. In the next chapter we shall use the Apache HBase Database in a Docker container.

CHAPTER 10

■ ■ ■

Using Apache HBase

Apache HBase is the Apache Hadoop database. Apache HBase is based on the wide column data store model with a table as the unit of storage. A table consists of one or more column families. Apache HBase is a schema-free NoSQL database. HBase stores data in the HDFS by default. In this chapter we shall use a Docker image to run Apache HBase in a Docker container. We shall use the svds/cdh Docker image, which we introduced in the Chapter 8.

> Setting the Environment
>
> Starting CDH
>
> Starting Interactive Shell
>
> Starting HBase Shell
>
> Creating an HBase Table
>
> Listing HBase Tables
>
> Getting a Single Table Row
>
> Getting a Single Row Column
>
> Scanning a Table
>
> Stopping CDH

Setting the Environment

The following software is required for this chapter.

> -Docker (version 1.8 used)
>
> -Docker Image for CDH

As in other chapters we have installed the software on an Amazon EC2 instance. SSH Login to the Amazon EC2 instance.

```
ssh -i "docker.pem" ec2-user@54.209.254.175
```

Start the Docker service.

```
sudo service docker start
```

Verify that Docker has started.

```
sudo service docker status
```

Download the svds/cdh Docker image if not already downloaded for the previous chapter.

```
sudo docker pull svds/cdh
```

The svds/cdh:latest Docker image gets downloaded as shown in Figure 10-1.

```
[ec2-user@ip-172-30-1-16 ~]$ sudo docker pull svds/cdh
Using default tag: latest
latest: Pulling from svds/cdh
de9c48daf08c: Pull complete
10de806794b2: Pull complete
031fd5268e85: Pull complete
0dc9ec408dd9: Pull complete
6adeac327f06: Pull complete
a4172715758c: Pull complete
6ec135e16988: Pull complete
d0aed77feb43: Pull complete
1e7f66f6f311: Pull complete
757082eae889: Pull complete
95119924abaa: Pull complete
4715b4ec211a: Pull complete
190d67765749: Pull complete
6bc9eaf71a3c: Pull complete
516bcbabdd00: Pull complete
c2ca5d25e887: Pull complete
81a9d08d9b11: Pull complete
8dc67cfb9d47: Pull complete
3f30741ab04b: Pull complete
b59a8b948d0b: Pull complete
6994ba23fe89: Pull complete
Digest: sha256:3e2a043497bdbb9b9b76f3193f830d255e1042ccb588b9052252818d7deaf83a
Status: Downloaded newer image for svds/cdh:latest
[ec2-user@ip-172-30-1-16 ~]$
```

Figure 10-1. *Downloading the svds/cdh Docker Image*

List the Docker images to verify that the svds/cdh image has been downloaded.

```
sudo docker images
```

Starting CDH

Start a Docker container to run the Apache Hadoop ecosystem frameworks, which include Apache HBase. Run the docker run command with the –d option, which starts the container in detached mode. The Docker container name is "cdh" as specified with the –name option.

```
sudo docker run  -d --name cdh svds/cdh
```

Docker container gets started as shown in Figure 10-2.

```
[ec2-user@ip-172-30-1-16 ~]$ sudo docker run  -d --name cdh svds/cdh
86f0cf0a5c8dd2d62878013bc47a1d9782538d8d93e4bceb4ea6e3ed3594add6
```

Figure 10-2. *Starting Docker Container*

List the running Docker containers.

```
sudo docker ps
```

The "cdh" container is listed as running as shown in Figure 10-3. The container id is also listed.

```
[ec2-user@ip-172-30-1-16 ~]$ sudo docker ps
CONTAINER ID         IMAGE               COMMAND              CREATED
    STATUS              PORTS
                    NAMES
86f0cf0a5c8d        svds/cdh                "cdh_startup_script.s"   25 seconds ago
    Up 24 seconds         8020/tcp, 8088/tcp, 8888/tcp, 9090/tcp, 11000/tcp, 1144
3/tcp, 19888/tcp    cdh
[ec2-user@ip-172-30-1-16 ~]$ █
```

Figure 10-3. *Listing the Running Docker Containers*

Starting Interactive Shell

Next, start an interactive terminal (tty) to run the HBase shell in.

```
sudo docker exec -it cdh bash
```

An interactive terminal gets started and the command prompt becomes root@86f0cf0a5c8d as shown in Figure 10-4.

```
[ec2-user@ip-172-30-1-16 ~]$ sudo docker exec -it cdh bash
root@86f0cf0a5c8d:/# []
```

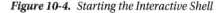

Figure 10-4. *Starting the Interactive Shell*

The interactive shell may also be started using the container id instead of the container name.

```
sudo docker exec -it 86f0cfoa5c8d bash
```

Starting HBase Shell

Next, start the HBase shell with the following command run in the interactive terminal.

```
bin/hbase shell
```

HBase shell gets started as shown in Figure 10-5.

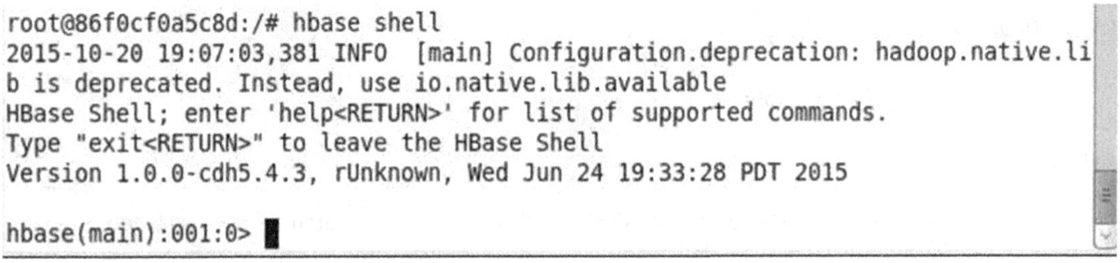

```
root@86f0cf0a5c8d:/# hbase shell
2015-10-20 19:07:03,381 INFO  [main] Configuration.deprecation: hadoop.native.li
b is deprecated. Instead, use io.native.lib.available
HBase Shell; enter 'help<RETURN>' for list of supported commands.
Type "exit<RETURN>" to leave the HBase Shell
Version 1.0.0-cdh5.4.3, rUnknown, Wed Jun 24 19:33:28 PDT 2015

hbase(main):001:0>
```

Figure 10-5. *Starting the HBase Shell*

Creating a HBase Table

Create an HBase table using the "create" command. In addition to the table name, provide the column family or column families and a dictionary of specifications for each column family. Optionally, provide a dictionary of table configuration. As an example, create a table called 'wlslog' with a column family called 'log'.

```
create 'wlslog' , 'log'
```

HBase table 'wlslog' gets created as shown in Figure 10-6.

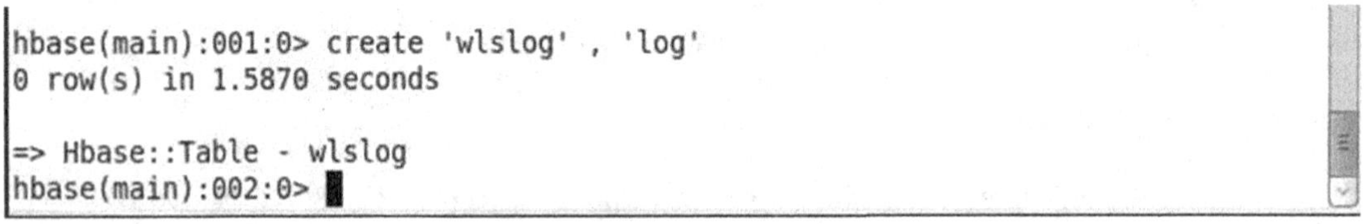

```
hbase(main):001:0> create 'wlslog' , 'log'
0 row(s) in 1.5870 seconds

=> Hbase::Table - wlslog
hbase(main):002:0>
```

Figure 10-6. *Creating an HBase Table*

Add cell values at table/row/column coordinates using the put command. Add 7 rows of data with the following put commands. Apache HBase and the other Apache Hadoop ecosystem software are designed for large quantities of data, which could be millions of rows of data, but only a sample of data is being added to demonstrate the use of Apache HBase.

```
put 'wlslog', 'log1', 'log:time_stamp', 'Apr-8-2014-7:06:16-PM-PDT'
put 'wlslog', 'log1', 'log:category', 'Notice'
put 'wlslog', 'log1', 'log:type', 'WeblogicServer'
put 'wlslog', 'log1', 'log:servername', 'AdminServer'
put 'wlslog', 'log1', 'log:code', 'BEA-000365'
put 'wlslog', 'log1', 'log:msg', 'Server state changed to STANDBY'

put 'wlslog', 'log2', 'log:time_stamp', 'Apr-8-2014-7:06:17-PM-PDT'
put 'wlslog', 'log2', 'log:category', 'Notice'
put 'wlslog', 'log2', 'log:type', 'WeblogicServer'
put 'wlslog', 'log2', 'log:servername', 'AdminServer'
put 'wlslog', 'log2', 'log:code', 'BEA-000365'
put 'wlslog', 'log2', 'log:msg', 'Server state changed to STARTING'

put 'wlslog', 'log3', 'log:time_stamp', 'Apr-8-2014-7:06:18-PM-PDT'
put 'wlslog', 'log3', 'log:category', 'Notice'
put 'wlslog', 'log3', 'log:type', 'WeblogicServer'
put 'wlslog', 'log3', 'log:servername', 'AdminServer'
put 'wlslog', 'log3', 'log:code', 'BEA-000365'
put 'wlslog', 'log3', 'log:msg', 'Server state changed to ADMIN'

put 'wlslog', 'log4', 'log:time_stamp', 'Apr-8-2014-7:06:19-PM-PDT'
put 'wlslog', 'log4', 'log:category', 'Notice'
put 'wlslog', 'log4', 'log:type', 'WeblogicServer'
put 'wlslog', 'log4', 'log:servername', 'AdminServer'
put 'wlslog', 'log4', 'log:code', 'BEA-000365'
put 'wlslog', 'log4', 'log:msg', 'Server state changed to RESUMING'

put 'wlslog', 'log5', 'log:time_stamp', 'Apr-8-2014-7:06:20-PM-PDT'
put 'wlslog', 'log5', 'log:category', 'Notice'
put 'wlslog', 'log5', 'log:type', 'WeblogicServer'
put 'wlslog', 'log5', 'log:servername', 'AdminServer'
put 'wlslog', 'log5', 'log:code', 'BEA-000331'
put 'wlslog', 'log5', 'log:msg', 'Started Weblogic AdminServer'

put 'wlslog', 'log6', 'log:time_stamp', 'Apr-8-2014-7:06:21-PM-PDT'
put 'wlslog', 'log6', 'log:category', 'Notice'
put 'wlslog', 'log6', 'log:type', 'WeblogicServer'
put 'wlslog', 'log6', 'log:servername', 'AdminServer'
put 'wlslog', 'log6', 'log:code', 'BEA-000365'
put 'wlslog', 'log6', 'log:msg', 'Server state changed to RUNNING'

put 'wlslog', 'log7', 'log:time_stamp', 'Apr-8-2014-7:06:22-PM-PDT'
put 'wlslog', 'log7', 'log:category', 'Notice'
put 'wlslog', 'log7', 'log:type', 'WeblogicServer'
put 'wlslog', 'log7', 'log:servername', 'AdminServer'
put 'wlslog', 'log7', 'log:code', 'BEA-000360'
put 'wlslog', 'log7', 'log:msg', 'Server started in RUNNING mode'
```

Data gets added to the 'wlslog' table as shown in Figure 10-7.

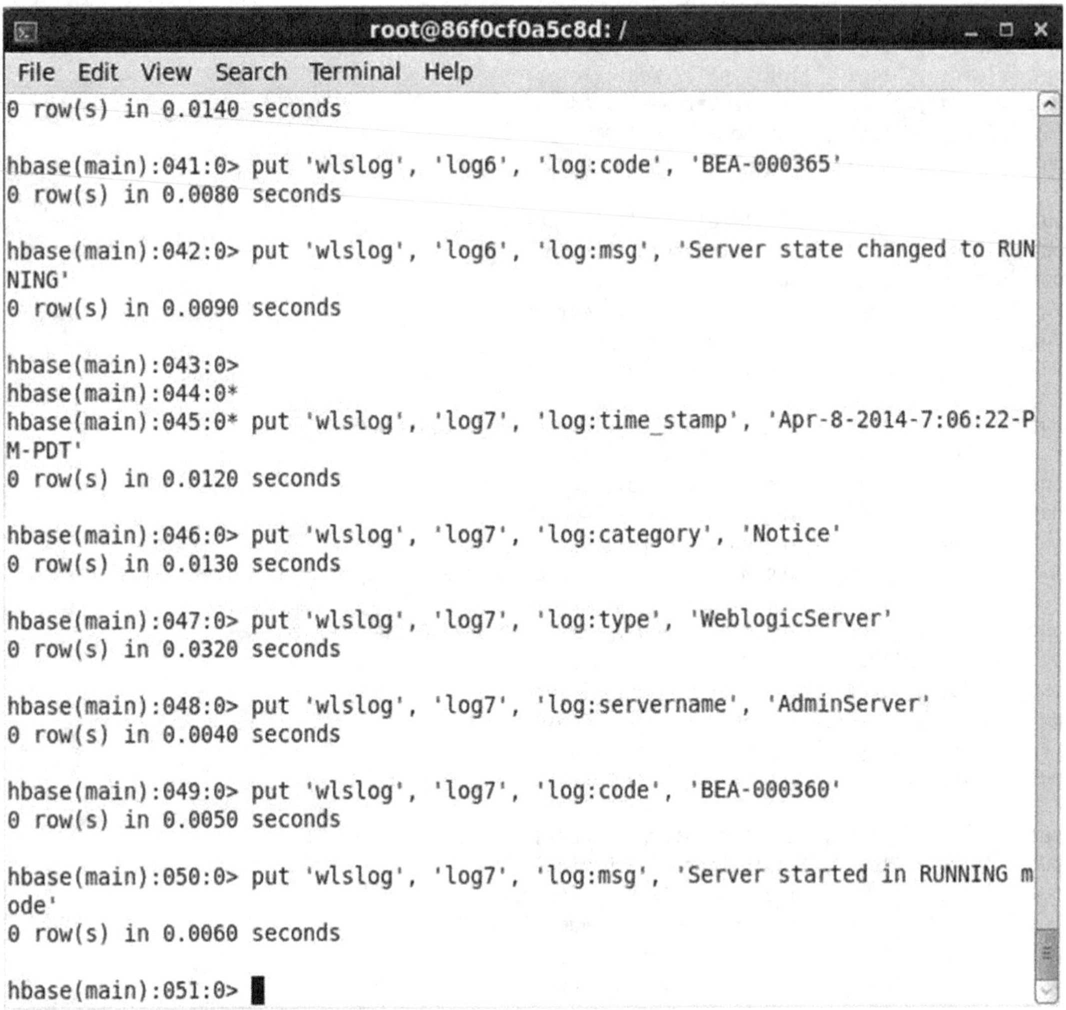
root@86f0cf0a5c8d: /
File Edit View Search Terminal Help
0 row(s) in 0.0140 seconds
hbase(main):041:0> put 'wlslog', 'log6', 'log:code', 'BEA-000365'
0 row(s) in 0.0080 seconds
hbase(main):042:0> put 'wlslog', 'log6', 'log:msg', 'Server state changed to RUN
NING'
0 row(s) in 0.0090 seconds
hbase(main):043:0>
hbase(main):044:0*
hbase(main):045:0* put 'wlslog', 'log7', 'log:time_stamp', 'Apr-8-2014-7:06:22-P
M-PDT'
0 row(s) in 0.0120 seconds
hbase(main):046:0> put 'wlslog', 'log7', 'log:category', 'Notice'
0 row(s) in 0.0130 seconds
hbase(main):047:0> put 'wlslog', 'log7', 'log:type', 'WeblogicServer'
0 row(s) in 0.0320 seconds
hbase(main):048:0> put 'wlslog', 'log7', 'log:servername', 'AdminServer'
0 row(s) in 0.0040 seconds
hbase(main):049:0> put 'wlslog', 'log7', 'log:code', 'BEA-000360'
0 row(s) in 0.0050 seconds
hbase(main):050:0> put 'wlslog', 'log7', 'log:msg', 'Server started in RUNNING m
ode'
0 row(s) in 0.0060 seconds
hbase(main):051:0>

Figure 10-7. *Adding Data to HBase Table*

Listing HBase Tables

List the tables with the following command run in HBase shell.

```
list
```

One table, the 'wlslog' table, gets listed as shown in Figure 10-8.

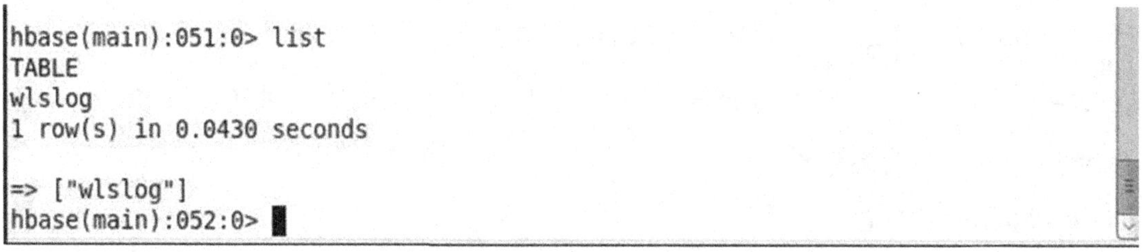

```
hbase(main):051:0> list
TABLE
wlslog
1 row(s) in 0.0430 seconds

=> ["wlslog"]
hbase(main):052:0> █
```

Figure 10-8. *Listing HBase Tables*

Getting A Single Table Row

The get command is used to get the data in a row or a column cell. Run the following get command to get the data in row 'log7' in table 'wlslog'.

```
get 'wlslog', 'log7'
```

A single row of data gets listed as shown in Figure 10-9.

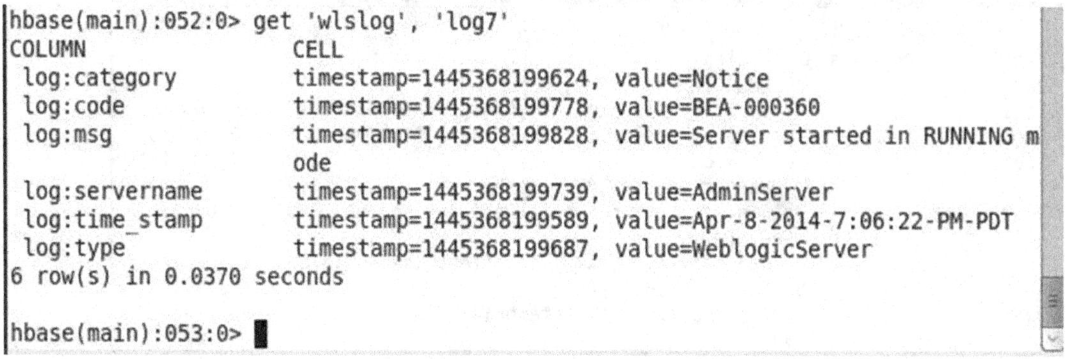

```
hbase(main):052:0> get 'wlslog', 'log7'
COLUMN                   CELL
 log:category            timestamp=1445368199624, value=Notice
 log:code                timestamp=1445368199778, value=BEA-000360
 log:msg                 timestamp=1445368199828, value=Server started in RUNNING m
                         ode
 log:servername          timestamp=1445368199739, value=AdminServer
 log:time_stamp          timestamp=1445368199589, value=Apr-8-2014-7:06:22-PM-PDT
 log:type                timestamp=1445368199687, value=WeblogicServer
6 row(s) in 0.0370 seconds

hbase(main):053:0> █
```

Figure 10-9. *Getting a Single Table Row*

Getting A Single Row Column

Optionally, a dictionary of columns may be supplied to the get command. For example, get the column data from the wlslog table from the 'log5' row in the log.msg column.

```
get  'wlslog', 'log5', {COLUMNS=>['log:msg']}
```

The log.msg column data from row 'log5' from table 'wlslog' gets output as shown in Figure 10-10.

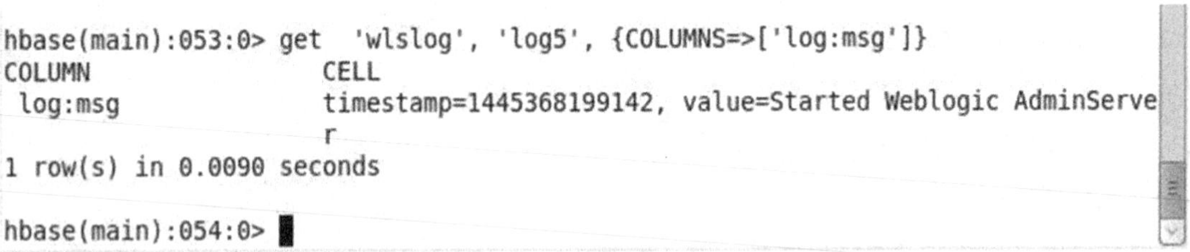

```
hbase(main):053:0> get 'wlslog', 'log5', {COLUMNS=>['log:msg']}
COLUMN                    CELL
 log:msg                    timestamp=1445368199142, value=Started Weblogic AdminServe
                            r
1 row(s) in 0.0090 seconds

hbase(main):054:0> █
```

Figure 10-10. Getting a Single Row Column Value

Scanning a Table

The scan command is used to scan a table to get all the data in the table. Optionally a dictionary of scanner specifications may be provided, which are omitted from the following command.

```
scan 'wlslog'
```

Row ➤ column data for each row gets output as shown in Figure 10-11.

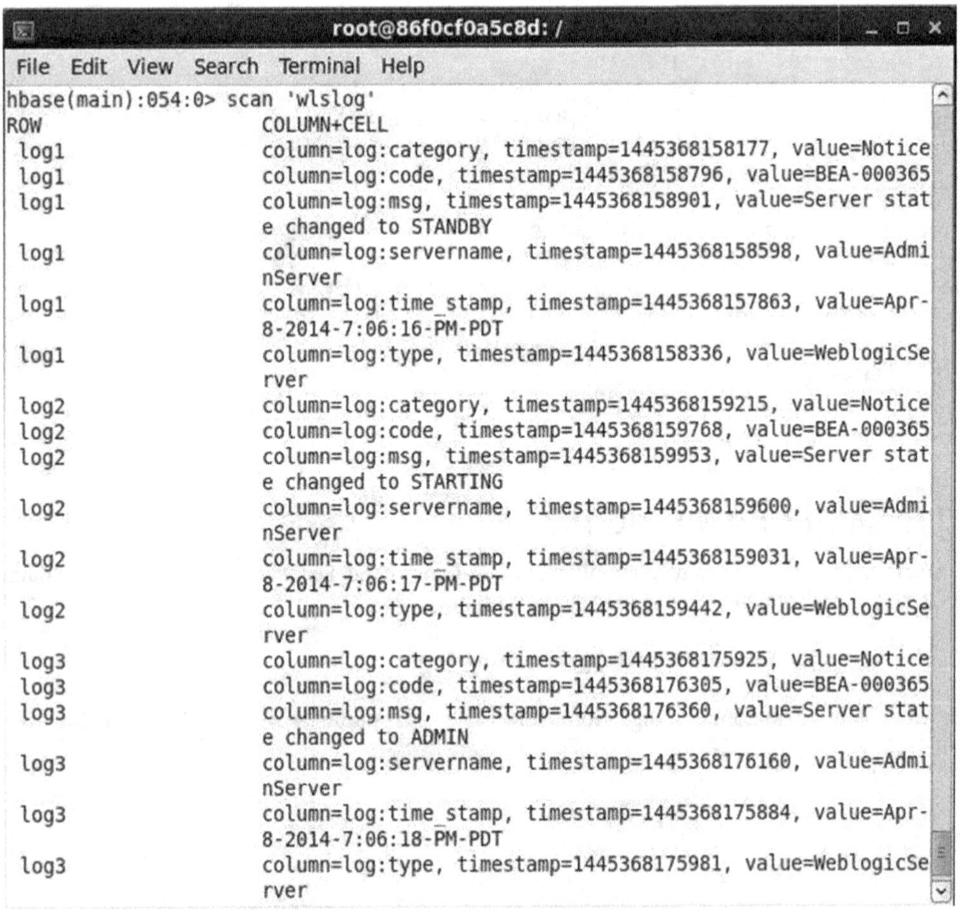

```
                         root@86f0cf0a5c8d: /                    _ □ ×
 File  Edit  View  Search  Terminal  Help
hbase(main):054:0> scan 'wlslog'
ROW                      COLUMN+CELL
 log1                     column=log:category, timestamp=1445368158177, value=Notice
 log1                     column=log:code, timestamp=1445368158796, value=BEA-000365
 log1                     column=log:msg, timestamp=1445368158901, value=Server stat
                          e changed to STANDBY
 log1                     column=log:servername, timestamp=1445368158598, value=Admi
                          nServer
 log1                     column=log:time_stamp, timestamp=1445368157863, value=Apr-
                          8-2014-7:06:16-PM-PDT
 log1                     column=log:type, timestamp=1445368158336, value=WeblogicSe
                          rver
 log2                     column=log:category, timestamp=1445368159215, value=Notice
 log2                     column=log:code, timestamp=1445368159768, value=BEA-000365
 log2                     column=log:msg, timestamp=1445368159953, value=Server stat
                          e changed to STARTING
 log2                     column=log:servername, timestamp=1445368159600, value=Admi
                          nServer
 log2                     column=log:time_stamp, timestamp=1445368159031, value=Apr-
                          8-2014-7:06:17-PM-PDT
 log2                     column=log:type, timestamp=1445368159442, value=WeblogicSe
                          rver
 log3                     column=log:category, timestamp=1445368175925, value=Notice
 log3                     column=log:code, timestamp=1445368176305, value=BEA-000365
 log3                     column=log:msg, timestamp=1445368176360, value=Server stat
                          e changed to ADMIN
 log3                     column=log:servername, timestamp=1445368176160, value=Admi
                          nServer
 log3                     column=log:time_stamp, timestamp=1445368175884, value=Apr-
                          8-2014-7:06:18-PM-PDT
 log3                     column=log:type, timestamp=1445368175981, value=WeblogicSe
                          rver
```

Figure 10-11. Scanning a HBase Table

The 7 rows of data get output as shown in Figure 10-12.

```
root@86f0cf0a5c8d: /                                      _ □ ×

File   Edit   View   Search   Terminal   Help

log5                    column=log:msg, timestamp=1445368199142, value=Started Web
                        logic AdminServer
log5                    column=log:servername, timestamp=1445368199067, value=Admi
                        nServer
log5                    column=log:time_stamp, timestamp=1445368198909, value=Apr-
                        8-2014-7:06:20-PM-PDT
log5                    column=log:type, timestamp=1445368199027, value=WeblogicSe
                        rver
log6                    column=log:category, timestamp=1445368199277, value=Notice
log6                    column=log:code, timestamp=1445368199497, value=BEA-000365
log6                    column=log:msg, timestamp=1445368199530, value=Server stat
                        e changed to RUNNING
log6                    column=log:servername, timestamp=1445368199459, value=Admi
                        nServer
log6                    column=log:time_stamp, timestamp=1445368199208, value=Apr-
                        8-2014-7:06:21-PM-PDT
log6                    column=log:type, timestamp=1445368199375, value=WeblogicSe
                        rver
log7                    column=log:category, timestamp=1445368199624, value=Notice
log7                    column=log:code, timestamp=1445368199778, value=BEA-000360
log7                    column=log:msg, timestamp=1445368199828, value=Server star
                        ted in RUNNING mode
log7                    column=log:servername, timestamp=1445368199739, value=Admi
                        nServer
log7                    column=log:time_stamp, timestamp=1445368199589, value=Apr-
                        8-2014-7:06:22-PM-PDT
log7                    column=log:type, timestamp=1445368199687, value=WeblogicSe
                        rver
7 row(s) in 0.4270 seconds

hbase(main):055:0> exit
root@86f0cf0a5c8d:/# ▊
```

Figure 10-12. Output from the scan Command

Stopping CDH

To stop the Docker container, run the docker stop command for the "cdh" container.

```
sudo docker stop cdh
```

Alternatively, the container id may be specified.

```
sudo docker stop  86f0cfoa5c8d
```

Summary

In this chapter we used a Docker image to run CDH frameworks in a Docker container. We started an interactive terminal and started an HBase shell in the tty. In the HBase shell, we used the create command to create a table. We used the put command to put data in the table. Subsequently, we used the get command to get the data added. We also ran the scan command to scan the complete table and list all the data in the table. In the next chapter we shall run Apache Sqoop in a Docker container.

CHAPTER 11

■ ■ ■

Using Apache Sqoop

Apache Sqoop is a Hadoop ecosystem framework for transferring bulk data from a relational database (RDBMS) to Hadoop Distributed File System (HDFS), Apache HBase, and Apache Hive. Sqoop also supports bulk data transfer from HDFS to a RDBMS. The direct data transfer paths supported by Sqoop are shown in Figure 11-1. Sqoop supports HSQLDB (version 1.8.0+), MySQL (5.0+), Oracle (10.2.0) and PostgreSQL (8.3+) and may also be usable with other relational databases such as IBM DB2 database and versions. Sqoop makes use of JDBC for data transfer and requires Java to be installed and the JDBC driver jar to be in the runtime classpath.

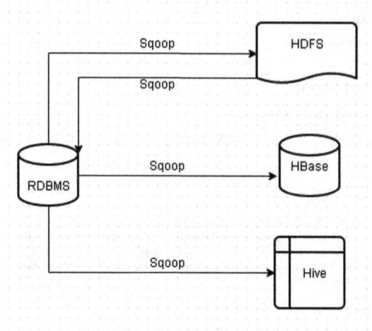

Figure 11-1. *Direct Transfer Paths supported by Sqoop*

In this chapter we shall use Apache Sqoop to import data into HDFS from MySQL database. We shall also export the data from HDFS back to a MySQL database table.

Setting the Environment

Starting Docker Containers

Starting Interactive Terminals

Creating a MySQL Tables

Adding MySQL JDBC Jar to Sqoop Classpath

Configuring Apache Hadoop

Importing MySQL Table Data into HDFS with Sqoop

Listing Data Imported into HDFS

Exporting from HDFS to MySQL with Sqoop

Querying Exported Data

Stopping and Removing Docker Containers

Setting the Environment

The following software is required for this chapter.

-Docker Engine (version 1.8)

-Docker image for MySQL Database

-Docker image for CDH

SSH connect to an Amazon EC2 instance.

```
ssh -i "docker.pem" ec2-user@54.175.13.99
```

Install Docker if not already installed as discussed in Chapter 1. Start the Docker service and verify that Docker has been started.

```
sudo service docker start
sudo service docker status
```

Download jdk-8u65-linux-x64.gz from http://www.oracle.com/technetwork/java/javase/downloads/jdk8-downloads-2133151.html. As JDK download requires a BSD license to be accepted, downloading with wget or similar software for downloading files makes the download command a non-standard command. Download jdk-8u65-linux-x64.gz using a browser and copy to the EC2 instance using a scp command such as the following.

```
scp -i "docker.pem" /jdk-8u65-linux-x64.gz ec2-user@54.175.13.99:/
```

We need to download two Docker images for this chapter because the Docker image for CDH, which includes Apache Sqoop, does not include MySQL Server. Download the mysql Docker image with the docker pull command.

```
sudo docker pull mysql
```

Download the svds/cdh Docker image.

```
sudo docker pull svds/cdh
```

List the Docker images with the `docker images` command.

```
sudo docker images
```

Both the `mysql` and `svds/cdh` Docker images should get listed as shown in Figure 11-2.

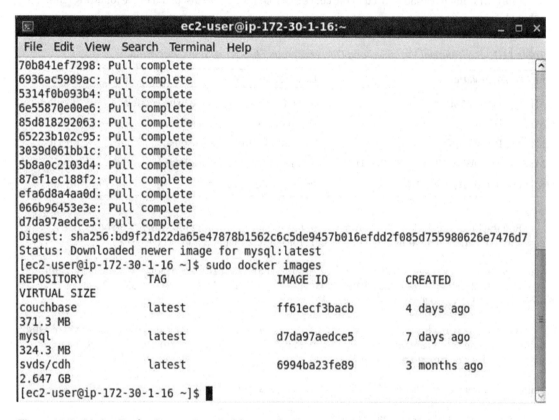

Figure 11-2. *Listing Docker Images Required for Apache Sqoop with MySQL Database*

Starting Docker Containers

Both the mysql and svds/cdh Docker images have been discussed in earlier chapters separately and used to start Docker containers. But, using the two Docker images is slightly different and requires the two Docker containers to be linked. In this section we shall start two separate Docker containers: `cdh` for the `cdh` Docker image, and `mysqldb` for the `mysql` Docker image. For the `mysqldb` container, create a directory for the data stored by MySQL and set its permissions to global (777).

```
sudo mkdir -p /mysql/data
sudo chmod -R 777 /mysql/data
```

153

The preceding commands are to be run when connected to the Amazon EC2 instance as shown in Figure 11-3.

```
[ec2-user@ip-172-30-1-16 ~]$ sudo mkdir -p /mysql/data
[ec2-user@ip-172-30-1-16 ~]$ sudo chmod -R 777 /mysql/data
```

Figure 11-3. *Creating Directory for MySQL Data*

The environment variables used in the docker run command are discussed in the following table, Table 11-1.

Table 11-1. *Environment Variables for a Docker container based on mysql Docker Image*

Environment Variable	Description	Value
MYSQL_DATABASE	MySQL database instance to be created.	mysqldb
MYSQL_USER	Username for the database created.	mysql
MYSQL_PASSWORD	Password for the database created.	mysql
MYSQL_ALLOW_EMPTY_PASSWORD	Is empty password to be allowed.	no
MYSQL_ROOT_PASSWORD	Password for "root" user.	mysql

Run the following docker run command to start a Docker container for MySQL Database. The environment variables are only set in the docker run command and not in the bash shell.

```
sudo docker run -v /mysql/data:/var/lib/mysql --name mysqldb -e MYSQL_DATABASE='mysqldb'
-e MYSQL_USER='mysql' -e MYSQL_PASSWORD='mysql' -e MYSQL_ALLOW_EMPTY_PASSWORD='no'
-e MYSQL_ROOT_PASSWORD='mysql' -d mysql
```

Run the following docker run command to start a Docker container for svds/cdh image software, which includes Apache Sqoop, and link the container with the mysqldb container running the MySQL database using the --link command parameter.

```
sudo docker run  -d --name cdh --link mysqldb svds/cdh
```

List the running Docker containers.

sudo docker ps

The output from the preceding commands is shown in Figure 11-4. Both the cdh and mysqldb containers are listed as started.

```
[ec2-user@ip-172-30-1-16 ~]$ sudo docker run -v /mysql/data:/var/lib/mysql --nam
e mysqldb -e MYSQL_DATABASE='mysqldb' -e MYSQL_USER='mysql' -e MYSQL_PASSWORD='m
ysql' -e MYSQL_ALLOW_EMPTY_PASSWORD='no' -e MYSQL_ROOT_PASSWORD='mysql' -d mysql
e414f8c41d0b931f4ea7eecd13d2c84ed8d50ea7c37e9f0078bcff56243d8d91
[ec2-user@ip-172-30-1-16 ~]$ sudo docker run  -d --name cdh -e JAVA_HOME='./jdk1
.8.0_65' --link mysqldb svds/cdh
49d774f8f1feae0c960999ced2025b48c115eb4d6b09cee21b931a3f989b431a
[ec2-user@ip-172-30-1-16 ~]$ sudo docker ps
CONTAINER ID          IMAGE                    COMMAND                 CREATED
     STATUS                PORTS
                      NAMES
49d774f8f1fe          svds/cdh                 "cdh_startup_script.s"  5 seconds ago
     Up 4 seconds             8020/tcp, 8088/tcp, 8888/tcp, 9090/tcp, 11000/tcp, 1144
3/tcp, 19888/tcp      cdh
e414f8c41d0b          mysql                    "/entrypoint.sh mysql"  18 seconds ago
     Up 18 seconds            3306/tcp
                      mysqldb
[ec2-user@ip-172-30-1-16 ~]$ █
```

Figure 11-4. *Starting Docker Containers for CDH and MySQL*

Starting Interactive Terminals

Having started the Docker containers, start the interactive terminals (tty) for the each of the Docker containers. Start the interactive shell for the mysqldb container with the following command.

```
sudo docker exec -it mysqldb bash
```

Start the interactive shell for the cdh container with the following command.

```
sudo docker exec -it cdh bash
```

Creating a MySQL Tables

In this section we shall login to the MySQL CLI and create a database table, which shall be imported into HDFS with Apache Sqoop. Run the following command to login into MySQL CLI.

```
mysql –u mysql –p
```

The mysql> prompt gets displayed as shown in Figure 11-5.

```
root@e414f8c41d0b:/# mysql -u mysql -p
Enter password:
Welcome to the MySQL monitor.  Commands end with ; or \g.
Your MySQL connection id is 4
Server version: 5.6.27 MySQL Community Server (GPL)

Copyright (c) 2000, 2015, Oracle and/or its affiliates. All rights reserved.

Oracle is a registered trademark of Oracle Corporation and/or its
affiliates. Other names may be trademarks of their respective
owners.

Type 'help;' or '\h' for help. Type '\c' to clear the current input statement.

mysql> █
```

Figure 11-5. *Starting the MySQL CLI Shell*

Set the database to use as "mysqldb".

```
use mysqldb
```

Grant all privileges on the mysqldb database to the mysql user with the GRANT option.

```
GRANT ALL PRIVILEGES ON mysqldb.* TO 'mysql'@'%' IDENTIFIED BY 'mysql' WITH GRANT OPTION;
```

Privileges get set on the mysqldb database as shown in Figure 11-6.

```
mysql> GRANT ALL PRIVILEGES ON mysqldb.* TO 'mysql'@'%' IDENTIFIED BY 'mysql' WI
TH GRANT OPTION;
Query OK, 0 rows affected (0.00 sec)

mysql> █
```

Figure 11-6. *Setting Privileges on mysqldb Database*

Next, create a database table called wlslog with columns time_stamp, category, type, servername, code and msg. The PRIMARY KEY column is required to be included for sqoop import tool to import data into HDFS. Run the following SQL command in MySQL CLI.

```
CREATE TABLE wlslog(time_stamp VARCHAR(255) PRIMARY KEY,category VARCHAR(255),type
VARCHAR(255),servername VARCHAR(255), code VARCHAR(255),msg VARCHAR(255));
```

A database table called wlslog gets created as shown in Figure 11-7.

```
mysql> CREATE TABLE wlslog(time_stamp VARCHAR(255) PRIMARY KEY,category VARCHAR(
255),type VARCHAR(255),servername VARCHAR(255), code VARCHAR(255),msg VARCHAR(25
5));
Query OK, 0 rows affected (0.02 sec)

mysql> █
```

Figure 11-7. *Creating a MySQL Database Table*

Add data to the wlslog table. Run the following INSERT SQL statements to add data to the wlslog table.

```
INSERT INTO wlslog(time_stamp,category,type,servername,code,msg) VALUES('Apr-8-2014-7:06:
16-PM-PDT','Notice','WebLogicServer','AdminServer','BEA-000365','Server state changed to
STANDBY');
INSERT INTO wlslog(time_stamp,category,type,servername,code,msg) VALUES('Apr-8-2014-7:06:
17-PM-PDT','Notice','WebLogicServer','AdminServer','BEA-000365','Server state changed to
STARTING');
INSERT INTO wlslog(time_stamp,category,type,servername,code,msg) VALUES('Apr-8-2014-7:06:
18-PM-PDT','Notice','WebLogicServer','AdminServer','BEA-000365','Server state changed to
ADMIN');
INSERT INTO wlslog(time_stamp,category,type,servername,code,msg) VALUES('Apr-8-2014-7:06:
19-PM-PDT','Notice','WebLogicServer','AdminServer','BEA-000365','Server state changed to
RESUMING');
INSERT INTO wlslog(time_stamp,category,type,servername,code,msg) VALUES('Apr-8-2014-
7:06:20-PM-PDT','Notice','WebLogicServer','AdminServer','BEA-000361','Started WebLogic
AdminServer');
INSERT INTO wlslog(time_stamp,category,type,servername,code,msg) VALUES('Apr-8-2014-7:06:
21-PM-PDT','Notice','WebLogicServer','AdminServer','BEA-000365','Server state changed to
RUNNING');
```

Output from the preceding SQL statements is shown in Figure 11-8.

157

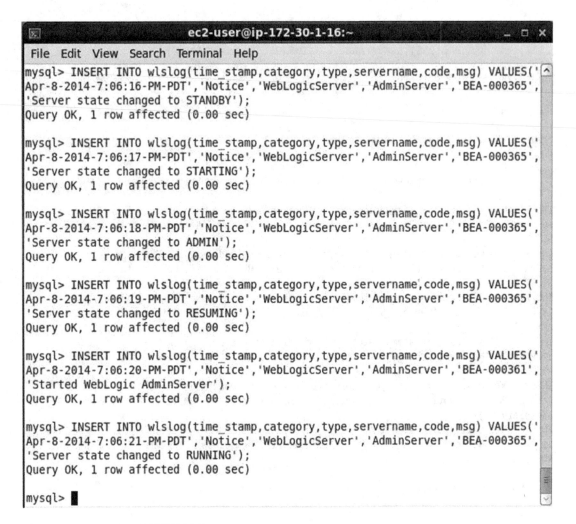

Figure 11-8. Running INSERT SQL Statements

Run the following SQL query to list the data added.

```
SELECT * FROM wlslog;
```

The 6 rows of data get listed as shown in Figure 11-9.

```
mysql> select * from wlslog;
+-------------------------------+----------+--------------------+---------------+----------
---+----------------------------------+
| time_stamp                    | category | type               | servername    | code
   | msg                              |
+-------------------------------+----------+--------------------+---------------+----------
---+----------------------------------+
| Apr-8-2014-7:06:16-PM-PDT | Notice   | WebLogicServer | AdminServer | BEA-0003
65 | Server state changed to STANDBY  |
| Apr-8-2014-7:06:17-PM-PDT | Notice   | WebLogicServer | AdminServer | BEA-0003
65 | Server state changed to STARTING |
| Apr-8-2014-7:06:18-PM-PDT | Notice   | WebLogicServer | AdminServer | BEA-0003
65 | Server state changed to ADMIN    |
| Apr-8-2014-7:06:19-PM-PDT | Notice   | WebLogicServer | AdminServer | BEA-0003
65 | Server state changed to RESUMING |
| Apr-8-2014-7:06:20-PM-PDT | Notice   | WebLogicServer | AdminServer | BEA-0003
61 | Started WebLogic AdminServer     |
| Apr-8-2014-7:06:21-PM-PDT | Notice   | WebLogicServer | AdminServer | BEA-0003
65 | Server state changed to RUNNING  |
+-------------------------------+----------+--------------------+---------------+----------
---+----------------------------------+
6 rows in set (0.00 sec)

mysql>
```

Figure 11-9. *Running a SQL Query*

We need to create another database table for the sqoop export tool to export data from HDFS into MySQL database. Because the wlslog table already has data create another table called WLSLOG_COPY, which has the same table definition as the wlslog table. Run the following SQL script in MySQL CLI.

```
CREATE TABLE WLSLOG_COPY(time_stamp VARCHAR(255) PRIMARY KEY,category VARCHAR(255),type
VARCHAR(255),servername VARCHAR(255), code VARCHAR(255),msg VARCHAR(255));
```

The WLSLOG_COPY table gets created as shown in Figure 11-10.

```
mysql> CREATE TABLE WLSLOG_COPY(time_stamp VARCHAR(255) PRIMARY KEY,category VAR
CHAR(255),type VARCHAR(255),servername VARCHAR(255), code VARCHAR(255),msg VARCH
AR(255));
Query OK, 0 rows affected (0.13 sec)

mysql> select * from WLSLOG_COPY;
Empty set (0.00 sec)

mysql>
```

Figure 11-10. *Creating MySQL Table WLSLOG_COPY*

Adding MySQL JDBC Jar to Sqoop Classpath

We need to add the MySQL JDBC jar to the Apache Sqoop classpath. Start the interactive terminal for the cdh container if not already started.

```
sudo docker exec -it cdh bash
```

In the interactive shell, download the mysql-connector-java-5.1.37.jar and copy the jar to the /usr/lib/ sqoop/lib directory.

```
wget http://central.maven.org/maven2/mysql/mysql-connector-java/5.1.37/
mysql-connector-java-5.1.37.jar
cp mysql-connector-java-5.1.37.jar /usr/lib/sqoop/lib
```

The output from the preceding commands is shown in Figure 11-11.

```
[ec2-user@ip-172-30-1-16 /]$ sudo docker exec -it cdh bash
root@6fba20d93011:/# wget http://central.maven.org/maven2/mysql/mysql-connector-
java/5.1.37/mysql-connector-java-5.1.37.jar
--2015-10-21 19:42:43--  http://central.maven.org/maven2/mysql/mysql-connector-j
ava/5.1.37/mysql-connector-java-5.1.37.jar
Resolving central.maven.org (central.maven.org)... 23.235.39.209
Connecting to central.maven.org (central.maven.org)|23.235.39.209|:80... connect
ed.
HTTP request sent, awaiting response... 200 OK
Length: 985600 (962K) [application/java-archive]
Saving to: 'mysql-connector-java-5.1.37.jar'

100%[=====================================>] 985,600      --.-K/s   in 0.1s

2015-10-21 19:42:43 (7.50 MB/s) - 'mysql-connector-java-5.1.37.jar' saved [98560
0/985600]

root@6fba20d93011:/# cp mysql-connector-java-5.1.37.jar /usr/lib/sqoop/lib
```

Figure 11-11. *Adding MySQL JDBC Jar to Sqoop Classpath*

Setting the JAVA_HOME Environment Variable

For the Apache Sqoop to run we need to set the JAVA_HOME environment variable. But, first we need to copy the jdk-8u65-linux-x64.gz file to the Docker container running the CDH frameworks including Apache Sqoop. We downloaded the jdk-8u65-linux-x64.gz earlier. Copy the jdk-8u65-linux-x64.gz file to the Docker container using the following command in which the container id is obtained from the output of the docker ps command in Figure 11-12.

```
sudo docker cp jdk-8u65-linux-x64.gz 49d774f8f1fe:/jdk-8u65-linux-x64.gz
```

```
[ec2-user@ip-172-30-1-16 ~]$ sudo docker cp jdk-8u65-linux-x64.gz 87e6f3577ace:/
jdk-8u65-linux-x64.gz
[ec2-user@ip-172-30-1-16 ~]$ ▌
```

Figure 11-12. *Copying the JDK gz File to Docker Container*

The jdk-8u65-linux-x64.gz file gets copied to the Docker container "cdh" as shown in Figure 11-12.

The preceding command is to be run from the Amazon EC2 instance. Start the interactive shell for the cdh container.

```
sudo docker exec -it cdh bash
```

List the files in the Docker container's root directory with the following command.

```
ls -l
```

The jdk-8u65-linux-x64.gz file gets listed as shown in Figure 11-13.

```
[ec2-user@ip-172-30-1-16 ~]$ sudo docker exec -it cdh bash
root@6fba20d93011:/# ls -l
total 177084
drwxr-xr-x.    2 root root      4096 Jul  5 13:33 bin
drwxr-xr-x.    2 root root      4096 Apr 10  2014 boot
drwxr-xr-x.    3 root root      4096 Jul  5 13:41 debian
drwxr-xr-x.    5 root root       360 Oct 21 19:35 dev
drwxr-xr-x.   88 root root      4096 Oct 21 19:35 etc
drwxr-xr-x.    2 root root      4096 Apr 10  2014 home
-rwxrwxrwx.    1 root root 181260798 Oct 21 18:31 jdk-8u65-linux-x64.gz
drwxr-xr-x.   12 root root      4096 Jun 12 11:35 lib
drwxr-xr-x.    2 root root      4096 Jun 12 11:35 lib64
drwxr-xr-x.    2 root root      4096 Jun 12 11:34 media
drwxr-xr-x.    2 root root      4096 Apr 10  2014 mnt
drwxr-xr-x.    2 root root      4096 Jun 12 11:34 opt
dr-xr-xr-x.  163 root root         0 Oct 21 19:35 proc
drwx------.    2 root root      4096 Jun 12 11:35 root
drwxr-xr-x.   19 root root      4096 Oct 21 19:36 run
drwxr-xr-x.    2 root root      4096 Jun 12 15:32 sbin
drwxr-xr-x.    2 root root      4096 Jun 12 11:34 srv
dr-xr-xr-x.   13 root root         0 Oct 21 16:36 sys
drwxrwxrwt.   24 root root      4096 Oct 21 19:36 tmp
drwxr-xr-x.   10 root root      4096 Jun 12 15:32 usr
drwxr-xr-x.   11 root root      4096 Jun 12 15:32 var
root@6fba20d93011:/# ▌
```

Figure 11-13. *Listing the files in Docker Container's root Directory*

Extract the jdk-8u65-linux-x64.gz file.

```
tar -xv jdk-8u65-linux-x64.gz
```

The .gz file gets extracted as shown in Figure 11-14.

```
root@6fba20d93011: /
File Edit View Search Terminal Help
jdk1.8.0_65/bin/jstat
jdk1.8.0_65/bin/ControlPanel
jdk1.8.0_65/bin/rmiregistry
jdk1.8.0_65/bin/appletviewer
jdk1.8.0_65/bin/javadoc
jdk1.8.0_65/bin/jdb
jdk1.8.0_65/bin/jjs
jdk1.8.0_65/bin/servertool
jdk1.8.0_65/bin/idlj
jdk1.8.0_65/bin/rmid
jdk1.8.0_65/bin/javapackager
jdk1.8.0_65/bin/policytool
jdk1.8.0_65/bin/javaws
jdk1.8.0_65/bin/unpack200
jdk1.8.0_65/bin/tnameserv
jdk1.8.0_65/bin/jmc.ini
jdk1.8.0_65/bin/jmap
jdk1.8.0_65/bin/serialver
jdk1.8.0_65/bin/wsgen
jdk1.8.0_65/bin/jrunscript
jdk1.8.0_65/bin/javah
jdk1.8.0_65/bin/javac
jdk1.8.0_65/bin/jvisualvm
jdk1.8.0_65/bin/jcontrol
jdk1.8.0_65/release
```

***Figure 11-14.** Extracting the JDK .gz File*

We need to set the JAVA_HOME environment variable in the hadoop-env.sh file. To find the directory for the hadoop-env.sh file run the following command.

```
find -name hadoop-env.sh
```

The different directories containing the hadoop-env.sh file get listed as shown in Figure 11-15.

```
root@49d774f8f1fe:/# find -name hadoop-env.sh
./usr/lib/hadoop-0.20-mapreduce/example-confs/conf.secure/hadoop-env.sh
./etc/hadoop/conf.pseudo/hadoop-env.sh
./etc/profile.d/hadoop-env.sh
```

***Figure 11-15.** Finding the hadoop-env.sh File*

Open the ./etc/hadoop/conf.psuedo/hadoop-env.sh file in a vi editor and add the following export statement.

```
export JAVA_HOME=./jdk1.8.0_65
```

The preceding statement in the hadoop-env.sh file is shown in Figure 11-16. Save the file with the :wq command.

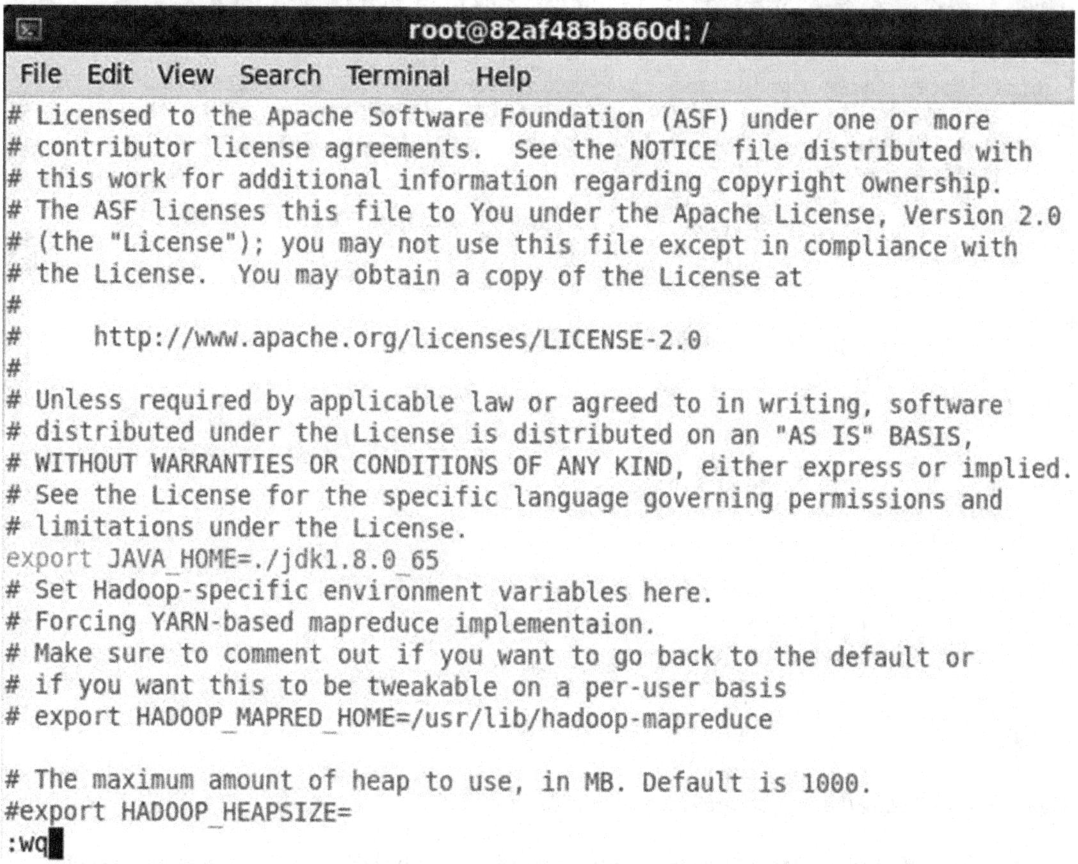

Figure 11-16. *Setting the JAVA_HOME Environment Variable*

Configuring Apache Hadoop

Apache Hadoop MapReduce framework may be started in one of the three modes: local, classic and yarn. In the "local" mode, MapReduce runs in a Java process. In the classic mode, MapReduce runs using the MapReduce1 framework. With the yarn mode, MapReduce runs using the MapReduce2 framework (also called YARN). The MapReduce framework to use is set in the mapreduce.framework.name setting in the mapred-site.xml configuration file, which is in the same directory as the hadoop-env.sh, the ./etc/hadoop/conf.psuedo directory. As yarn and classic frameworks require more RAM than the local, set the mapreduce.framework.name to local.

```
<property>
        <name>mapreduce.framework.name</name>
        <value>local</value>
    </property>
```

The mapreduce.framework.name setting is shown in Figure 11.17.

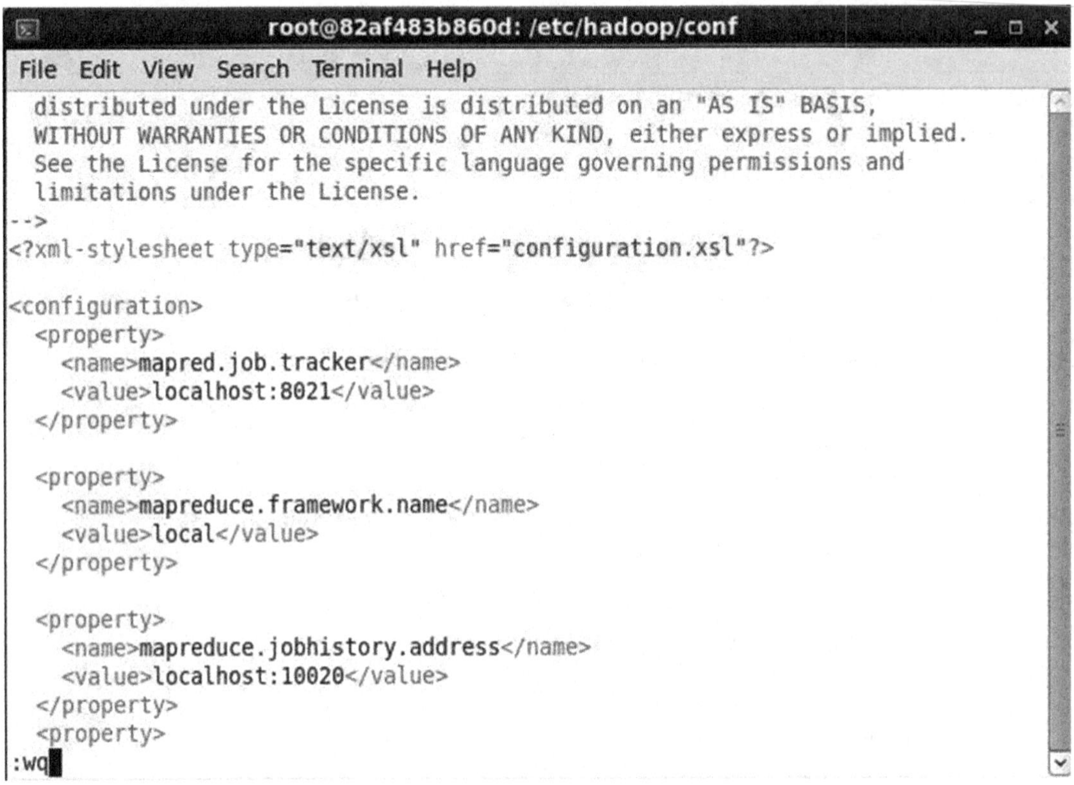

Figure 11-17. *Setting the MapReduce Framework to local*

Also set the following (Table 11-2) configuration properties in the hdfs-site.xml configuration file.

Table 11-2. *Configuration Properties for hdfs-site.xml*

Configuration Property	Description	Value
dfs.permissions.superusergroup	Sets the super user group	hadoop
dfs.namenode.name.dir	Sets the NameNode storage directory	file:///data/1/dfs/nn
dfs.replication	Sets the replication level	1
dfs.permissions	Whether permissions are to be checked	false

The hdfs-site.xml configuration settings are listed below.

```
<configuration>
 <property>
   <name>dfs.permissions.superusergroup</name>
   <value>hadoop</value>
 </property>
 <property>
   <name>dfs.namenode.name.dir</name>
   <value>file:///data/1/dfs/nn</value>
 </property>
 <property>
   <name>dfs.replication</name>
   <value>1</value>
 </property>
 <property>
   <name>dfs.permissions</name>
   <value>false</value>
 </property>
</configuration>
```

The hdfs-site.xml configuration file is shown in Figure 11-18.

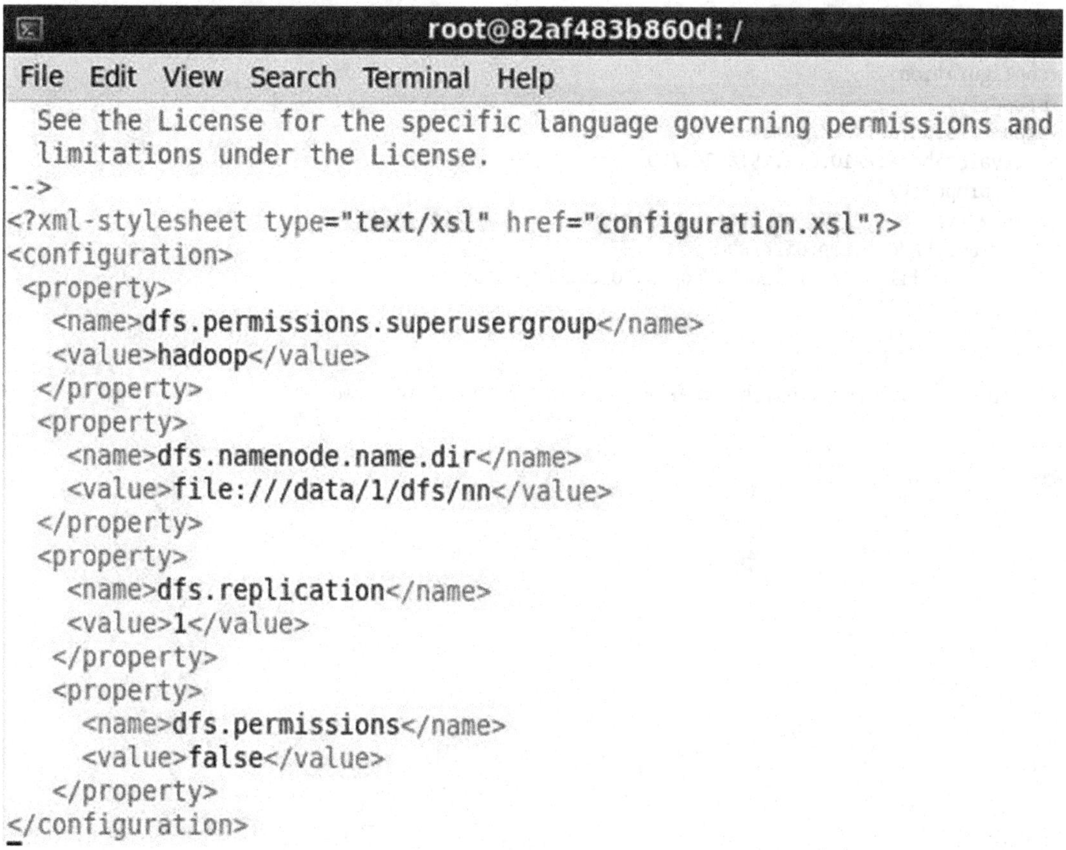

Figure 11-18. The hdfs-site.xml Configuration File

We need to create the NameNode storage directory set in the `dfs.namenode.name.dir` property. Create the `/data/1/dfs/nn` directory and set its permissions to global (777).

```
sudo mkdir -p /data/1/dfs/nn
sudo chmod -R 777 /data/1/dfs/nn
```

Create the user group hadoop and a user hadoop.

```
groupadd hadoop
useradd hadoop
```

We need to set the following (Table 11-3) configuration properties in the `core-site.xml` file.

Table 11-3. *Configuration Properties for core-site.xml*

Configuration Property	Description	Value
fs.defaultFS	The NameNode URI	hdfs://localhost:8020
hadoop.tmp.dir	The Hadoop temporary directory	file:///var/lib/hadoop-0.20/cache

The `core-site.xml` configuration settings are listed:

```
<configuration>
<property>
  <name>fs.defaultFS</name>
    <value>hdfs://10.0.2.15:8020</value>
    </property>
 <property>
    <name>hadoop.tmp.dir</name>
    <value>file:///var/lib/hadoop-0.20/cache</value>
  </property>
</configuration>
```

The `core-site.xml` file is shown in Figure 11-19. Save the file with `:wq`.

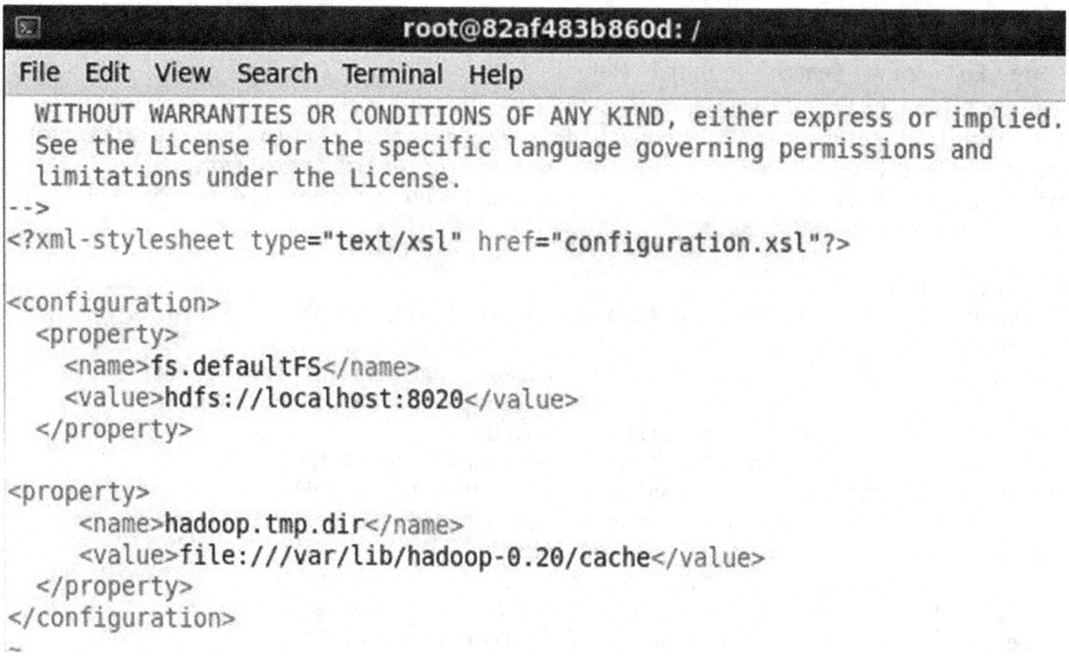

```
[»_]                    root@82af483b860d: /
File  Edit  View  Search  Terminal  Help
WITHOUT WARRANTIES OR CONDITIONS OF ANY KIND, either express or implied.
See the License for the specific language governing permissions and
limitations under the License.
-->
<?xml-stylesheet type="text/xsl" href="configuration.xsl"?>

<configuration>
  <property>
    <name>fs.defaultFS</name>
    <value>hdfs://localhost:8020</value>
  </property>

<property>
    <name>hadoop.tmp.dir</name>
    <value>file:///var/lib/hadoop-0.20/cache</value>
  </property>
</configuration>
~
```

Figure 11-19. *The core-site.xml Configuration File*

Create the directory set in the hadoop.tmp.dir directory and set its permissions to global (777).

```
mkdir -p /var/lib/hadoop-0.20/cache
chmod -R 777  /var/lib/hadoop-0.20/cache
```

We also need to set the permissions of the / directory in HDFS to global (777) with the following command.

```
sudo -u hdfs hdfs dfs -chmod 777 /
```

Importing MySQL Table Data into HDFS with Sqoop

In this section we shall use the sqoop import command to import MySQL database table data to the HDFS. The different commands supported by the sqoop tool may be listed by running the sqoop help command from the interactive shell for the cdh container as shown in Figure 11-20. The import command is used to import a table from a relational database to HDFS.

```
┌─────────────────────────────────────────────────────────────────────────────┐
│ ▨                      root@f24264039d44: /                          ─  □     │
├─────────────────────────────────────────────────────────────────────────────┤
│ File  Edit  View  Search  Terminal  Help                                      │
│ root@f24264039d44:/# sqoop help                                               │
│ Warning: /usr/lib/sqoop/../accumulo does not exist! Accumulo imports will fail.│
│ Please set $ACCUMULO_HOME to the root of your Accumulo installation.           │
│ 15/10/21 17:39:57 INFO sqoop.Sqoop: Running Sqoop version: 1.4.5-cdh5.4.3      │
│ usage: sqoop COMMAND [ARGS]                                                    │
│                                                                               │
│ Available commands:                                                           │
│   codegen            Generate code to interact with database records          │
│   create-hive-table  Import a table definition into Hive                      │
│   eval               Evaluate a SQL statement and display the results         │
│   export             Export an HDFS directory to a database table             │
│   help               List available commands                                  │
│   import             Import a table from a database to HDFS                    │
│   import-all-tables  Import tables from a database to HDFS                     │
│   import-mainframe   Import datasets from a mainframe server to HDFS           │
│   job                Work with saved jobs                                      │
│   list-databases     List available databases on a server                     │
│   list-tables        List available tables in a database                      │
│   merge              Merge results of incremental imports                     │
│   metastore          Run a standalone Sqoop metastore                         │
│   version            Display version information                              │
│                                                                               │
│ See 'sqoop help COMMAND' for information on a specific command.                │
│ root@f24264039d44:/# █                                                        │
└─────────────────────────────────────────────────────────────────────────────┘
```

Figure 11-20. *Running the sqoop help Command*

Running the sqoop import command requires the code to be generated for accessing the relational database. The code may be generated directly while the sqoop import command is run or before the sqoop import command is run using the sqoop codegen command. Run the following sqoop codegen command to generate the code to interact with the database records.

```
sudo -u hdfs sqoop codegen --connect "jdbc:mysql://e414f8c41d0b:3306/mysqldb"  --password "mysql" --username "mysql" --table "wlslog"
```

The –u hdfs specifies the user as hdfs. The command parameters are discussed in Table 11-4.

Table 11-4. *Command Parameters for the hdfs Command*

Parameter	Description	Value
--connect	The connection url to connect to MySQL database. The hostname is the container id in which MySQL is run.	"jdbc:mysql://e414f8c41d0b:3306/mysqldb"
--password	Password to connect to MySQL. It is recommended to use a non-root user.	"mysql"
--username	Username to connect to MySQL.	"mysql"
--table	MySQL table from which to import from	"wlslog"

The code required to interact with the database gets generated in the wlslog.jar file as shown in Figure 11-21.

```
root@08b338cb2a90:/# sudo -u hdfs sqoop codegen --connect "jdbc:mysql://e414f8c4
1d0b:3306/mysqldb"  --password "mysql" --username "mysql" --table "wlslog"
Warning: /usr/lib/sqoop/../accumulo does not exist! Accumulo imports will fail.
Please set $ACCUMULO_HOME to the root of your Accumulo installation.
15/10/22 00:05:54 INFO sqoop.Sqoop: Running Sqoop version: 1.4.5-cdh5.4.3
15/10/22 00:05:54 WARN tool.BaseSqoopTool: Setting your password on the command-
line is insecure. Consider using -P instead.
15/10/22 00:05:55 INFO manager.MySQLManager: Preparing to use a MySQL streaming
resultset.
15/10/22 00:05:55 INFO tool.CodeGenTool: Beginning code generation
15/10/22 00:05:56 INFO manager.SqlManager: Executing SQL statement: SELECT t.* F
ROM `wlslog` AS t LIMIT 1
15/10/22 00:05:56 INFO manager.SqlManager: Executing SQL statement: SELECT t.* F
ROM `wlslog` AS t LIMIT 1
15/10/22 00:05:57 INFO orm.CompilationManager: HADOOP_MAPRED_HOME is /usr/lib/ha
doop-mapreduce
Note: /tmp/sqoop-hdfs/compile/6348ef9539c8ad2bee9ba1875a62c923/wlslog.java uses
or overrides a deprecated API.
Note: Recompile with -Xlint:deprecation for details.
15/10/22 00:06:03 INFO orm.CompilationManager: Writing jar file: /tmp/sqoop-hdfs
/compile/6348ef9539c8ad2bee9ba1875a62c923/wlslog.jar
root@08b338cb2a90:/# 
```

Figure 11-21. *Output from the codegen Command*

Next, run the sqoop import command as user hdfs. Add the wlslog.jar file in the classpath with the -libjars option.

```
sudo -u hdfs sqoop import -libjars /tmp/sqoop-hdfs/compile/6348ef9539c8ad2bee9ba1875a6
2c923/wlslog.jar  --connect "jdbc:mysql://e414f8c41d0b:3306/mysqldb"  --password "mysql"
--username "mysql" --table "wlslog" --columns "time_stamp,category,type,servername,code,msg"
--target-dir "/mysql/import" –verbose
```

The other command parameters are discussed in Table 11-5.

Table 11-5. *Command Parameters for sqoop import*

Parameter	Description	Value
--connect	The connection url to connect to MySQL database. The hostname is the container id in which MySQL is run.	"jdbc:mysql://e414f8c41d0b:3306/mysqldb"
--password	Password to connect to MySQL. It is recommended to use a non-root user.	"mysql"
--username	Username to connect to MySQL.	"mysql"
--columns	Columns to be imported	"time_stamp,category,type,servername,code,msg"
--table	MySQL table from which to import from	"wlslog"
--target-dir	The HDFS directory in which to import	"/mysql/import"

The output from the `sqoop import` command is shown in Figure 11-22.

Figure 11-22. *Output from sqoop import*

The detailed output from the sqoop import command is listed:

```
root@08b338cb2a90:/# sudo -u hdfs sqoop import -libjars /tmp/sqoop-hdfs/compile/6348ef95
39c8ad2bee9ba1875a62c923/wlslog.jar  --connect "jdbc:mysql://e414f8c41d0b:3306/mysqldb"
--password "mysql" --username "mysql" --table "wlslog" --columns "time_stamp,category,type,s
ervername,code,msg" --target-dir "/mysql/import" -verbose
15/10/22 00:07:07 INFO sqoop.Sqoop: Running Sqoop version: 1.4.5-cdh5.4.3
ConnManager
15/10/22 00:07:10 INFO tool.CodeGenTool: Beginning code generation
15/10/22 00:07:10 DEBUG manager.SqlManager: Execute getColumnInfoRawQuery : SELECT t.* FROM
`wlslog` AS t LIMIT 1
15/10/22 00:07:10 DEBUG manager.SqlManager: No connection paramenters specified. Using
regular API for making connection.
15/10/22 00:07:11 DEBUG manager.SqlManager: Using fetchSize for next query: -2147483648
15/10/22 00:07:11 INFO manager.SqlManager: Executing SQL statement: SELECT t.* FROM `wlslog`
AS t LIMIT 1
15/10/22 00:07:11 DEBUG manager.SqlManager: Found column time_stamp of type [12, 255, 0]
15/10/22 00:07:11 DEBUG manager.SqlManager: Found column category of type [12, 255, 0]
15/10/22 00:07:11 DEBUG manager.SqlManager: Found column type of type [12, 255, 0]
15/10/22 00:07:11 DEBUG manager.SqlManager: Found column servername of type [12, 255, 0]
15/10/22 00:07:11 DEBUG manager.SqlManager: Found column code of type [12, 255, 0]
15/10/22 00:07:11 DEBUG manager.SqlManager: Found column msg of type [12, 255, 0]
15/10/22 00:07:11 DEBUG orm.ClassWriter: selected columns:
15/10/22 00:07:11 DEBUG orm.ClassWriter:    time_stamp
15/10/22 00:07:11 DEBUG orm.ClassWriter:    category
15/10/22 00:07:11 DEBUG orm.ClassWriter:    type
15/10/22 00:07:11 DEBUG orm.ClassWriter:    servername
15/10/22 00:07:11 DEBUG orm.ClassWriter:    code
15/10/22 00:07:11 DEBUG orm.ClassWriter:    msg
15/10/22 00:07:11 DEBUG manager.SqlManager: Using fetchSize for next query: -2147483648
15/10/22 00:07:11 INFO manager.SqlManager: Executing SQL statement: SELECT t.* FROM `wlslog`
AS t LIMIT 1
15/10/22 00:07:11 DEBUG manager.SqlManager: Found column time_stamp of type VARCHAR
15/10/22 00:07:11 DEBUG manager.SqlManager: Found column category of type VARCHAR
15/10/22 00:07:11 DEBUG manager.SqlManager: Found column type of type VARCHAR
15/10/22 00:07:11 DEBUG manager.SqlManager: Found column servername of type VARCHAR
15/10/22 00:07:11 DEBUG manager.SqlManager: Found column code of type VARCHAR
15/10/22 00:07:11 DEBUG manager.SqlManager: Found column msg of type VARCHAR
15/10/22 00:07:11 DEBUG orm.ClassWriter: Writing source file: /tmp/sqoop-hdfs/compile/3c3425
a2eecf819af8fe8f4eabd40468/wlslog.java
15/10/22 00:07:11 DEBUG orm.ClassWriter: Table name: wlslog
15/10/22 00:07:11 DEBUG orm.ClassWriter: Columns: time_stamp:12, category:12, type:12,
servername:12, code:12, msg:12,
15/10/22 00:07:11 DEBUG orm.ClassWriter: sourceFilename is wlslog.java
15/10/22 00:07:11 DEBUG orm.CompilationManager: Found existing /tmp/sqoop-hdfs/compile/3c342
5a2eecf819af8fe8f4eabd40468/
15/10/22 00:07:11 INFO orm.CompilationManager: HADOOP_MAPRED_HOME is /usr/lib/hadoop-mapreduce
15/10/22 00:07:11 DEBUG orm.CompilationManager: Returning jar file path /usr/lib/hadoop-
mapreduce/hadoop-mapreduce-client-core.jar:/usr/lib/hadoop-mapreduce/hadoop-mapreduce-
client-core-2.6.0-cdh5.4.3.jar
```

15/10/22 00:07:17 DEBUG orm.CompilationManager: Could not rename /tmp/sqoop-hdfs/compile/3c3
425a2eecf819af8fe8f4eabd40468/wlslog.java to /./wlslog.java
15/10/22 00:07:17 INFO orm.CompilationManager: Writing jar file: /tmp/sqoop-hdfs/compile/3c3
425a2eecf819af8fe8f4eabd40468/wlslog.jar
15/10/22 00:07:17 DEBUG orm.CompilationManager: Scanning for .class files in directory:
/tmp/sqoop-hdfs/compile/3c3425a2eecf819af8fe8f4eabd40468
15/10/22 00:07:17 DEBUG orm.CompilationManager: Got classfile: /tmp/sqoop-hdfs/compile/3c342
5a2eecf819af8fe8f4eabd40468/wlslog.class -> wlslog.class
15/10/22 00:07:17 DEBUG orm.CompilationManager: Finished writing jar file /tmp/sqoop-hdfs/co
mpile/3c3425a2eecf819af8fe8f4eabd40468/wlslog.jar
15/10/22 00:07:17 WARN manager.MySQLManager: It looks like you are importing from mysql.
15/10/22 00:07:17 WARN manager.MySQLManager: This transfer can be faster! Use the --direct
15/10/22 00:07:17 WARN manager.MySQLManager: option to exercise a MySQL-specific fast path.
15/10/22 00:07:17 INFO manager.MySQLManager: Setting zero DATETIME behavior to convertToNull
(mysql)
15/10/22 00:07:17 DEBUG manager.MySQLManager: Rewriting connect string to jdbc:mysql:
//e414f8c41d0b:3306/mysqldb?zeroDateTimeBehavior=convertToNull
15/10/22 00:07:17 DEBUG manager.CatalogQueryManager: Retrieving primary key for table
'wlslog' with query SELECT column_name FROM INFORMATION_SCHEMA.COLUMNS WHERE TABLE_SCHEMA =
(SELECT SCHEMA()) AND TABLE_NAME = 'wlslog' AND COLUMN_KEY = 'PRI'
15/10/22 00:07:17 DEBUG manager.CatalogQueryManager: Retrieving primary key for table
'wlslog' with query SELECT column_name FROM INFORMATION_SCHEMA.COLUMNS WHERE TABLE_SCHEMA =
(SELECT SCHEMA()) AND TABLE_NAME = 'wlslog' AND COLUMN_KEY = 'PRI'
15/10/22 00:07:17 INFO mapreduce.ImportJobBase: Beginning import of wlslog
15/10/22 00:07:17 INFO Configuration.deprecation: mapred.job.tracker is deprecated. Instead,
use mapreduce.jobtracker.address
15/10/22 00:07:17 INFO Configuration.deprecation: mapred.jar is deprecated. Instead, use
mapreduce.job.jar
15/10/22 00:07:17 DEBUG db.DBConfiguration: Securing password into job credentials store
15/10/22 00:07:17 DEBUG mapreduce.DataDrivenImportJob: Using table class: wlslog
15/10/22 00:07:17 DEBUG mapreduce.DataDrivenImportJob: Using InputFormat: class com.
cloudera.sqoop.mapreduce.db.DataDrivenDBInputFormat
15/10/22 00:07:18 INFO Configuration.deprecation: mapred.map.tasks is deprecated. Instead,
use mapreduce.job.maps
15/10/22 00:07:19 INFO jvm.JvmMetrics: Initializing JVM Metrics with processName=JobTracker,
sessionId=
15/10/22 00:07:20 DEBUG db.DBConfiguration: Fetching password from job credentials store
15/10/22 00:07:20 INFO db.DBInputFormat: Using read commited transaction isolation
15/10/22 00:07:20 DEBUG db.DataDrivenDBInputFormat: Creating input split with lower bound
'1=1' and upper bound '1=1'
15/10/22 00:07:20 INFO mapreduce.JobSubmitter: number of splits:1
15/10/22 00:07:21 INFO mapreduce.JobSubmitter: Submitting tokens for job:
job_local2065078437_0001
15/10/22 00:07:25 INFO mapreduce.Job: The url to track the job: http://localhost:8080/
15/10/22 00:07:25 INFO mapreduce.Job: Running job: job_local2065078437_0001
15/10/22 00:07:25 INFO mapred.LocalJobRunner: OutputCommitter set in config null
15/10/22 00:07:25 INFO output.FileOutputCommitter: File Output Committer Algorithm version is 1
15/10/22 00:07:25 INFO mapred.LocalJobRunner: OutputCommitter is org.apache.hadoop.
mapreduce.lib.output.FileOutputCommitter
15/10/22 00:07:26 INFO mapred.LocalJobRunner: Waiting for map tasks

15/10/22 00:07:26 INFO mapred.LocalJobRunner: Starting task: attempt_local2065078437_0001
_m_000000_0
15/10/22 00:07:26 INFO output.FileOutputCommitter: File Output Committer Algorithm version is 1
15/10/22 00:07:26 INFO mapred.Task: Using ResourceCalculatorProcessTree : [ ]
15/10/22 00:07:26 DEBUG db.DBConfiguration: Fetching password from job credentials store
15/10/22 00:07:26 INFO db.DBInputFormat: Using read commited transaction isolation
15/10/22 00:07:26 INFO mapred.MapTask: Processing split: 1=1 AND 1=1
15/10/22 00:07:26 DEBUG db.DataDrivenDBInputFormat: Creating db record reader for db product: MYSQL
15/10/22 00:07:26 INFO mapreduce.Job: Job job_local2065078437_0001 running in uber mode : false
15/10/22 00:07:26 INFO mapreduce.Job: map 0% reduce 0%
15/10/22 00:07:27 INFO db.DBRecordReader: Working on split: 1=1 AND 1=1
15/10/22 00:07:27 DEBUG db.DataDrivenDBRecordReader: Using query: SELECT `time_stamp`,
`category`, `type`, `servername`, `code`, `msg` FROM `wlslog` AS `wlslog` WHERE (1=1) AND (1=1)
15/10/22 00:07:27 DEBUG db.DBRecordReader: Using fetchSize for next query: -2147483648
15/10/22 00:07:27 INFO db.DBRecordReader: Executing query: SELECT `time_stamp`, `category`,
`type`, `servername`, `code`, `msg` FROM `wlslog` AS `wlslog` WHERE (1=1) AND (1=1)
15/10/22 00:07:27 DEBUG mapreduce.AutoProgressMapper: Instructing auto-progress thread to quit.
15/10/22 00:07:27 DEBUG mapreduce.AutoProgressMapper: Waiting for progress thread shutdown…
15/10/22 00:07:27 INFO mapreduce.AutoProgressMapper: Auto-progress thread is finished.
keepGoing=false
15/10/22 00:07:27 DEBUG mapreduce.AutoProgressMapper: Progress thread shutdown detected.
15/10/22 00:07:27 INFO mapred.LocalJobRunner:
15/10/22 00:07:27 INFO mapred.Task: Task:attempt_local2065078437_0001_m_000000_0 is done.
And is in the process of committing
15/10/22 00:07:27 INFO mapred.LocalJobRunner:
15/10/22 00:07:27 INFO mapred.Task: Task attempt_local2065078437_0001_m_000000_0 is allowed
to commit now
15/10/22 00:07:27 INFO output.FileOutputCommitter: Saved output of task 'attempt_loca
l2065078437_0001_m_000000_0' to hdfs://localhost:8020/mysql/import/_temporary/0/task_
local2065078437_0001_m_000000
15/10/22 00:07:27 INFO mapred.LocalJobRunner: map
15/10/22 00:07:27 INFO mapred.Task: Task 'attempt_local2065078437_0001_m_000000_0' done.
15/10/22 00:07:27 INFO mapred.LocalJobRunner: Finishing task: attempt_local2065078437_0001
_m_000000_0
15/10/22 00:07:27 INFO mapred.LocalJobRunner: map task executor complete.
15/10/22 00:07:28 INFO mapreduce.Job: map 100% reduce 0%
15/10/22 00:07:28 INFO mapreduce.Job: Job job_local2065078437_0001 completed successfully
15/10/22 00:07:28 INFO mapreduce.Job: Counters: 23
        File System Counters
                FILE: Number of bytes read=17796154
                FILE: Number of bytes written=18238016
                FILE: Number of read operations=0
                FILE: Number of large read operations=0
                FILE: Number of write operations=0
                HDFS: Number of bytes read=0
                HDFS: Number of bytes written=615
                HDFS: Number of read operations=4
                HDFS: Number of large read operations=0
                HDFS: Number of write operations=3
        Map-Reduce Framework
                Map input records=6

```
                    Map output records=6
                    Input split bytes=87
                    Spilled Records=0
                    Failed Shuffles=0
                    Merged Map outputs=0
                    GC time elapsed (ms)=306
                    CPU time spent (ms)=0
                    Physical memory (bytes) snapshot=0
                    Virtual memory (bytes) snapshot=0
                    Total committed heap usage (bytes)=138571776
            File Input Format Counters
                    Bytes Read=0
            File Output Format Counters
                    Bytes Written=615
15/10/22 00:07:28 INFO mapreduce.ImportJobBase: Transferred 615 bytes in 9.6688 seconds
(63.6064 bytes/sec)
15/10/22 00:07:28 INFO mapreduce.ImportJobBase: Retrieved 6 records.
root@08b338cb2a90:/#
```

Listing Data Imported into HDFS

To list the files generated with the sqoop import tool in the /mysql/import directory, run the following command.

```
sudo -u hdfs hdfs dfs -ls /mysql/import
```

Two files get listed: _SUCCESS, which indicates that the sqoop import command completed successfully, and part-m-00000, which has the data imported as shown in Figure 11-23.

```
root@08b338cb2a90:/# sudo -u hdfs hdfs dfs -ls /mysql/import
Found 2 items
-rw-r--r--   1 hdfs supergroup          0 2015-10-22 00:07 /mysql/import/_SUCCES
S
-rw-r--r--   1 hdfs supergroup        615 2015-10-22 00:07 /mysql/import/part-m-
00000
root@08b338cb2a90:/# █
```

Figure 11-23. *Listing Files Generated by sqoop import*

List the data in the data file part-m-00000 with the following command.

```
sudo -u hdfs hdfs dfs -cat /mysql/import/part-m-00000
```

The data imported with the sqoop import tool gets listed as shown in Figure 11-24.

```
root@08b338cb2a90:/# sudo -u hdfs hdfs dfs -cat /mysql/import/part-m-00000
Apr-8-2014-7:06:16-PM-PDT,Notice,WebLogicServer,AdminServer,BEA-000365,Server st
ate changed to STANDBY
Apr-8-2014-7:06:17-PM-PDT,Notice,WebLogicServer,AdminServer,BEA-000365,Server st
ate changed to STARTING
Apr-8-2014-7:06:18-PM-PDT,Notice,WebLogicServer,AdminServer,BEA-000365,Server st
ate changed to ADMIN
Apr-8-2014-7:06:19-PM-PDT,Notice,WebLogicServer,AdminServer,BEA-000365,Server st
ate changed to RESUMING
Apr-8-2014-7:06:20-PM-PDT,Notice,WebLogicServer,AdminServer,BEA-000361,Started W
ebLogic AdminServer
Apr-8-2014-7:06:21-PM-PDT,Notice,WebLogicServer,AdminServer,BEA-000365,Server st
ate changed to RUNNING
root@08b338cb2a90:/# ▌
```

Figure 11-24. Listing Data imported by Sqoop

Exporting from HDFS to MySQL with Sqoop

Next, we shall export the data imported into HDFS back to MySQL database. In general the sqoop export tool exports a set of files from HDFS back to an RDBMS where the target table exists already in the database and the input files will be read and parsed into a set of records according to the delimiters specified in the "user-specified" values.

The code required to interact with the database may be generated during the sqoop export command or before the sqoop export command. We shall generate the code before running the sqoop export command using the sqoop codegen command as follows.

```
sudo -u hdfs sqoop codegen --connect "jdbc:mysql://e414f8c41d0b:3306/mysqldb"   --password
"mysql" --username "mysql" --table "WLSLOG_COPY"
```

The command parameters are the same as for the sqoop codegen command run before the sqoop import command except the table name is WLSLOG_COPY instead of wlslog. The code required by the sqoop export command gets generated in the WLSLOG_COPY.jar file as shown in Figure 11-25.

```
root@08b338cb2a90:/# sudo -u hdfs sqoop codegen --connect "jdbc:mysql://e414f8c4
1d0b:3306/mysqldb"  --password "mysql" --username "mysql" --table "WLSLOG_COPY"
Warning: /usr/lib/sqoop/../accumulo does not exist! Accumulo imports will fail.
Please set $ACCUMULO_HOME to the root of your Accumulo installation.
15/10/22 00:12:29 INFO sqoop.Sqoop: Running Sqoop version: 1.4.5-cdh5.4.3
15/10/22 00:12:29 WARN tool.BaseSqoopTool: Setting your password on the command-
line is insecure. Consider using -P instead.
15/10/22 00:12:29 INFO manager.MySQLManager: Preparing to use a MySQL streaming
resultset.
15/10/22 00:12:29 INFO tool.CodeGenTool: Beginning code generation
15/10/22 00:12:30 INFO manager.SqlManager: Executing SQL statement: SELECT t.* F
ROM `WLSLOG_COPY` AS t LIMIT 1
15/10/22 00:12:31 INFO manager.SqlManager: Executing SQL statement: SELECT t.* F
ROM `WLSLOG_COPY` AS t LIMIT 1
15/10/22 00:12:31 INFO orm.CompilationManager: HADOOP_MAPRED_HOME is /usr/lib/ha
doop-mapreduce
Note: /tmp/sqoop-hdfs/compile/047d0687acbb2298370a7b461cdfdd2e/WLSLOG_COPY.java
uses or overrides a deprecated API.
Note: Recompile with -Xlint:deprecation for details.
15/10/22 00:12:37 INFO orm.CompilationManager: Writing jar file: /tmp/sqoop-hdfs
/compile/047d0687acbb2298370a7b461cdfdd2e/WLSLOG_COPY.jar
root@08b338cb2a90:/# █
```

Figure 11-25. *Running the sqoop codegen Command*

Next, run the sqoop export command adding the WLSLOG_COPY.jar in the classpath with the –libjars option. The other command parameters are the same as the sqoop import command except the –table being "WLSLOG_COPY" and the --export-dir option replacing the --target-dir. The directory in the --export-dir option should be the same as the directory in the --data-dir option for the sqoop import command.

```
sudo -u hdfs sqoop export  -libjars /tmp/sqoop-hdfs/compile/047d0687acbb2298370a7b461cdfdd
2e/WLSLOG_COPY.jar --connect "jdbc:mysql://e414f8c41d0b:3306/mysqldb"  --password "mysql"
--username "mysql"  --export-dir "/mysql/import" --table "WLSLOG_COPY"  --verbose
```

The output from the sqoop export command is shown in Figure 11-26.

```
root@08b338cb2a90: /                                    _  □  )
File  Edit  View  Search  Terminal  Help
15/10/22 00:14:13 INFO mapreduce.Job: Counters: 23
        File System Counters
                FILE: Number of bytes read=71190614
                FILE: Number of bytes written=72948608
                FILE: Number of read operations=0
                FILE: Number of large read operations=0
                FILE: Number of write operations=0
                HDFS: Number of bytes read=4068
                HDFS: Number of bytes written=0
                HDFS: Number of read operations=86
                HDFS: Number of large read operations=0
                HDFS: Number of write operations=0
        Map-Reduce Framework
                Map input records=6
                Map output records=6
                Input split bytes=576
                Spilled Records=0
                Failed Shuffles=0
                Merged Map outputs=0
                GC time elapsed (ms)=0
                CPU time spent (ms)=0
                Physical memory (bytes) snapshot=0
                Virtual memory (bytes) snapshot=0
                Total committed heap usage (bytes)=576782336
        File Input Format Counters
                Bytes Read=0
        File Output Format Counters
                Bytes Written=0
15/10/22 00:14:13 INFO mapreduce.ExportJobBase: Transferred 3.9727 KB in 8.722 s
econds (466.4067 bytes/sec)
15/10/22 00:14:13 INFO mapreduce.ExportJobBase: Exported 6 records.
root@08b338cb2a90:/# []
```

Figure 11-26. Output from the sqoop export command

The detailed output from the sqoop export command is listed:

```
root@08b338cb2a90:/# sudo -u hdfs sqoop export  -libjars /tmp/sqoop-hdfs/compile/047d0687a
cbb2298370a7b461cdfdd2e/WLSLOG_COPY.jar --connect "jdbc:mysql://e414f8c41d0b:3306/mysqldb"
--password "mysql" --username "mysql"  --export-dir "/mysql/import" --table "WLSLOG_COPY"
--verbose
15/10/22 00:13:52 INFO sqoop.Sqoop: Running Sqoop version: 1.4.5-cdh5.4.3
15/10/22 00:13:54 INFO tool.CodeGenTool: Beginning code generation
15/10/22 00:13:54 DEBUG manager.SqlManager: Execute getColumnInfoRawQuery : SELECT t.* FROM
`WLSLOG_COPY` AS t LIMIT 1
15/10/22 00:13:54 DEBUG manager.SqlManager: No connection paramenters specified. Using
regular API for making connection.
```

```
15/10/22 00:13:55 DEBUG manager.SqlManager: Using fetchSize for next query: -2147483648
15/10/22 00:13:55 INFO manager.SqlManager: Executing SQL statement: SELECT t.* FROM
`WLSLOG_COPY` AS t LIMIT 1
15/10/22 00:13:55 DEBUG manager.SqlManager: Found column time_stamp of type [12, 255, 0]
15/10/22 00:13:55 DEBUG manager.SqlManager: Found column category of type [12, 255, 0]
15/10/22 00:13:55 DEBUG manager.SqlManager: Found column type of type [12, 255, 0]
15/10/22 00:13:55 DEBUG manager.SqlManager: Found column servername of type [12, 255, 0]
15/10/22 00:13:55 DEBUG manager.SqlManager: Found column code of type [12, 255, 0]
15/10/22 00:13:55 DEBUG manager.SqlManager: Found column msg of type [12, 255, 0]
15/10/22 00:13:55 DEBUG orm.ClassWriter: selected columns:
15/10/22 00:13:55 DEBUG orm.ClassWriter:    time_stamp
15/10/22 00:13:55 DEBUG orm.ClassWriter:    category
15/10/22 00:13:55 DEBUG orm.ClassWriter:    type
15/10/22 00:13:55 DEBUG orm.ClassWriter:    servername
15/10/22 00:13:55 DEBUG orm.ClassWriter:    code
15/10/22 00:13:55 DEBUG orm.ClassWriter:    msg
15/10/22 00:13:55 DEBUG manager.SqlManager: Using fetchSize for next query: -2147483648
15/10/22 00:13:55 INFO manager.SqlManager: Executing SQL statement: SELECT t.* FROM
`WLSLOG_COPY` AS t LIMIT 1
15/10/22 00:13:55 DEBUG manager.SqlManager: Found column time_stamp of type VARCHAR
15/10/22 00:13:55 DEBUG manager.SqlManager: Found column category of type VARCHAR
15/10/22 00:13:55 DEBUG manager.SqlManager: Found column type of type VARCHAR
15/10/22 00:13:55 DEBUG manager.SqlManager: Found column servername of type VARCHAR
15/10/22 00:13:55 DEBUG manager.SqlManager: Found column code of type VARCHAR
15/10/22 00:13:55 DEBUG manager.SqlManager: Found column msg of type VARCHAR
15/10/22 00:13:55 DEBUG orm.ClassWriter: Writing source file: /tmp/sqoop-hdfs/compile/715ce1
218221b63dfffd800222f863f0/WLSLOG_COPY.java
15/10/22 00:13:55 DEBUG orm.ClassWriter: Table name: WLSLOG_COPY
15/10/22 00:13:55 DEBUG orm.ClassWriter: Columns: time_stamp:12, category:12, type:12,
servername:12, code:12, msg:12,
15/10/22 00:13:55 DEBUG orm.ClassWriter: sourceFilename is WLSLOG_COPY.java
15/10/22 00:13:55 DEBUG orm.CompilationManager: Found existing /tmp/sqoop-hdfs/compile/715ce
1218221b63dfffd800222f863f0/
15/10/22 00:13:55 INFO orm.CompilationManager: HADOOP_MAPRED_HOME is /usr/lib/hadoop-mapreduce
15/10/22 00:13:55 DEBUG orm.CompilationManager: Returning jar file path /usr/lib/hadoop-
mapreduce/hadoop-mapreduce-client-core.jar:/usr/lib/hadoop-mapreduce/hadoop-mapreduce-
client-core-2.6.0-cdh5.4.3.jar
15/10/22 00:14:02 INFO mapreduce.ExportJobBase: Beginning export of WLSLOG_COPY
15/10/22 00:14:02 INFO Configuration.deprecation: mapred.job.tracker is deprecated. Instead,
use mapreduce.jobtracker.address
15/10/22 00:14:02 INFO Configuration.deprecation: mapred.jar is deprecated. Instead, use
mapreduce.job.jar
15/10/22 00:14:04 DEBUG mapreduce.JobBase: Using InputFormat: class org.apache.sqoop.
mapreduce.ExportInputFormat
15/10/22 00:14:04 DEBUG db.DBConfiguration: Securing password into job credentials store
15/10/22 00:14:04 INFO jvm.JvmMetrics: Initializing JVM Metrics with processName=JobTracker,
sessionId=
15/10/22 00:14:06 INFO input.FileInputFormat: Total input paths to process : 1
15/10/22 00:14:06 DEBUG mapreduce.ExportInputFormat: Target numMapTasks=4
15/10/22 00:14:06 DEBUG mapreduce.ExportInputFormat: Total input bytes=615
15/10/22 00:14:06 DEBUG mapreduce.ExportInputFormat: maxSplitSize=153
```

```
15/10/22 00:14:06 INFO input.FileInputFormat: Total input paths to process : 1
15/10/22 00:14:06 DEBUG mapreduce.ExportInputFormat: Generated splits:
15/10/22 00:14:06 DEBUG mapreduce.ExportInputFormat:    Paths:/mysql/import/
part-m-00000:0+153 Locations:08b338cb2a90:;
15/10/22 00:14:06 DEBUG mapreduce.ExportInputFormat:    Paths:/mysql/import/
part-m-00000:153+153 Locations:08b338cb2a90:;
15/10/22 00:14:06 DEBUG mapreduce.ExportInputFormat:    Paths:/mysql/import/
part-m-00000:306+153 Locations:08b338cb2a90:;
15/10/22 00:14:06 DEBUG mapreduce.ExportInputFormat:    Paths:/mysql/import/
part-m-00000:459+78,/mysql/import/part-m-00000:537+78 Locations:08b338cb2a90:;
15/10/22 00:14:06 INFO mapreduce.JobSubmitter: number of splits:4
15/10/22 00:14:06 INFO Configuration.deprecation: mapred.map.tasks.speculative.execution is
deprecated. Instead, use mapreduce.map.speculative
15/10/22 00:14:06 INFO mapreduce.JobSubmitter: Submitting tokens for job:
job_local1198888838_0001
15/10/22 00:14:11 INFO mapreduce.Job: The url to track the job: http://localhost:8080/
15/10/22 00:14:11 INFO mapreduce.Job: Running job: job_local1198888838_0001
15/10/22 00:14:11 INFO mapred.LocalJobRunner: OutputCommitter set in config null
15/10/22 00:14:11 INFO mapred.LocalJobRunner: OutputCommitter is org.apache.sqoop.mapreduce.
NullOutputCommitter
15/10/22 00:14:11 INFO mapred.LocalJobRunner: Waiting for map tasks
15/10/22 00:14:11 INFO mapred.LocalJobRunner: Starting task: attempt_local1198888838_0001
_m_000000_0
15/10/22 00:14:11 DEBUG mapreduce.CombineShimRecordReader: ChildSplit operates on:
hdfs://localhost:8020/mysql/import/part-m-00000
15/10/22 00:14:11 DEBUG db.DBConfiguration: Fetching password from job credentials store
15/10/22 00:14:12 DEBUG mapreduce.CombineShimRecordReader: ChildSplit operates on:
hdfs://localhost:8020/mysql/import/part-m-00000
15/10/22 00:14:12 DEBUG mapreduce.AutoProgressMapper: Instructing auto-progress thread to quit.
15/10/22 00:14:12 DEBUG mapreduce.AutoProgressMapper: Waiting for progress thread shutdown...
15/10/22 00:14:12 INFO mapreduce.AutoProgressMapper: Auto-progress thread is finished.
keepGoing=false
15/10/22 00:14:12 DEBUG mapreduce.AutoProgressMapper: Progress thread shutdown detected.
15/10/22 00:14:12 INFO mapred.LocalJobRunner:
15/10/22 00:14:12 DEBUG mapreduce.AsyncSqlOutputFormat: Committing transaction of 1 statements
15/10/22 00:14:12 INFO mapred.Task: Task:attempt_local1198888838_0001_m_000000_0 is done.
And is in the process of committing
15/10/22 00:14:12 INFO mapred.LocalJobRunner: map
15/10/22 00:14:12 INFO mapred.Task: Task 'attempt_local1198888838_0001_m_000000_0' done.
15/10/22 00:14:12 INFO mapred.LocalJobRunner: Finishing task: attempt_local1198888838_0001
_m_000000_0
15/10/22 00:14:12 INFO mapred.LocalJobRunner: Starting task: attempt_local1198888838_0001
_m_000001_0
15/10/22 00:14:12 INFO mapred.Task:  Using ResourceCalculatorProcessTree : [ ]
15/10/22 00:14:12 INFO mapred.MapTask: Processing split: Paths:/mysql/import/
part-m-00000:0+153
15/10/22 00:14:12 DEBUG mapreduce.CombineShimRecordReader: ChildSplit operates on:
hdfs://localhost:8020/mysql/import/part-m-00000
15/10/22 00:14:12 DEBUG db.DBConfiguration: Fetching password from job credentials store
15/10/22 00:14:12 DEBUG mapreduce.AutoProgressMapper: Instructing auto-progress thread to quit.
15/10/22 00:14:12 DEBUG mapreduce.AutoProgressMapper: Waiting for progress thread shutdown...
```

```
15/10/22 00:14:12 INFO mapreduce.AutoProgressMapper: Auto-progress thread is finished.
keepGoing=false
15/10/22 00:14:12 DEBUG mapreduce.AutoProgressMapper: Progress thread shutdown detected.
15/10/22 00:14:12 INFO mapred.LocalJobRunner:
15/10/22 00:14:12 DEBUG mapreduce.AsyncSqlOutputFormat: Committing transaction of 1
statements
15/10/22 00:14:12 INFO mapred.Task: Task:attempt_local1198888838_0001_m_000001_0 is done.
And is in the process of committing
15/10/22 00:14:12 INFO mapred.LocalJobRunner: map
15/10/22 00:14:12 INFO mapred.Task: Task 'attempt_local1198888838_0001_m_000001_0' done.
15/10/22 00:14:12 INFO mapred.LocalJobRunner: Finishing task: attempt_local1198888838_0001
_m_000001_0
15/10/22 00:14:12 INFO mapred.LocalJobRunner: Starting task: attempt_local1198888838_0001
_m_000002_0
15/10/22 00:14:12 INFO mapreduce.Job: Job job_local1198888838_0001 running in uber mode : false
15/10/22 00:14:12 INFO mapred.Task:  Using ResourceCalculatorProcessTree : [ ]
15/10/22 00:14:12 INFO mapred.MapTask: Processing split: Paths:/mysql/import/
part-m-00000:153+153
15/10/22 00:14:12 DEBUG mapreduce.CombineShimRecordReader: ChildSplit operates on:
hdfs://localhost:8020/mysql/import/part-m-00000
15/10/22 00:14:12 INFO mapreduce.Job:  map 100% reduce 0%
15/10/22 00:14:12 DEBUG db.DBConfiguration: Fetching password from job credentials store
15/10/22 00:14:12 DEBUG mapreduce.AutoProgressMapper: Instructing auto-progress thread to quit.
15/10/22 00:14:12 DEBUG mapreduce.AutoProgressMapper: Waiting for progress thread shutdown...
15/10/22 00:14:12 INFO mapreduce.AutoProgressMapper: Auto-progress thread is finished.
keepGoing=false
15/10/22 00:14:12 DEBUG mapreduce.AutoProgressMapper: Progress thread shutdown detected.
15/10/22 00:14:12 INFO mapred.LocalJobRunner:
15/10/22 00:14:12 DEBUG mapreduce.AsyncSqlOutputFormat: Committing transaction of 1
statements
15/10/22 00:14:12 INFO mapred.Task: Task:attempt_local1198888838_0001_m_000002_0 is done.
And is in the process of committing
15/10/22 00:14:12 INFO mapred.LocalJobRunner: map
15/10/22 00:14:12 INFO mapred.Task: Task 'attempt_local1198888838_0001_m_000002_0' done.
15/10/22 00:14:12 INFO mapred.LocalJobRunner: Finishing task: attempt_local1198888838_0001
_m_000002_0
15/10/22 00:14:12 INFO mapred.LocalJobRunner: Starting task: attempt_local1198888838_0001
_m_000003_0
15/10/22 00:14:12 INFO mapred.Task:  Using ResourceCalculatorProcessTree : [ ]
15/10/22 00:14:12 INFO mapred.MapTask: Processing split: Paths:/mysql/import/
part-m-00000:306+153
15/10/22 00:14:12 DEBUG mapreduce.CombineShimRecordReader: ChildSplit operates on:
hdfs://localhost:8020/mysql/import/part-m-00000
15/10/22 00:14:12 DEBUG db.DBConfiguration: Fetching password from job credentials store
15/10/22 00:14:12 DEBUG mapreduce.AutoProgressMapper: Instructing auto-progress thread to quit.
15/10/22 00:14:12 DEBUG mapreduce.AutoProgressMapper: Waiting for progress thread shutdown...
15/10/22 00:14:12 INFO mapreduce.AutoProgressMapper: Auto-progress thread is finished.
keepGoing=false
15/10/22 00:14:12 DEBUG mapreduce.AutoProgressMapper: Progress thread shutdown detected.
15/10/22 00:14:12 INFO mapred.LocalJobRunner:
15/10/22 00:14:12 DEBUG mapreduce.AsyncSqlOutputFormat: Committing transaction of 1 statements
```

```
15/10/22 00:14:12 INFO mapred.Task: Task:attempt_local1198888838_0001_m_000003_0 is done.
And is in the process of committing
15/10/22 00:14:12 INFO mapred.LocalJobRunner: map
15/10/22 00:14:12 INFO mapred.Task: Task 'attempt_local1198888838_0001_m_000003_0' done.
15/10/22 00:14:12 INFO mapred.LocalJobRunner: Finishing task: attempt_local1198888838_0001
_m_000003_0
15/10/22 00:14:12 INFO mapred.LocalJobRunner: map task executor complete.
15/10/22 00:14:13 INFO mapreduce.Job: Job job_local1198888838_0001 completed successfully
15/10/22 00:14:13 INFO mapreduce.Job: Counters: 23
        File System Counters
                FILE: Number of bytes read=71190614
                FILE: Number of bytes written=72948608
                FILE: Number of read operations=0
                FILE: Number of large read operations=0
                FILE: Number of write operations=0
                HDFS: Number of bytes read=4068
                HDFS: Number of bytes written=0
                HDFS: Number of read operations=86
                HDFS: Number of large read operations=0
                HDFS: Number of write operations=0
        Map-Reduce Framework
                Map input records=6
                Map output records=6
                Input split bytes=576
                Spilled Records=0
                Failed Shuffles=0
                Merged Map outputs=0
                GC time elapsed (ms)=0
                CPU time spent (ms)=0
                Physical memory (bytes) snapshot=0
                Virtual memory (bytes) snapshot=0
                Total committed heap usage (bytes)=576782336
        File Input Format Counters
                Bytes Read=0
        File Output Format Counters
                Bytes Written=0
15/10/22 00:14:13 INFO mapreduce.ExportJobBase: Transferred 3.9727 KB in 8.722 seconds
(466.4067 bytes/sec)
15/10/22 00:14:13 INFO mapreduce.ExportJobBase: Exported 6 records.
root@08b338cb2a90:/#
```

Querying Exported Data

Having exported from HDFS to MySQL, use the following SELECT statement in MySQL CLI to query the data exported.

```
select * from WLSLOG_COPY;
```

The six rows of data exported get listed as shown in Figure 11-27.

```
ec2-user@ip-172-30-1-16:~                          _ □ ×

File  Edit  View  Search  Terminal  Help
mysql> select * from WLSLOG_COPY;
+-----------------------------+----------+-----------------+--------------+---------
---+-----------------------------------+
| time_stamp                  | category | type            | servername   | code
   | msg                               |
+-----------------------------+----------+-----------------+--------------+---------
---+-----------------------------------+
| Apr-8-2014-7:06:16-PM-PDT | Notice   | WebLogicServer  | AdminServer  | BEA-0003
65 | Server state changed to STANDBY   |
| Apr-8-2014-7:06:17-PM-PDT | Notice   | WebLogicServer  | AdminServer  | BEA-0003
65 | Server state changed to STARTING  |
| Apr-8-2014-7:06:18-PM-PDT | Notice   | WebLogicServer  | AdminServer  | BEA-0003
65 | Server state changed to ADMIN     |
| Apr-8-2014-7:06:19-PM-PDT | Notice   | WebLogicServer  | AdminServer  | BEA-0003
65 | Server state changed to RESUMING  |
| Apr-8-2014-7:06:20-PM-PDT | Notice   | WebLogicServer  | AdminServer  | BEA-0003
61 | Started WebLogic AdminServer      |
| Apr-8-2014-7:06:21-PM-PDT | Notice   | WebLogicServer  | AdminServer  | BEA-0003
65 | Server state changed to RUNNING   |
+-----------------------------+----------+-----------------+--------------+---------
---+-----------------------------------+
6 rows in set (0.00 sec)

mysql> █
```

Figure 11-27. Querying Exported Data in WLSLOG_COPY

Stopping and Removing Docker Containers

To remove the mysqldb and cdh containers the containers have to be first stopped. Stop the mysqldb container with the docker stop command.

```
sudo docker stop mysqldb
```

Remove the mysqldb container with the docker rm command.

```
sudo docker rm mysqldb
```

The mysqldb container gets stopped and removed as shown in Figure 11-28.

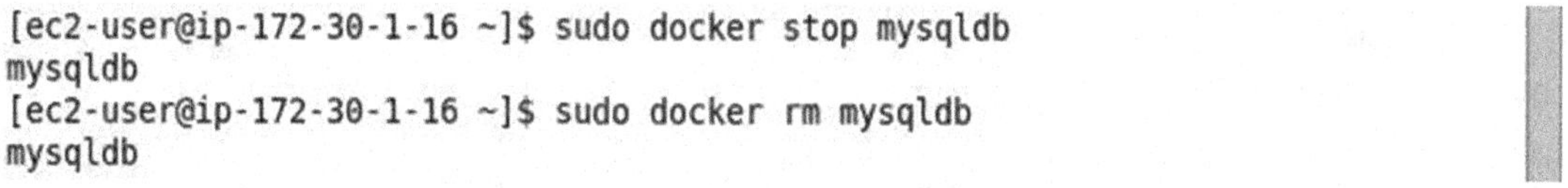

```
[ec2-user@ip-172-30-1-16 ~]$ sudo docker stop mysqldb
mysqldb
[ec2-user@ip-172-30-1-16 ~]$ sudo docker rm mysqldb
mysqldb
```

Figure 11-28. *Stopping and Removing Docker Container for MySQL Database*

Similarly stop and remove the cdh container.

```
sudo docker stop cdh
sudo docker rm cdh
```

The cdh container gets stopped and removed as shown in Figure 11-29.

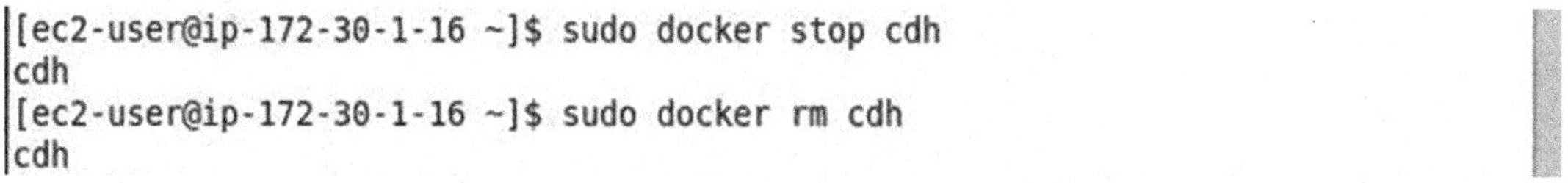

```
[ec2-user@ip-172-30-1-16 ~]$ sudo docker stop cdh
cdh
[ec2-user@ip-172-30-1-16 ~]$ sudo docker rm cdh
cdh
```

Figure 11-29. *Stopping and Removing Docker Container for CDH*

Summary

In this chapter we used Docker images for CDH and MySQL database to run two separate, but linked, Docker containers. We created a MySQL database in the Docker container and ran the sqoop import tool in the CDH container to import data from MySQL to HDFS. Subsequently we ran the sqoop export tool to export from HDFS to MySQL database. In the next chapter we shall discuss Apache Kafka.

CHAPTER 12

■ ■ ■

Using Apache Kafka

Apache Kafka is a messaging system based on the publish-subscribe model. A Kafka cluster consists of one or more servers called brokers. Kafka keeps messages categorized by "topics". Producers produce messages and publish the messages to topics. Consumers subscribe to specific topic/s and consume feeds of messages published to the topic/s. The messages published to a topic do not have to be consumed as produced and are stored in the topic for a configurable duration. A consumer may choose to consume the messages in a topic from the beginning. Apache ZooKeeper server is used to coordinate a Kafka cluster. The Kafka architecture is illustrated in Figure 12-1.

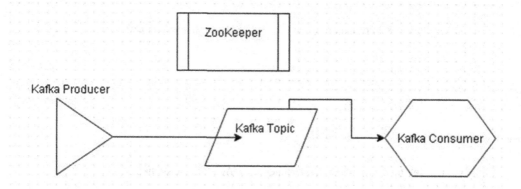

Figure 12-1. *Apache Kafka Architecture*

Apache Kafka is not directly based on Apache Hadoop nor does it make use of Apache Hadoop. But Kafka could be used as an Apache Flume source, channel, or sink. In this chapter we shall make use of a Docker image to run Apache Kafka in a Docker container. This chapter has the following sections.

> Setting the Environment
>
> Starting Docker Containers for Apache Kafka
>
> Finding IP Addresses
>
> Listing the Kafka Logs
>
> Creating a Kafka Topic
>
> Starting the Kafka Producer

Starting the Kafka Consumer

Producing and Consuming Messages

Stopping and Removing the Docker Containers

Setting the Environment

The following software is required for this chapter.

-Docker (version 1.8)

-Docker image for Apache ZooKeeper (version latest)

-Docker image for Apache Kafka (version latest)

Connect to an Amazon EC2 instance on which the software is to be installed; the Public IP Address would be different for different users.

```
ssh -i "docker.pem" ec2-user@52.91.168.33
```

Install Docker and start the Docker service.

```
sudo service docker start
```

An OK message indicates that Docker has been started as shown in Figure 12-2.

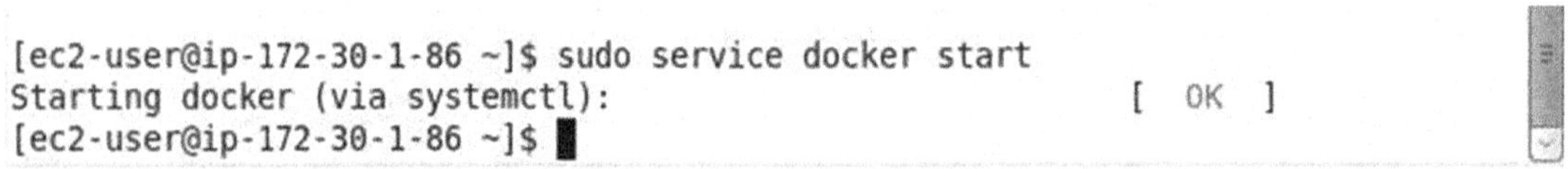

```
[ec2-user@ip-172-30-1-86 ~]$ sudo service docker start
Starting docker (via systemctl):                        [  OK  ]
[ec2-user@ip-172-30-1-86 ~]$
```

Figure 12-2. *Starting Docker Service*

Download the Docker image dockerkafka/zookeeper for Apache ZooKeeper.

```
sudo docker pull dockerkafka/zookeeper
```

The Docker image gets downloaded as shown in Figure 12-3.

Figure 12-3. *Downloading dockerkafka/zookeeper Docker Image*

The dockerkafka/zookeeper image has been selected for download because a corresponding dockerkafka/kafka image is also available. Download the Docker image dockerkafka/kafka also.

```
sudo  docker pull dockerkafka/kafka
```

Docker image dockerkafka/kafka gets downloaded as shown in Figure 12-4.

```
[ec2-user@ip-172-30-1-86 ~]$ sudo  docker pull dockerkafka/kafka
Using default tag: latest
latest: Pulling from dockerkafka/kafka
0b12df66f608: Pull complete
b9c1c5f483f7: Pull complete
afc814718fc0: Pull complete
3832c01b8067: Pull complete
ba9b095d3962: Pull complete
3f8a97ec9e67: Pull complete
e05e4800a34e: Pull complete
dc269adc7d73: Pull complete
203ad8afa4f7: Pull complete
cdcc5e2eb027: Pull complete
4f75aa83c1e2: Pull complete
ded5f5a542e6: Pull complete
e5e30918403e: Pull complete
a8bce79e2431: Pull complete
cb16f24e3554: Pull complete
7696a5ea6c29: Pull complete
776a0ad98c89: Pull complete
04dfaf166381: Pull complete
44bbba2bdad8: Pull complete
a98340b715b2: Pull complete
dba5e17df2c6: Pull complete
Digest: sha256:57be79cd7617b96db9ba6856b0a872fd951a57728825b958475c300dbccc6a7e
Status: Downloaded newer image for dockerkafka/kafka:latest
[ec2-user@ip-172-30-1-86 ~]$
```

Figure 12-4. *Downloading the dockerkafka/kafka Docker Image*

Starting Docker Containers for Apache Kafka

We need to start both Apache ZooKeeper and Apache Kafka containers as both are required for a Kafka cluster. First, start a Docker container for Apache ZooKeeper using the following docker run command in which the port for ZooKeeper is set to 2181. The Docker container is started in detached mode with the –d option.

```
sudo docker run -d --name zookeeper -p 2181:2181  dockerkafka/zookeeper
```

Next, start the Docker container for the Kafka server using the dockerkafka/kafka image. Specify the port for the Kafka server as 9092 and link the Kafka container with the container running the ZooKeeper using –link parameter.

```
sudo docker run --name kafka  -p 9092:9092 --link zookeeper:zookeeper  dockerkafka/kafka
```

List the running containers with the docker ps command.

```
sudo docker ps
```

The two containers, one for Apache ZooKeeper and the other for Apache Kafka get listed as shown in Figure 12-5.

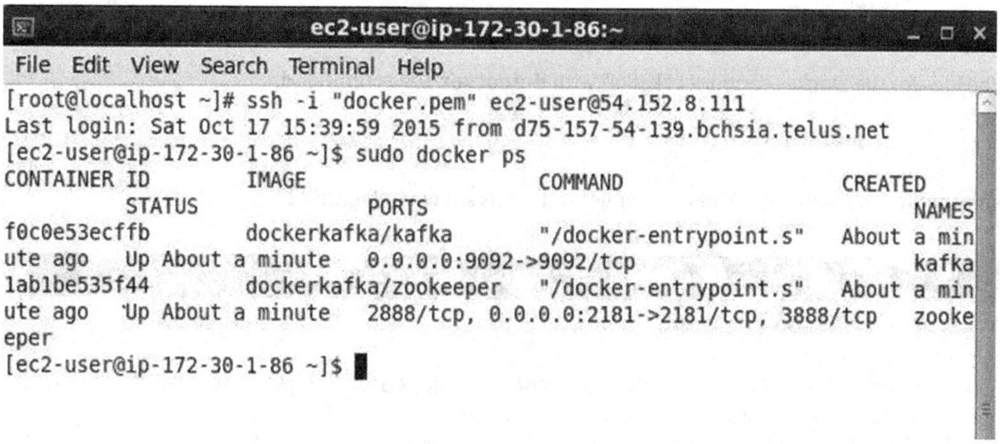

Figure 12-5. *Listing Running Docker Containers*

Finding IP Addresses

To run the Kakfa Producer and Consumer, we need to find the IP address of the Docker container running the ZooKeeper and IP address of the Docker container running the Kafka server. Run the following two commands to export the ZK_IP and KAFKA_IP environment variables.

```
export ZK_IP=$(sudo docker inspect --format '{{ .NetworkSettings.IPAddress }}' zookeeper)
export KAFKA_IP=$(sudo docker inspect --format '{{ .NetworkSettings.IPAddress }}' kafka)
```

Subsequently, echo the ZK_IP and KAFKA_IP variables. The ZK_IP is output as 172.17.0.1 and the KAFKA_IP is output as *172.17.0.2* as shown in Figure 12-6. We shall use these IP addresses in subsequent sections.

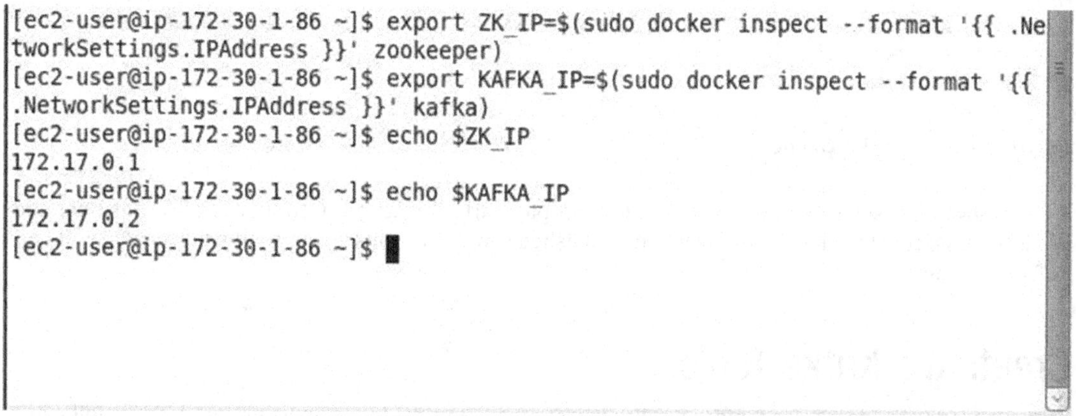

Figure 12-6. *Finding IP Addresses for Zookeeper and Kafka Servers*

Listing the Kafka Logs

Output the logs for the Docker container "kafka" with the docker logs command.

```
sudo docker logs -f kafka
```

The output indicates that the Kafka server got started as shown in Figure 12-7.

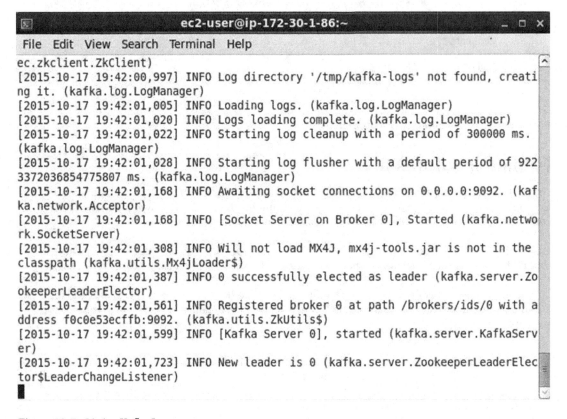

Figure 12-7. *Listing Kafka Logs*

In subsequent sections we shall create a Kafka topic, start a Kafka producer, start a Kafka consumer and produce messages at the Kafka Producer to be published at a Kafka topic, and consume the messages at the Kafka Consumer.

Creating a Kafka Topic

First, we need to create a Kafka topic to publish messages to. Start the interactive terminal with the following command.

```
sudo docker exec -it kafka bash
```

Create a Kafka topic in the interactive terminal with the kafka-topics.sh –create command. Specify the topic to create with the –topic option as "test". Specify the ZooKeeper address as the IP address for the ZooKeeper obtained earlier and set in the environment variable ZK_IP. Specify the ZooKeeper port as 2181. The number of partitions is set to 1 with the --partitions option, and the replication factor is set to 1 with the --replication-factor option.

```
kafka-topics.sh --create --topic test --zookeeper 172.17.0.1:2181 --replication-factor 1
--partitions 1
```

The output from the command is Created topic "test" as shown in Figure 12-8.

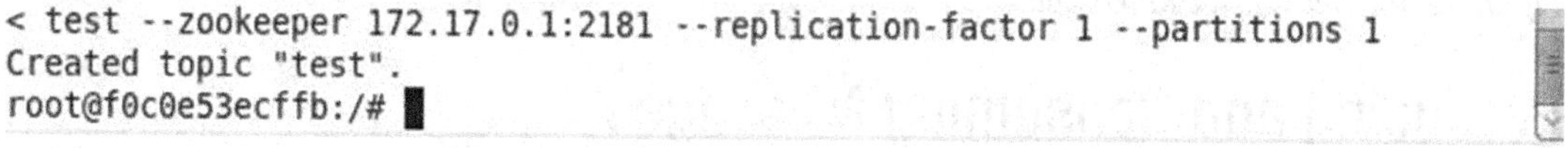

```
< test --zookeeper 172.17.0.1:2181 --replication-factor 1 --partitions 1
Created topic "test".
root@f0c0e53ecffb:/# ▌
```

Figure 12-8. *Creating a Kafka topic*

Starting the Kafka Producer

Next, start the Kafka producer with the following command from an interactive terminal for the "kafka" container running the Kafka server. The broker list is specified as 172.17.0.2:9092 in which the IP address is the environment variable KAFKA_IP exported earlier. The port Kafka server listens on is 9092. The topic to which the messages are to be published is set with the –topic option as "test".

```
kafka-console-producer.sh --topic test --broker-list 172.17.0.2:9092
```

Kafka producer console gets started as shown in Figure 12-9.

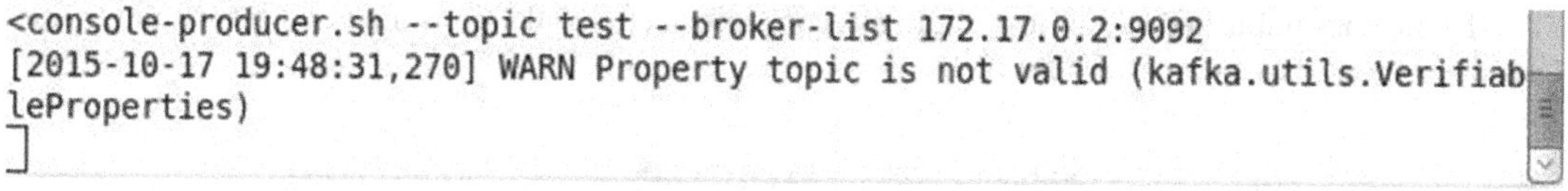

```
<console-producer.sh --topic test --broker-list 172.17.0.2:9092
[2015-10-17 19:48:31,270] WARN Property topic is not valid (kafka.utils.Verifiab
leProperties)
]
```

Figure 12-9. *Starting the Kafka Producer*

Starting the Kafka Consumer

For the Kafka Consumer console we need to start another interactive terminal for the "kafka" container.

```
sudo docker exec -it kafka bash
```

Run the following command to start the Kafka consumer console to consume messages published to the "test" topic as specified with the –topic option. The ZooKeeper host:port is set with the –zookeeper option to 172.17.0.1:2181 in which the IP Address is the environment variable ZK_IP and the port is 2181. The --from-beginning option implies that messages are to be consumed from the beginning.

```
kafka-console-consumer.sh --topic test --from-beginning --zookeeper 172.17.0.1:2181
```

The Kafka consumer console gets started as shown in Figure 12-10.

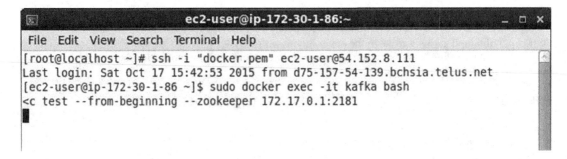

Figure 12-10. *Starting the Kafka Consumer*

Producing and Consuming Messages

In this section we shall publish messages from the Kafka Producer to the Kafka topic "test" configured when we started the Producer, and consume the messages at the Kafka consumer also subscribed to the "test" topic.

Publish a message "Hello Kafka from Docker" at the Producer console as shown in Figure 12-11. Click on Enter to navigate to the next line in the console.

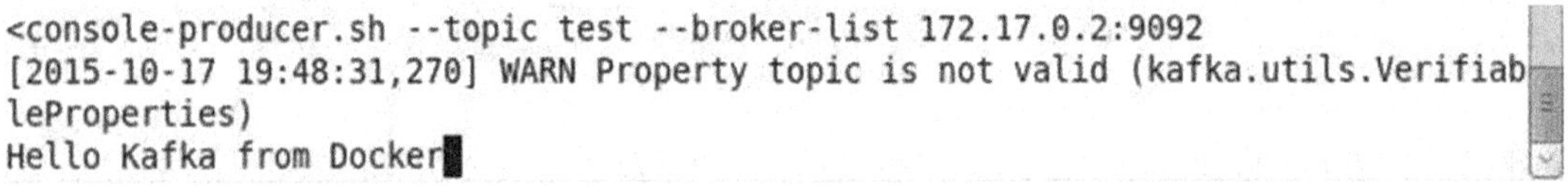

```
<console-producer.sh --topic test --broker-list 172.17.0.2:9092
[2015-10-17 19:48:31,270] WARN Property topic is not valid (kafka.utils.Verifiab
leProperties)
Hello Kafka from Docker
```

Figure 12-11. *Producing a Message at the Kafka Producer*

The message published to the "test" topic gets consumed at the Kafka Consumer and gets output in the Consumer console as shown in Figure 12-12.

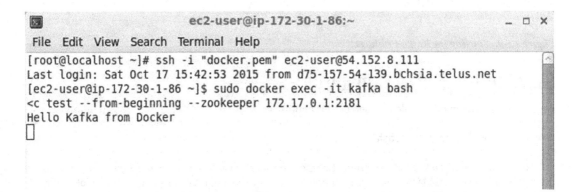

Figure 12-12. *Consuming Messages at the Consumer*

Similarly, publish more messages to the "test" topic from the Kafka Producer as shown in Figure 12-13.

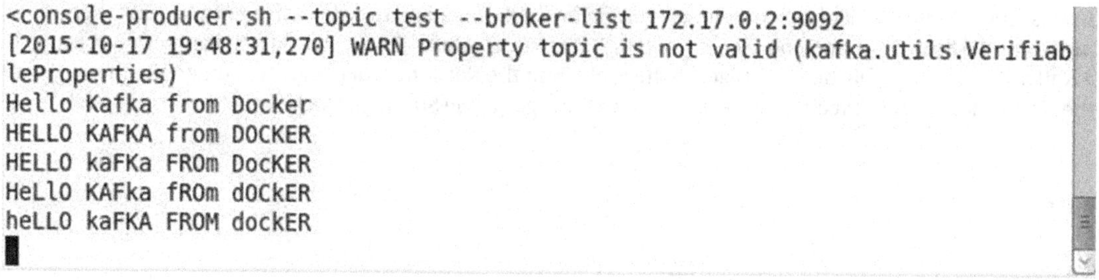

```
<console-producer.sh --topic test --broker-list 172.17.0.2:9092
[2015-10-17 19:48:31,270] WARN Property topic is not valid (kafka.utils.Verifiab
leProperties)
Hello Kafka from Docker
HELLO KAFKA from DOCKER
HELLO kaFKa FROm DocKER
HeLlO KAFka fROm dOCkER
heLLO kaFKA FROM dockER
```

Figure 12-13. *Producing More Messages at the Producer*

The messages get output at the Kafka Consumer console as shown in Figure 12-14.

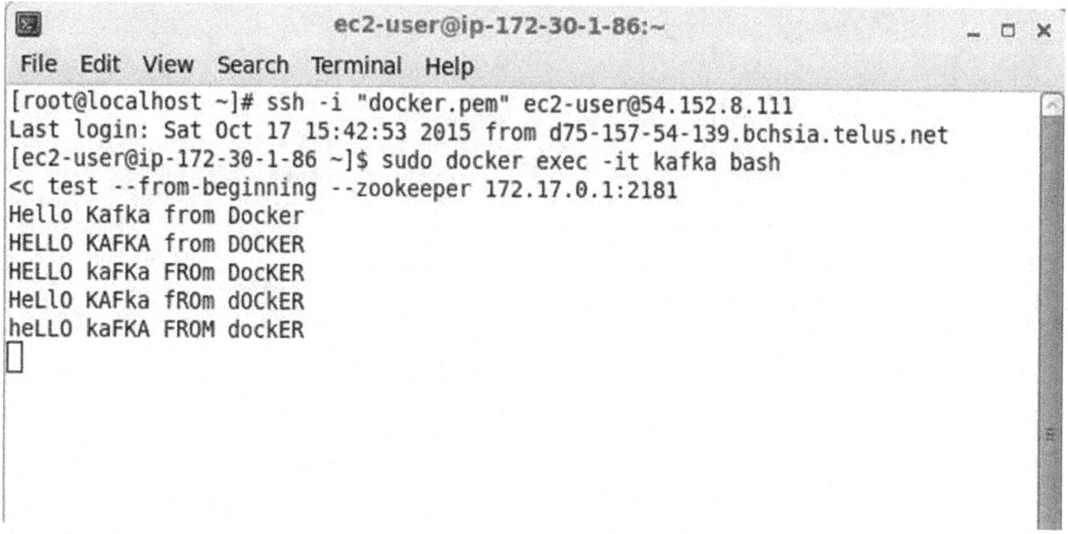

```
ec2-user@ip-172-30-1-86:~                                    _  □  ✕

File  Edit  View  Search  Terminal  Help
[root@localhost ~]# ssh -i "docker.pem" ec2-user@54.152.8.111
Last login: Sat Oct 17 15:42:53 2015 from d75-157-54-139.bchsia.telus.net
[ec2-user@ip-172-30-1-86 ~]$ sudo docker exec -it kafka bash
<c test --from-beginning --zookeeper 172.17.0.1:2181
Hello Kafka from Docker
HELLO KAFKA from DOCKER
HELLO kaFKa FROm DocKER
HeLlO KAFka fROm dOCkER
heLLO kaFKA FROM dockER
```

Figure 12-14. *Consumming Messages*

Stopping and Removing the Docker Containers

To stop the Docker containers, run the docker stop command. Stop the "kafka" container as follows.

```
sudo docker stop kafka
```

The "kafka" container may be removed with the docker rm command.

```
sudo docker rm kafka
```

Similarly, stop and remove the Docker container "zookeeper".

```
sudo docker stop zookeeper
sudo docker rm zookeeper
```

Summary

In this chapter we used Docker containers for Apache ZooKeeper and Apache Kafka to run a Kafka server process linked to an Apache ZooKeeper process. We created a Kafka Topic, started a Kafka producer, started a Kafka Consumer, published messages to the topic from the Kafka producer and consumed the messages at the Consumer. In the next chapter we shall discuss using Apache Solr with Docker.

■ ■ ■

Using Apache Solr

Apache Solr is an open source search platform built on Apache Lucene, a text search engine library. Apache Solr is scalable and reliable and provides indexing and querying service. Cloudera Search is based on Apache Solr. In this chapter we shall use the official Docker image for Apache Solr to run Apache Solr in a Docker container. This chapter has the following sections.

> Setting the Environment
>
> Starting Docker Container for Apache Solr Server
>
> Starting Interactive Shell
>
> Logging in to the Solr Admin Console
>
> Creating a Core Admin Index
>
> Loading Sample Data
>
> Querying Apache Solr in Solr Admin Console
>
> Querying Apache Solr using REST API Client
>
> Deleting Data
>
> Listing Logs
>
> Stopping Apache Solr Server

Setting the Environment

The following software is required for this chapter.

> -Docker Engine (version 1.8)
>
> -Docker image for Apache Solr

We will use an Amazon EC2 instance based on the Ubuntu Server 14.04 LTS (HVM), SSD Volume Type - ami-d05e75b8. Login to the Amazon EC2 instance with the user name "ubuntu" and the public IP address of the Amazon EC2 instance.

```
ssh -i "docker.pem" ubuntu@54.208.53.110
```

Ubuntu instance on Amazon EC2 gets logged in to as shown in Figure 13-1.

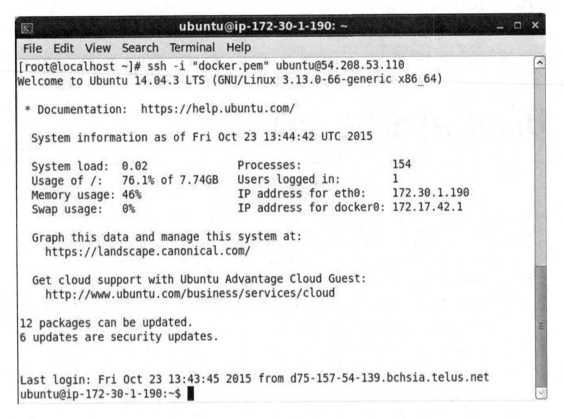

Figure 13-1. Logging in to Ubuntu on AmazonEC2

Install Docker on Ubuntu as discussed in Chapter 1. Start the Docker service. If Docker is already started, a message "start: Job is already running: docker" gets output.

```
sudo service docker start
```

Docker service status may be output with the following command.

```
sudo service docker status
```

A message indicating that a docker process is running gets output as shown in Figure 13-2.

```
ubuntu@ip-172-30-1-190:~$ sudo service docker start
start: Job is already running: docker
ubuntu@ip-172-30-1-190:~$ sudo service docker status
docker start/running, process 898
ubuntu@ip-172-30-1-190:~$
```

Figure 13-2. Starting and Finding Docker Service Status

Next, download the official Docker image for Apache Solr with the `docker pull` command.

```
sudo docker pull solr
```

The Docker image gets downloaded as shown in Figure 13-3.

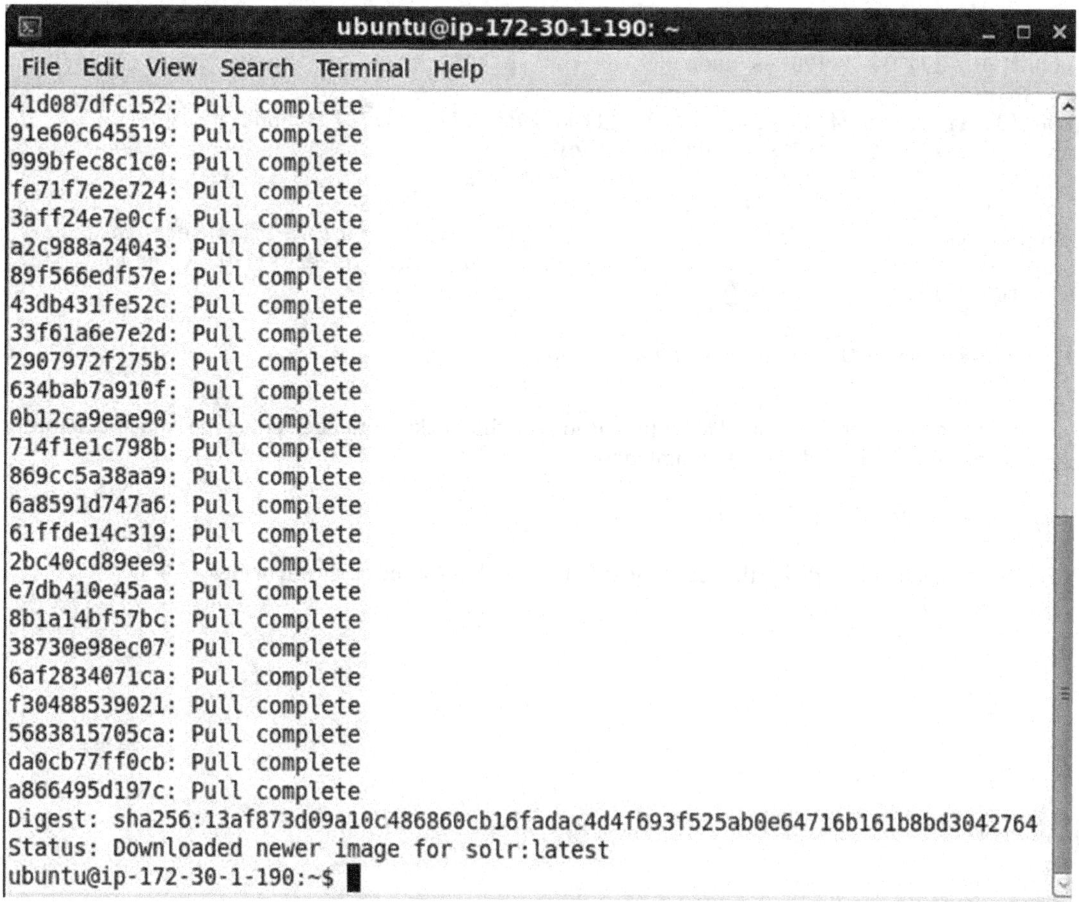
ubuntu@ip-172-30-1-190: ~
File Edit View Search Terminal Help
41d087dfc152: Pull complete
91e60c645519: Pull complete
999bfec8c1c0: Pull complete
fe71f7e2e724: Pull complete
3aff24e7e0cf: Pull complete
a2c988a24043: Pull complete
89f566edf57e: Pull complete
43db431fe52c: Pull complete
33f61a6e7e2d: Pull complete
2907972f275b: Pull complete
634bab7a910f: Pull complete
0b12ca9eae90: Pull complete
714f1e1c798b: Pull complete
869cc5a38aa9: Pull complete
6a8591d747a6: Pull complete
61ffde14c319: Pull complete
2bc40cd89ee9: Pull complete
e7db410e45aa: Pull complete
8b1a14bf57bc: Pull complete
38730e98ec07: Pull complete
6af2834071ca: Pull complete
f30488539021: Pull complete
5683815705ca: Pull complete
da0cb77ff0cb: Pull complete
a866495d197c: Pull complete
Digest: sha256:13af873d09a10c486860cb16fadac4d4f693f525ab0e64716b161b8bd3042764
Status: Downloaded newer image for solr:latest
ubuntu@ip-172-30-1-190:~$

Figure 13-3. *Downloading Docker Image solr*

Starting Docker Container for Apache Solr Server

To start Apache Solr server run the `docker run` command with port specified with `-p` as 8983. Specify the container name with `-name` option as "solr_on_docker," which is arbitrary. The `-d` command parameter makes the Docker container run in a detached mode.

```
sudo docker run -p 8983:8983  -d --name  solr_on_docker  solr
```

List the running Docker containers with the docker ps command.

```
sudo docker ps
```

The Docker container running Apache Solr get listed including the container id assigned to the container as shown in Figure 13-4.

```
ubuntu@ip-172-30-1-190:~$ sudo docker run -p 8983:8983  -d --name  solr_on_docke
r  solr
8061f79d1f1631ad824f659e54c2d3ee08e11f5da296f1377c3a0a78263bebd4
ubuntu@ip-172-30-1-190:~$ sudo docker ps
CONTAINER ID        IMAGE               COMMAND               CREATED
    STATUS              PORTS               NAMES
8061f79d1f16        solr                "/opt/solr/bin/solr -"  4 seconds ago
    Up 3 seconds        0.0.0.0:8983->8983/tcp   solr_on_docker
ubuntu@ip-172-30-1-190:~$ █
```

Figure 13-4. *Starting Docker Container for Apache Solr*

Run the docker logs command to output the logs for the Docker container. Either the container name or container id may be used in docker commands.

```
sudo docker logs -f 8061f79d1f16
```

The container logs indicate that the Apache Solr server has started as shown in Figure 13-5.

```
┌──────────────────────────────────────────────────────────────────────┐
│ ⊠            ubuntu@ip-172-30-1-190: ~                    _  □  ×      │
├──────────────────────────────────────────────────────────────────────┤
│  File  Edit  View  Search  Terminal  Help                             │
│ 1234 WARN  (main) [   ] o.a.s.c.SolrResourceLoader No files added to classloader⌃│
│ from lib: lib (resolved as: /opt/solr/server/solr/lib).               │
│ 1260 INFO  (main) [   ] o.a.s.h.c.HttpShardHandlerFactory created with socketTim│
│ eout : 600000,connTimeout : 60000,maxConnectionsPerHost : 20,maxConnections : 10│
│ 000,corePoolSize : 0,maximumPoolSize : 2147483647,maxThreadIdleTime : 5,sizeOfQu│
│ eue : -1,fairnessPolicy : false,useRetries : false,                   │
│ 1583 INFO  (main) [   ] o.a.s.u.UpdateShardHandler Creating UpdateShardHandler H│
│ TTP client with params: socketTimeout=600000&connTimeout=60000&retry=true       │
│ 1585 INFO  (main) [   ] o.a.s.l.LogWatcher SLF4J impl is org.slf4j.impl.Log4jLog│
│ gerFactory                                                            │
│ 1586 INFO  (main) [   ] o.a.s.l.LogWatcher Registering Log Listener [Log4j (org.│
│ slf4j.impl.Log4jLoggerFactory)]                                       │
│ 1588 INFO  (main) [   ] o.a.s.c.CoreContainer Security conf doesn't exist. Skipp│
│ ing setup for authorization module.                                  │
│ 1588 INFO  (main) [   ] o.a.s.c.CoreContainer No authentication plugin used.    │
│ 1626 INFO  (main) [   ] o.a.s.c.CoresLocator Looking for core definitions undern│
│ eath /opt/solr/server/solr                                           │
│ 1632 INFO  (main) [   ] o.a.s.c.CoresLocator Found 0 core definitions            │
│ 1635 INFO  (main) [   ] o.a.s.s.SolrDispatchFilter user.dir=/opt/solr/server     │
│ 1635 INFO  (main) [   ] o.a.s.s.SolrDispatchFilter SolrDispatchFilter.init() don│
│ e                                                                     │
│ 1648 INFO  (main) [   ] o.e.j.s.h.ContextHandler Started o.e.j.w.WebAppContext@5│
│ 7fffcd7{/solr,file:/opt/solr/server/solr-webapp/webapp/,AVAILABLE}{/opt/solr/ser│
│ ver/solr-webapp/webapp}                                              │
│ 1659 INFO  (main) [   ] o.e.j.s.ServerConnector Started ServerConnector@ad48334{│
│ HTTP/1.1}{0.0.0.0:8983}                                               │
│ 1659 INFO  (main) [   ] o.e.j.s.Server Started @2075ms                │
│ █                                                                   ⌄ │
└──────────────────────────────────────────────────────────────────────┘
```

Figure 13-5. *Listing Docker Container Log*

Starting the Interactive Shell

Start the interactive shell for the Docker container as user "solr."

```
sudo docker exec -it –user=solr solr_on_docker bash
```

The interactive shell (or tty) gets started as shown in Figure 13-6.

```
ubuntu@ip-172-30-1-190:~$ sudo docker exec -it --user=solr solr_on_docker bash
solr@8061f79d1f16:/opt/solr$ █
```

Figure 13-6. *Starting TTY*

Apache Solr commands may be run in the interactive terminal.

Logging in to the Solr Admin Console

If the Docker container running the Apache Solr server is running on a different host than the Admin Console, use the public DNS name of the Amazon EC2 instance running the Docker engine and the Docker container. Obtain the public DNS from the Amazon EC2 Management Console. The public DNS is ec2-54-208-53-110.compute-1.amazonaws.com as shown in Figure 13-7.

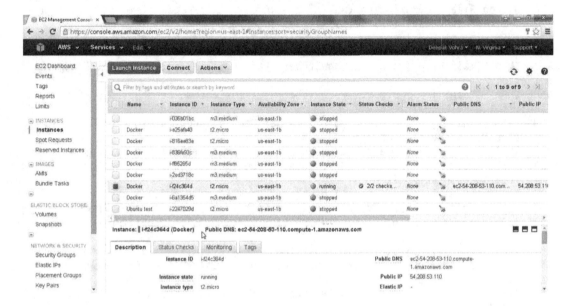

Figure 13-7. *Finding the Public DNS*

Use the URL http://ec2-54-208-53-110.compute-1.amazonaws.com:8983/ to access the Apache Solr Admin Console. The Dashboard is shown in Figure 13-8.

Figure 13-8. *Logging in to Solr Admin Console*

Creating a Core Index

Next, create a core, an index for the data to be stored in Apache Solr. From the tty run the bin/solr create_core command to create a core called gettingstarted.

```
bin/solr create_core -c gettingstarted
```

A new core called "gettingstarted" gets created as shown in Figure 13-9.

```
ubuntu@ip-172-30-1-190:~$ sudo docker exec -it --user=solr solr_on_docker bash
solr@8061f79d1f16:/opt/solr$ bin/solr create_core -c gettingstarted

Setup new core instance directory:
/opt/solr/server/solr/gettingstarted

Creating new core 'gettingstarted' using command:
http://localhost:8983/solr/admin/cores?action=CREATE&name=gettingstarted&instanc
eDir=gettingstarted

{
  "responseHeader":{
    "status":0,
    "QTime":2102},
  "core":"gettingstarted"}


solr@8061f79d1f16:/opt/solr$
```

Figure 13-9. *Creating a Core called "gettingstarted"*

In the Solr Admin Console, select Core Admin as shown in Figure 13-10.

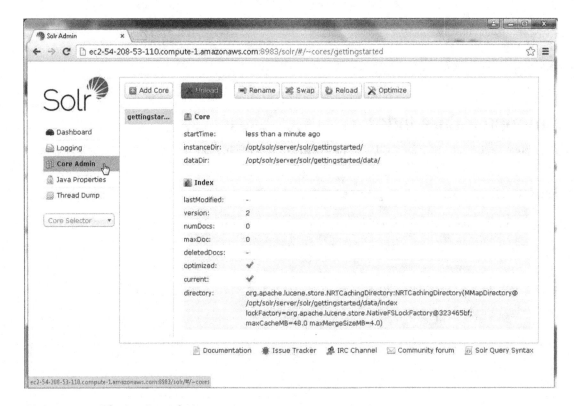

Figure 13-10. *Selecting Core Admin*

In the Core Selector, select the gettingstarted core as shown in Figure 13-11.

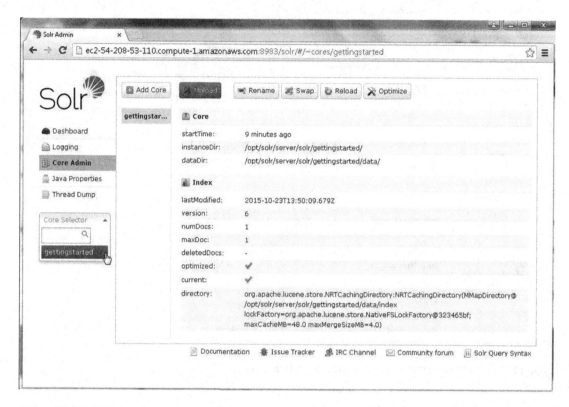

Figure 13-11. *Selecting the gettingstarted Core*

Select Overview tab in the margin as shown in Figure 13-12. The index stats get listed such as the version, Num Docs, Max Doc, and Deleted.

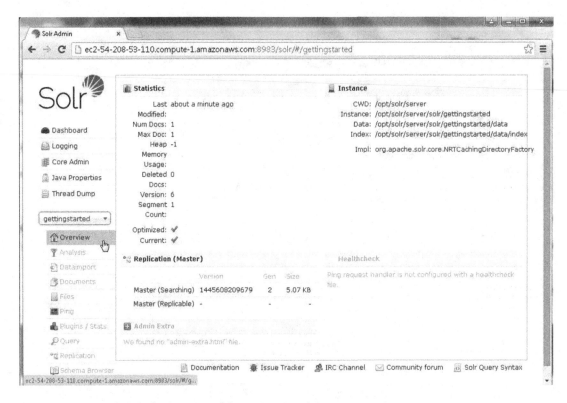

Figure 13-12. Displaying the Overview of the gettingstarted Core

Loading Sample Data

Apache Solr supports indexing of documents in XML, JSON and CSV formats. We shall index using the
XML format. The root element is required to be <add/> and each document must be enclosed in the
element. The id field is required. We shall index the following XML format document. Store the document as
solr.xml.

```
<add>
<doc>
  <field name="id">SOLR1000</field>
  <field name="name">Solr, the Enterprise Search Server</field>
  <field name="manu">Apache Software Foundation</field>
  <field name="cat">software</field>
  <field name="cat">search</field>
  <field name="features">Advanced Full-Text Search Capabilities using Lucene</field>
  <field name="features">Optimized for High Volume Web Traffic</field>
  <field name="features">Standards Based Open Interfaces - XML and HTTP</field>
  <field name="features">Comprehensive HTML Administration Interfaces</field>
  <field name="features">Scalability - Efficient Replication to other Solr Search Servers</field>
  <field name="features">Flexible and Adaptable with XML configuration and Schema</field>
  <field name="features">Good unicode support: h&#xE9;llo (hello with an accent over the e)</field>
  <field name="price">0</field>
```

```
<field name="popularity">10</field>
<field name="inStock">true</field>
<field name="incubationdate_dt">2006-01-17T00:00:00.000Z</field>
</doc>
</add>
```

Copy the solr.xml to the /opt/solr directory in the Docker container. Run the following docker cp command from the Ubuntu host, not the Docker container, to copy the solr.xml document to the Docker container with id 8061f79d1f16, which is running the Apache Solr server. The container id may be obtained from the output of the docker ps command.

```
sudo docker cp solr.xml 8061f79d1f16:/opt/solr/solr.xml
```

The solr.xml document gets copied to the /opt/solr directory in the Docker container as shown in Figure 13-13.

```
ubuntu@ip-172-30-1-190:~$ sudo docker cp solr.xml 8061f79d1f16:/opt/solr/solr.xml
l
ubuntu@ip-172-30-1-190:~$ ▮
```

Figure 13-13. *Copying solr.xml to DockerContainer*

Start the interactive terminal (tty) with the following command.

```
sudo docker exec -it –user=solr solr_on_docker bash
```

From the /opt/solr directory run the following command to list the files and directories in the directory. The solr.xml should get listed as shown in Figure 13-14.

```
solr@8061f79d1f16:/opt/solr$ ls -l
total 1164
-rw-r--r--  1 solr solr 503614 Sep 16 19:07 CHANGES.txt
-rw-r--r--  1 solr solr  12646 Aug 12 09:16 LICENSE.txt
-rw-r--r--  1 solr solr 566457 Sep  9 11:31 LUCENE_CHANGES.txt
-rw-r--r--  1 solr solr  26529 Aug 12 09:16 NOTICE.txt
-rw-r--r--  1 solr solr   7167 Aug 12 09:16 README.txt
drwxr-xr-x  3 solr solr   4096 Oct 16 23:08 bin
drwxr-xr-x 13 solr solr   4096 Sep 16 20:20 contrib
drwxr-xr-x  4 solr solr   4096 Oct 16 23:08 dist
drwxr-xr-x 19 solr solr   4096 Oct 16 23:08 docs
drwxr-xr-x  7 solr solr   4096 Oct 16 23:08 example
drwxr-xr-x  2 solr solr  36864 Oct 16 23:08 licenses
drwxr-xr-x 13 solr solr   4096 Oct 23 13:42 server
-rwxrwxr-x  1 root root   1048 Oct 23 13:44 solr.xml
solr@8061f79d1f16:/opt/solr$ ▮
```

Figure 13-14. *Listing the solr.xml File in Docker Container*

Run the following command to post the solr.xml to the gettingstarted index.

```
docker exec -it --user=solr solr_on_docker bin/post -c gettingstarted ./solr.xml
```

The solr.xml file gets indexed as shown in Figure 13-15.

```
solr@8061f79d1f16:/opt/solr$ bin/post -c gettingstarted ./solr.xml
java -classpath /opt/solr/dist/solr-core-5.3.1.jar -Dauto=yes -Dc=gettingstarted
  -Ddata=files org.apache.solr.util.SimplePostTool ./solr.xml
SimplePostTool version 5.0.0
Posting files to [base] url http://localhost:8983/solr/gettingstarted/update...
Entering auto mode. File endings considered are xml,json,csv,pdf,doc,docx,ppt,pp
tx,xls,xlsx,odt,odp,ods,ott,otp,ots,rtf,htm,html,txt,log
POSTing file solr.xml (application/xml) to [base]
1 files indexed.
COMMITting Solr index changes to http://localhost:8983/solr/gettingstarted/updat
e...
Time spent: 0:00:00.402
solr@8061f79d1f16:/opt/solr$ ▮
```

Figure 13-15. *indexing solr.xml*

Querying Apache Solr in Solr Admin Console

The indexed document may be queried from the Solr Admin console. Select the Query tab as shown in Figure 13-16.

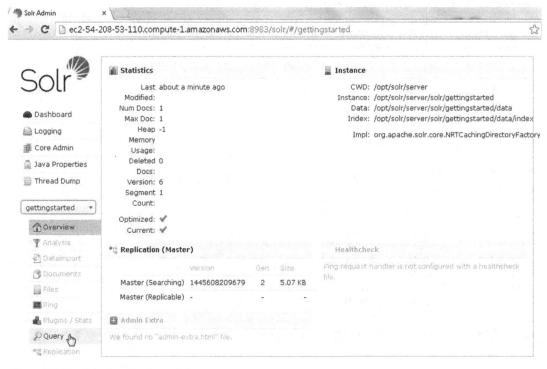

Figure 13-16. *Selecting the Query tab*

The Request-Handler (qt) should be set to /select and the query should be set to *.* to select all documents in the index as shown in Figure 13-17. The start index is set to 0 and the number of rows to select is set to 10. The wt (response writer) is set to json to return the queried documents in JSON format. Other supported formats are XML and CSV.

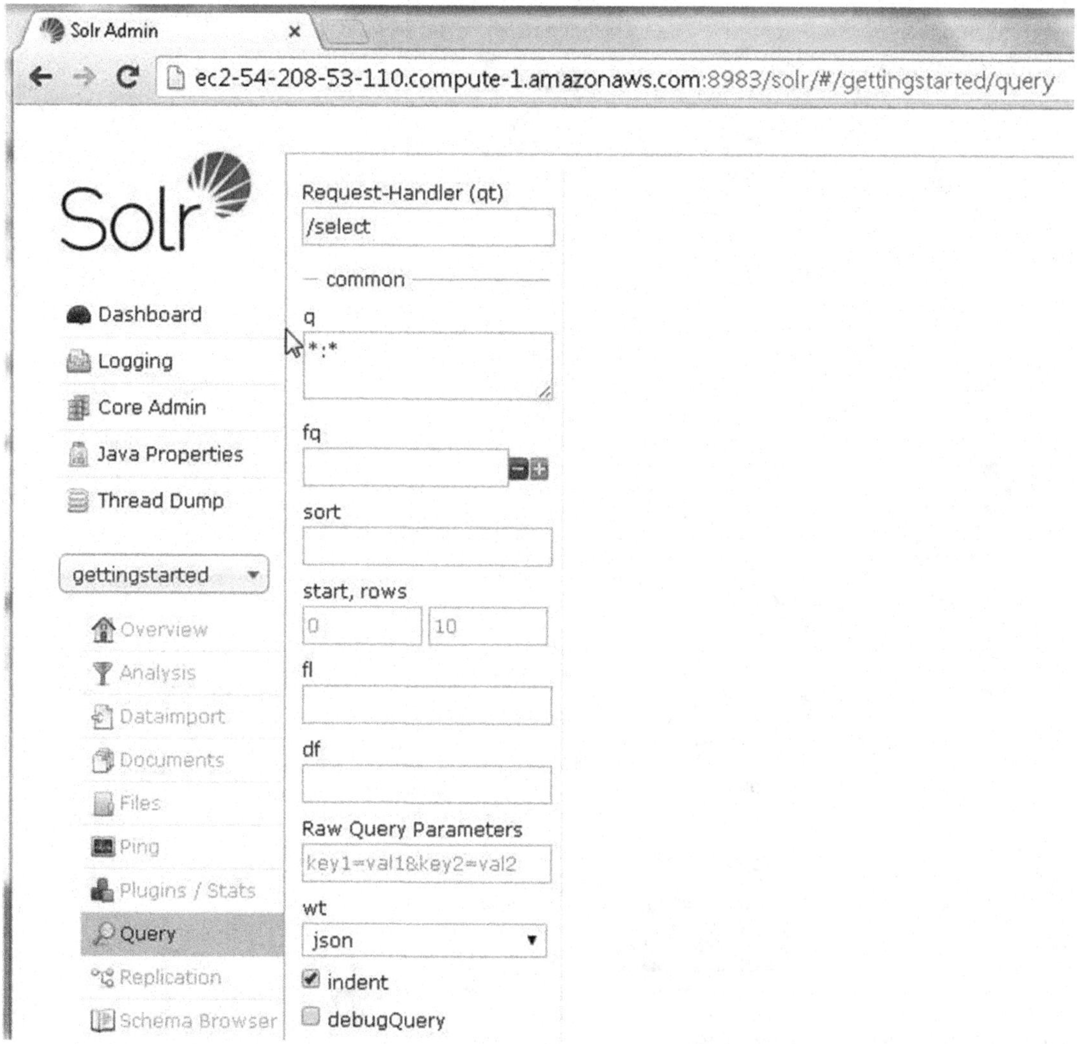

Figure 13-17. *The /select Request Handler*

Click on Execute Query as shown in Figure 13-18.

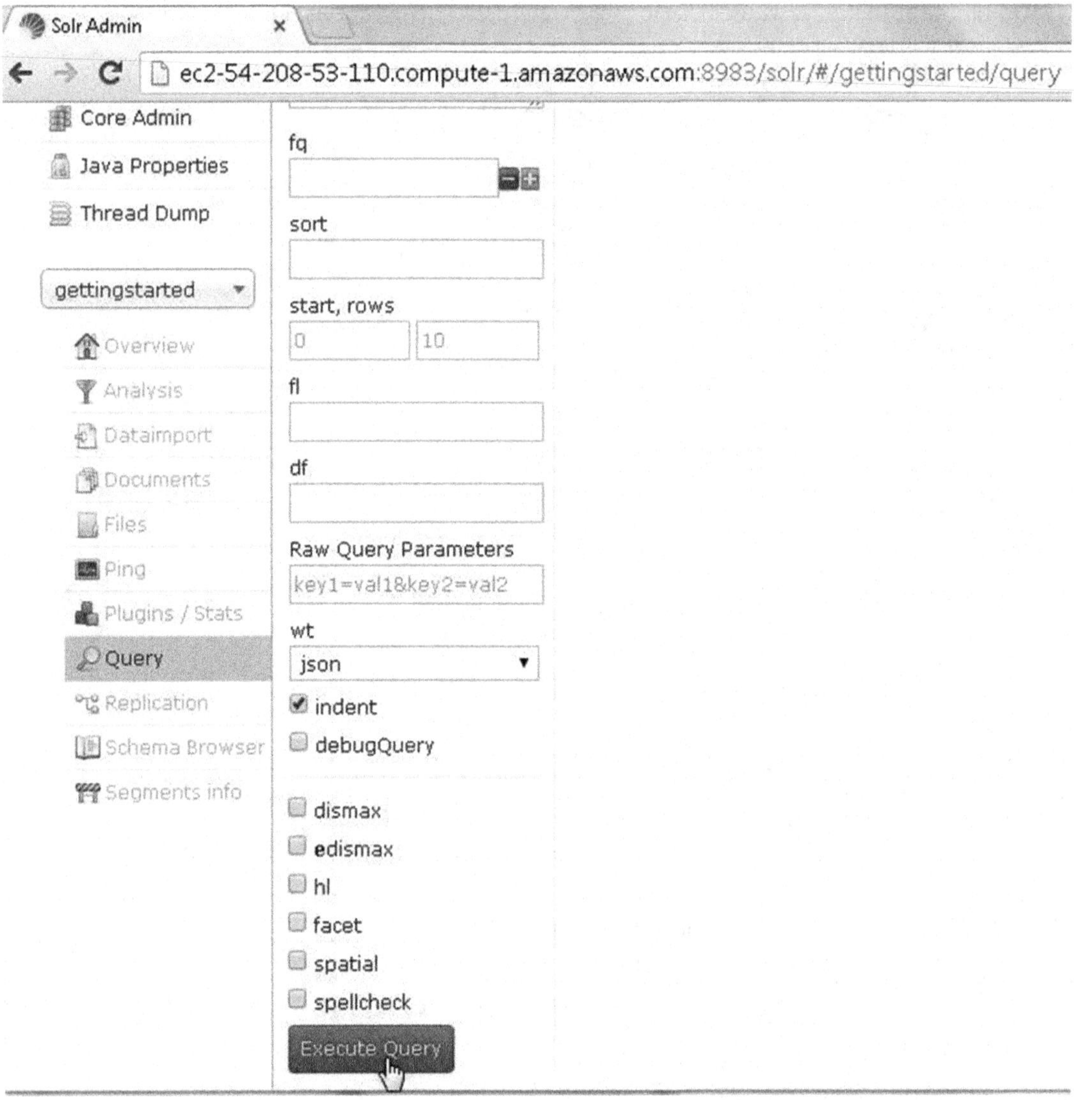

Figure 13-18. *Clicking on Execute Query*

The query result gets returned as JSON as shown in Figure 13-19.

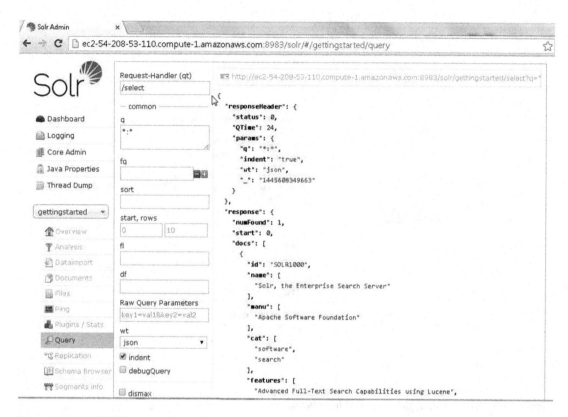

Figure 13-19. *JSON Response from Query*

The *version* field gets added to the JSON document returned as shown in Figure 13-20.

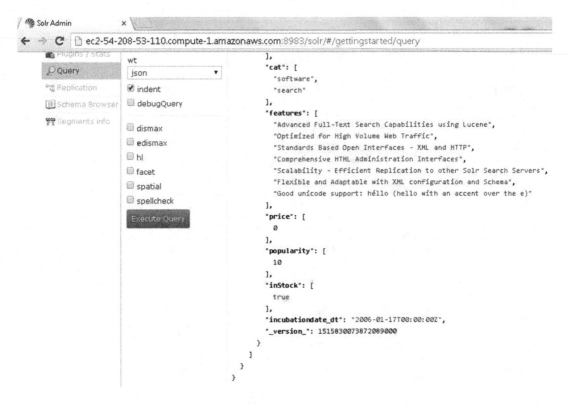

Figure 13-20. *The _version_ field added automatically*

Querying Apache Solr using REST API Client

The Apache Solr indexed documents may also be accessed using the REST client such as curl. For example, query all the documents in the gettingstarted index using the following curl command run from the interactive terminal for the "solr" container.

```
curl http://ec2-54-208-53-110.compute-1.amazonaws.com:8983/solr/gettingstarted/select?q=*%3A
*&wt=json&indent=true
```

All the documents indexed in the gettingstarted index get output as shown in Figure 13-21.

```
<.com:8983/solr/gettingstarted/select?q=*%3A*&wt=json&indent=true"
{
  "responseHeader":{
    "status":0,
    "QTime":1,
    "params":{
      "q":"*:*",
      "indent":"true",
      "wt":"json"}},
  "response":{"numFound":1,"start":0,"docs":[
      {
        "id":"SOLR1000",
        "name":["Solr, the Enterprise Search Server"],
        "manu":["Apache Software Foundation"],
        "cat":["software",
          "search"],
        "features":["Advanced Full-Text Search Capabilities using Lucene",
          "Optimized for High Volume Web Traffic",
          "Standards Based Open Interfaces - XML and HTTP",
          "Comprehensive HTML Administration Interfaces",
          "Scalability - Efficient Replication to other Solr Search Servers",
          "Flexible and Adaptable with XML configuration and Schema",
          "Good unicode support: héllo (hello with an accent over the e)"],
        "price":[0],
        "popularity":[10],
        "inStock":[true],
        "incubationdate_dt":"2006-01-17T00:00:00Z",
        "_version_":1515830073872089088}]
  }}
solr@8061f79d1f16:/opt/solr$ █
```

Figure 13-21. *Running a REST Client Query*

As another example, query all documents with "Lucene" in the document.

```
curl "http://ec2-54-208-53-110.compute-1.amazonaws.com:8983/solr/gettingstarted/select?wt=js
on&indent=true&q=Lucene"
```

As the single document indexed has "Lucene" in it the document gets returned as shown in Figure 13-22.

```
<.com:8983/solr/gettingstarted/select?wt=json&indent=true&q=Lucene"
{
  "responseHeader":{
    "status":0,
    "QTime":9,
    "params":{
      "q":"Lucene",
      "indent":"true",
      "wt":"json"}},
  "response":{"numFound":1,"start":0,"docs":[
      {
        "id":"SOLR1000",
        "name":["Solr, the Enterprise Search Server"],
        "manu":["Apache Software Foundation"],
        "cat":["software",
          "search"],
        "features":["Advanced Full-Text Search Capabilities using Lucene",
          "Optimized for High Volume Web Traffic",
          "Standards Based Open Interfaces - XML and HTTP",
          "Comprehensive HTML Administration Interfaces",
          "Scalability - Efficient Replication to other Solr Search Servers",
          "Flexible and Adaptable with XML configuration and Schema",
          "Good unicode support: héllo (hello with an accent over the e)"],
        "price":[0],
        "popularity":[10],
        "inStock":[true],
        "incubationdate_dt":"2006-01-17T00:00:00Z",
        "_version_":1515830073872089088}]
  }}
solr@8061f79d1f16:/opt/solr$
```

Figure 13-22. *Running a REST Client Query using term 'Lucene'*

To query for a document with text in a specific field use the `field=text` format in the q parameter. For example, search for all documents with "Lucene" in the "name" field.

```
curl "http://ec2-54-208-53-110.compute-1.amazonaws.com:8983/solr/gettingstarted/select?wt=js
on&indent=true&q=name:Lucene"
```

As the name field of the single document in the index does not include "Lucene" no document gets returned as shown in Figure 13-23.

```
<.com:8983/solr/gettingstarted/select?wt=json&indent=true&q=name:Lucene"
{
  "responseHeader":{
    "status":0,
    "QTime":0,
    "params":{
      "q":"name:Lucene",
      "indent":"true",
      "wt":"json"}},
  "response":{"numFound":0,"start":0,"docs":[]
  }}
solr@8061f79d1f16:/opt/solr$
```

Figure 13-23. *Running a REST Client Query with "Lucene" in "name" Field*

A phrase search may also be performed using the REST client. For example search for the phrase "Enterprise Search".

```
curl "http://ec2-54-208-53-110.compute-1.amazonaws.com:8983/solr/gettingstarted/select?wt=js
on&indent=true&q=\"Enterprise+Search\""
```

As the single document has 'Enterprise Search' in it, the document gets returned as shown in Figure 13-24.

```
<ted/select?wt=json&indent=true&q=\"Enterprise+Search\""
{
  "responseHeader":{
    "status":0,
    "QTime":8,
    "params":{
      "q":"\"Enterprise Search\"",
      "indent":"true",
      "wt":"json"}},
  "response":{"numFound":1,"start":0,"docs":[
      {
        "id":"SOLR1000",
        "name":["Solr, the Enterprise Search Server"],
        "manu":["Apache Software Foundation"],
        "cat":["software",
          "search"],
        "features":["Advanced Full-Text Search Capabilities using Lucene",
          "Optimized for High Volume Web Traffic",
          "Standards Based Open Interfaces - XML and HTTP",
          "Comprehensive HTML Administration Interfaces",
          "Scalability - Efficient Replication to other Solr Search Servers",
          "Flexible and Adaptable with XML configuration and Schema",
          "Good unicode support: héllo (hello with an accent over the e)"],
        "price":[0],
        "popularity":[10],
        "inStock":[true],
        "incubationdate_dt":"2006-01-17T00:00:00Z",
        "_version_":15158300738720890088}]
  }}
solr@8061f79d1f16:/opt/solr$ ▮
```

Figure 13-24. *Running a REST Query using a Phrase*

Deleting Data

To delete a document run the same tool, the post tool, as used to post a document. Specify the document id to delete using the XML `<delete><id></id></delete>`. The index to delete from is specified with the –c option.

```
bin/post -c gettingstarted -d "<delete><id>SOLR1000</id></delete>"
```

The single document indexed, which has the id SOLR1000, gets deleted as shown in Figure 13-25.

```
<$ bin/post -c gettingstarted -d "<delete><id>SOLR1000</id></delete>"
java -classpath /opt/solr/dist/solr-core-5.3.1.jar -Dauto=yes -Dc=gettingstarted
 -Ddata=args org.apache.solr.util.SimplePostTool <delete><id>SOLR1000</id></dele
te>
SimplePostTool version 5.0.0
POSTing args to http://localhost:8983/solr/gettingstarted/update...
COMMITting Solr index changes to http://localhost:8983/solr/gettingstarted/updat
e...
Time spent: 0:00:00.043
solr@8061f79d1f16:/opt/solr$ ▮
```

Figure 13-25. *Deleting a Single Document*

Subsequently, run the same curl command as run before to search for all documents.

```
curl http://ec2-54-208-53-110.compute-1.amazonaws.com:8983/solr/gettingstarted/select?q=*%3A
*&wt=json&indent=true
```

No document gets found as shown in Figure 13-26 as the only document indexed has been deleted.

```
<$ bin/post -c gettingstarted -d "<delete><id>SOLR1000</id></delete>"
java -classpath /opt/solr/dist/solr-core-5.3.1.jar -Dauto=yes -Dc=gettingstarted
 -Ddata=args org.apache.solr.util.SimplePostTool <delete><id>SOLR1000</id></dele
te>
SimplePostTool version 5.0.0
POSTing args to http://localhost:8983/solr/gettingstarted/update...
COMMITting Solr index changes to http://localhost:8983/solr/gettingstarted/updat
e...
Time spent: 0:00:00.043
<.com:8983/solr/gettingstarted/select?q=*%3A*&wt=json&indent=true"
{
  "responseHeader":{
    "status":0,
    "QTime":0,
    "params":{
      "q":"*:*",
      "indent":"true",
      "wt":"json"}},
  "response":{"numFound":0,"start":0,"docs":[]
  }}
solr@8061f79d1f16:/opt/solr$ ▮
```

Figure 13-26. *REST Query does not list any Document after deleting the only document*

Run a query in the Solr Admin Console after deleting the only indexed document and no document gets returned as indicated by numFound field value of 0 in the JSON document returned as shown in Figure 13-27.

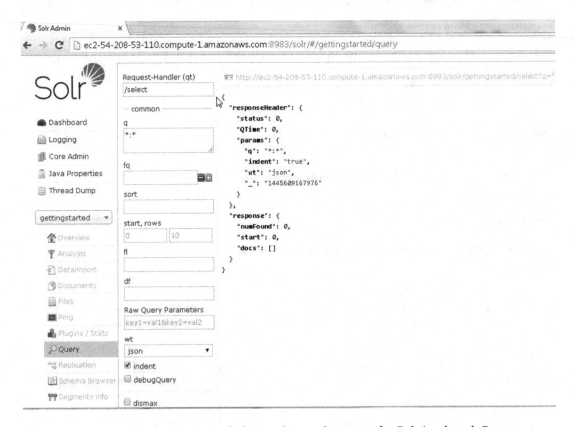

Figure 13-27. *Query in Sole Admin Console does not list any document after Deleting the only Document*

Listing Logs

The Docker container logs for all commands run on the Apache Solr server may be output using the docker logs command.

```
sudo docker logs -f solr_on_docker
```

The Docker container logs get output as shown in Figure 13-28.

```
ubuntu@ip-172-30-1-190: ~                                    _  □  ×

File  Edit  View  Search  Terminal  Help
1093597 ERROR (qtp5592464-13) [    x:gettingstarted] o.a.s.h.a.ShowFileRequestHan
dler Can not find: admin-extra.menu-bottom.html [/opt/solr/server/solr/gettingst
arted/conf/admin-extra.menu-bottom.html]
1093597 INFO  (qtp5592464-13) [    x:gettingstarted] o.a.s.c.S.Request [gettingst
arted] webapp=/solr path=/admin/file params={file=admin-extra.menu-bottom.html&c
ontentType=text/html;charset%3Dutf-8&_=1445608278871} status=404 QTime=0
1093745 INFO  (qtp5592464-17) [    x:gettingstarted] o.a.s.c.S.Request [gettingst
arted] webapp=/solr path=/admin/luke params={show=index&numTerms=0&wt=json&_=144
5608279098} status=0 QTime=0
1093751 INFO  (qtp5592464-16) [    x:gettingstarted] o.a.s.c.S.Request [gettingst
arted] webapp=/solr path=/replication params={wt=json&command=details&_=14456082
79103} status=0 QTime=1
1093834 INFO  (qtp5592464-20) [    x:gettingstarted] o.a.s.c.S.Request [gettingst
arted] webapp=/solr path=/admin/system params={wt=json&_=1445608279105} status=0
 QTime=4
1093845 ERROR (qtp5592464-19) [    x:gettingstarted] o.a.s.h.a.ShowFileRequestHan
dler Can not find: admin-extra.html [/opt/solr/server/solr/gettingstarted/conf/a
dmin-extra.html]
1093845 INFO  (qtp5592464-19) [    x:gettingstarted] o.a.s.c.S.Request [gettingst
arted] webapp=/solr path=/admin/file params={file=admin-extra.html&_=14456082791
07} status=404 QTime=0
1093852 INFO  (qtp5592464-18) [    x:gettingstarted] o.a.s.c.S.Request [gettingst
arted] webapp=/solr path=/admin/ping params={action=status&wt=json&_=14456082791
08} status=503 QTime=0
1164309 INFO  (qtp5592464-15) [    x:gettingstarted] o.a.s.c.S.Request [gettingst
arted] webapp=/solr path=/select params={q=*:*&indent=true&wt=json&_=14456083496
63} hits=1 status=0 QTime=24
```

Figure 13-28. *Listing Docker Container Logs*

Stopping Apache Solr Server

The running Docker containers may be listed with the docker ps command. The solr_on_docker container is listed as running as shown in Figure 13-29.

```
ubuntu@ip-172-30-1-190:~$ sudo docker ps
CONTAINER ID        IMAGE               COMMAND              CREATED
    STATUS              PORTS               NAMES
8061f79d1f16        solr                "/opt/solr/bin/solr -"   36 minutes ago
    Up 36 minutes       0.0.0.0:8983->8983/tcp   solr on docker
```

Figure 13-29. *Listing Running Docker Containers*

To stop the solr_on_docker container run the docker stop command as shown in Figure 13-30.

```
sudo docker stop solr_on_docker
```

```
ubuntu@ip-172-30-1-190:~$ sudo docker stop solr_on_docker
solr_on_docker
ubuntu@ip-172-30-1-190:~$ sudo docker ps
CONTAINER ID       IMAGE              COMMAND            CREATED
STATUS             PORTS              NAMES
```

***Figure 13-30.** Stopping Docker Container for Apache Solr*

Run the docker ps command to list the running Docker containers again. The solr_on_docker container does not get listed.

The Docker image still gets listed with the docker images command as shown in Figure 13-31.

```
ubuntu@ip-172-30-1-190:~$ sudo docker images
REPOSITORY         TAG                IMAGE ID           CREATED
VIRTUAL SIZE
couchbase          latest             ff61ecf3bacb       6 days ago
371.3 MB
solr               latest             a866495d197c       6 days ago
740.2 MB
hello-world        latest             0a6ba66e537a       9 days ago
960 B
ubuntu@ip-172-30-1-190:~$ 
```

***Figure 13-31.** Listing Docker Image for a stopped Docker Container*

If the Docker image is to be removed, first the Docker container solr_on_docker has to be removed after being stopped.

```
sudo docker rm solr_on_docker
sudo docker rm solr
```

Summary

In this chapter we used the official Docker image for Apache Solr to run the Apache Solr server in a Docker container. We created a core index and posted a document to the index. Subsequently, we queried the document from the Solr Admin Console and also the REST client tool curl. In the next chapter we shall discuss Apache Spark with Docker.

■ ■ ■

Using Apache Spark

Apache Spark is a data processing engine for large data sets. Apache Spark is much faster (up to 100 times faster in memory) than Apache Hadoop MapReduce. In cluster mode, Spark applications run as independent processes coordinated by the SparkContext object in the driver program, which is the main program. The SparkContext may connect to several types of cluster managers to allocate resources to Spark applications. The supported cluster managers include the Standalone cluster manager, Mesos and YARN. Apache Spark is designed to access data from varied data sources including the HDFS, Apache HBase and NoSQL databases such as Apache Cassandra and MongoDB. In this chapter we shall use the same CDH Docker image that we used for several of the Apache Hadoop frameworks including Apache Hive and Apache HBase. We shall run an Apache Spark Master in cluster mode using the YARN cluster manager in a Docker container.

> Setting the Environment
>
> Running the Docker Container for CDH
>
> Running Apache Spark Job in yarn-cluster Mode
>
> Running Apache Spark Job in yarn-client Mode
>
> Running the Apache Spark Shell

Setting the Environment

The following software is required for this chapter.

> -Docker Engine (version 1.8)
>
> -Docker image for Apache Spark

Connect to an Amazon EC2 instance using the public IP address for the instance. The public IP address may be found from the Amazon EC2 Console as explained in Appendix A.

```
ssh -i "docker.pem" ec2-user@54.208.146.254
```

Start the Docker service and verify status as started.

```
sudo service docker start
sudo service docker status
```

Download the Docker image for CDH, the svds/cdh image if not already downloaded for an earlier chapter.

```
sudo docker pull svds/cdh
```

Docker image svds/cdh gets downloaded as shown in Figure 14-1.

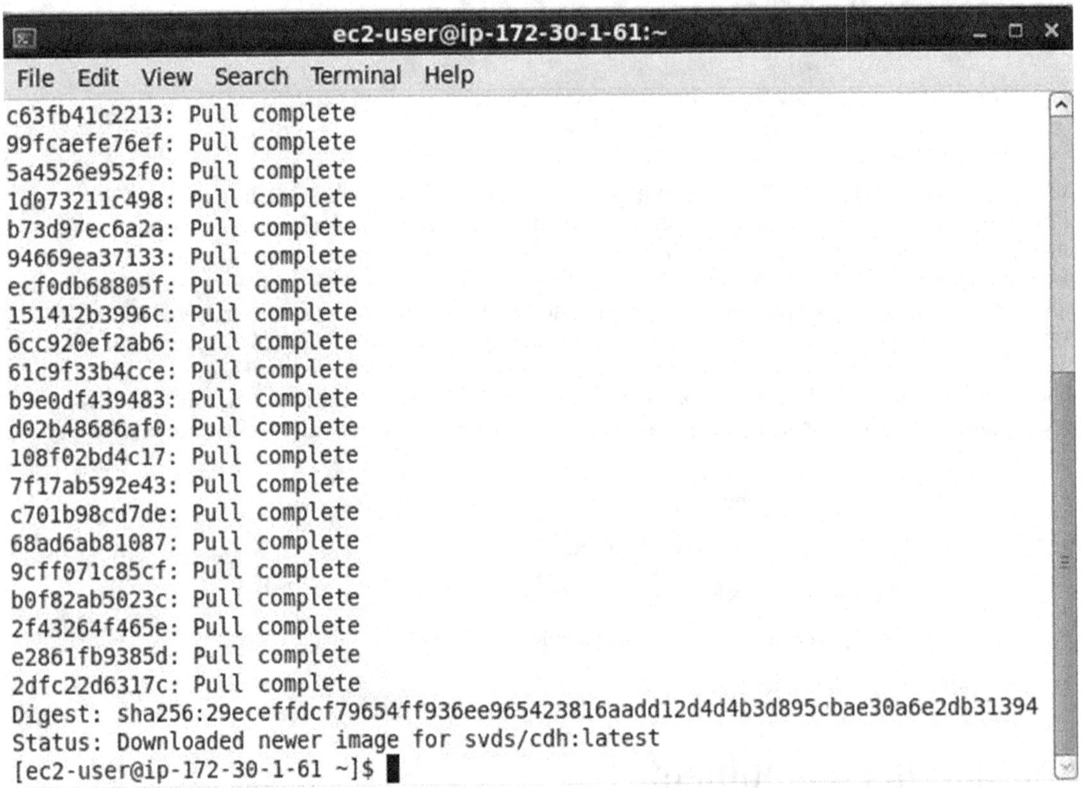

```
ec2-user@ip-172-30-1-61:~

File  Edit  View  Search  Terminal  Help
c63fb41c2213: Pull complete
99fcaefe76ef: Pull complete
5a4526e952f0: Pull complete
1d073211c498: Pull complete
b73d97ec6a2a: Pull complete
94669ea37133: Pull complete
ecf0db68805f: Pull complete
151412b3996c: Pull complete
6cc920ef2ab6: Pull complete
61c9f33b4cce: Pull complete
b9e0df439483: Pull complete
d02b48686af0: Pull complete
108f02bd4c17: Pull complete
7f17ab592e43: Pull complete
c701b98cd7de: Pull complete
68ad6ab81087: Pull complete
9cff071c85cf: Pull complete
b0f82ab5023c: Pull complete
2f43264f465e: Pull complete
e2861fb9385d: Pull complete
2dfc22d6317c: Pull complete
Digest: sha256:29eceffdcf79654ff936ee965423816aadd12d4d4b3d895cbae30a6e2db31394
Status: Downloaded newer image for svds/cdh:latest
[ec2-user@ip-172-30-1-61 ~]$
```

Figure 14-1. Downloading svds/cdh Docker Image

Running the Docker Container for CDH

Start a Docker container for the CDH frameworks using the Apache Spark Master port as 8088.

```
sudo docker run  -p 8088 -d --name cdh svds/cdh
```

List the running Docker containers.

```
sudo docker ps
```

CDH processes including Apache Spark get started and the container cdh gets listed as running as shown in Figure 14-2.

```
[ec2-user@ip-172-30-1-61 ~]$ sudo docker run  -p 8088 -d --name cdh svds/cdh
4b4780802318f23004530e41322d7f01f9719c59c7310a58dc03a15612cb9755
[ec2-user@ip-172-30-1-61 ~]$ sudo docker ps
CONTAINER ID        IMAGE               COMMAND                CREATED
    STATUS            PORTS
                        NAMES
4b4780802318        svds/cdh            "cdh_startup_script.s"  11 seconds ago
    Up 10 seconds       8020/tcp, 8888/tcp, 9090/tcp, 11000/tcp, 11443/tcp, 198
88/tcp, 0.0.0.0:32768->8088/tcp   cdh
```

Figure 14-2. *Starting Docker Container for CDH including Apache Spark*

Start an interactive terminal for the cdh container.

```
sudo docker exec -it cdh bash
```

The interactive terminal gets started as shown in Figure 14-3.

```
[ec2-user@ip-172-30-1-61 ~]$ sudo docker exec -it cdh bash
root@4fbf325c6ecd:/# █
```

Figure 14-3. *Starting the TTY*

In YARN mode, a Spark application may be submitted to a cluster in *yarn-cluster* mode or *yarn-client* mode. In the yarn-cluster mode, the Apache Spark driver runs inside an Application Master, which is managed by the YARN. In yarn-client mode. The Spark driver runs in the client process outside of YARN and the Application Master is used only for requesting resources from YARN. The --master parameter is yarn-cluster or yarn-client based on the mode of application submission. In yarn-client mode the Spark driver logs to the console.

We shall run a Spark application using each of the application submission modes. We shall use the example application org.apache.spark.examples.SparkPi.

Running Apache Spark Job in yarn-cluster Mode

To submit the Spark application SparkPi in yarn-cluster mode using 1000 iterations, run the following spark-submit command with the --master parameter as yarn-cluster.

```
spark-submit --master yarn-cluster --class org.apache.spark.examples.SparkPi /usr/lib/spark/
examples/lib/spark-examples-1.3.0-cdh5.4.7-hadoop2.6.0-cdh5.4.7.jar 1000
```

The preceding command is run from the interactive terminal as shown in Figure 14-4.

```
[ec2-user@ip-172-30-1-61 ~]$ sudo docker exec -it cdh bash
root@4b4780802318:/# spark-submit --master yarn-cluster --class org.apache.spark
.examples.SparkPi /usr/lib/spark/examples/lib/spark-examples-1.3.0-cdh5.4.7-hado
op2.6.0-cdh5.4.7.jar 1000
```

Figure 14-4. Submitting the Spark Application in yarn-cluster Mode

The output from the Spark application is shown in Figure 14-5.

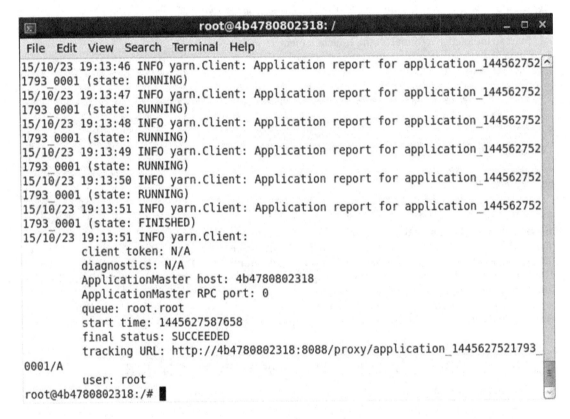

Figure 14-5. Output from Spark Job in yarn-cluster Mode

A more detailed output from the spark-submit command is listed:

```
spark-submit --master yarn-cluster --class org.apache.spark.examples.SparkPi /usr/lib/spark/
examples/lib/spark-examples-1.3.0-cdh5.4.7-hadoop2.6.0-cdh5.4.7.jar 1000
15/10/23 19:12:52 WARN util.NativeCodeLoader: Unable to load native-hadoop library for your
platform... using builtin-java classes where applicable
15/10/23 19:12:54 INFO client.RMProxy: Connecting to ResourceManager at /0.0.0.0:8032
15/10/23 19:12:56 INFO yarn.Client: Requesting a new application from cluster with 1
NodeManagers
15/10/23 19:12:56 INFO yarn.Client: Verifying our application has not requested more than
the maximum memory capability of the cluster (8192 MB per container)
```

15/10/23 19:12:56 INFO yarn.Client: Will allocate AM container, with 896 MB memory including 384 MB overhead
15/10/23 19:12:56 INFO yarn.Client: Setting up container launch context for our AM
15/10/23 19:12:56 INFO yarn.Client: Preparing resources for our AM container
15/10/23 19:12:59 WARN shortcircuit.DomainSocketFactory: The short-circuit local reads feature cannot be used because libhadoop cannot be loaded.
15/10/23 19:12:59 INFO yarn.Client: Uploading resource file:/usr/lib/spark/lib/spark-assembly-1.3.0-cdh5.4.7-hadoop2.6.0-cdh5.4.7.jar -> hdfs://localhost:8020/user/root/.sparkStaging/application_1445627521793_0001/spark-assembly-1.3.0-cdh5.4.7-hadoop2.6.0-cdh5.4.7.jar
15/10/23 19:13:05 INFO yarn.Client: Uploading resource file:/usr/lib/spark/examples/lib/spark-examples-1.3.0-cdh5.4.7-hadoop2.6.0-cdh5.4.7.jar -> hdfs://localhost:8020/user/root/.sparkStaging/application_1445627521793_0001/spark-examples-1.3.0-cdh5.4.7-hadoop2.6.0-cdh5.4.7.jar
15/10/23 19:13:06 INFO yarn.Client: Setting up the launch environment for our AM container
15/10/23 19:13:07 INFO spark.SecurityManager: Changing view acls to: root
15/10/23 19:13:07 INFO spark.SecurityManager: Changing modify acls to: root
15/10/23 19:13:07 INFO spark.SecurityManager: SecurityManager: authentication disabled; ui acls disabled; users with view permissions: Set(root); users with modify permissions: Set(root)
15/10/23 19:13:07 INFO yarn.Client: Submitting application 1 to ResourceManager
15/10/23 19:13:08 INFO impl.YarnClientImpl: Submitted application application_1445627521793_0001
15/10/23 19:13:09 INFO yarn.Client: Application report for application_1445627521793_0001 (state: ACCEPTED)
15/10/23 19:13:09 INFO yarn.Client:
         client token: N/A
         diagnostics: N/A
         ApplicationMaster host: N/A
         ApplicationMaster RPC port: -1
         queue: root.root
         start time: 1445627587658
         final status: UNDEFINED
         tracking URL: http://4b4780802318:8088/proxy/application_1445627521793_0001/
         user: root
15/10/23 19:13:10 INFO yarn.Client: Application report for application_1445627521793_0001 (state: ACCEPTED)
15/10/23 19:13:11 INFO yarn.Client: Application report for application_1445627521793_0001 (state: ACCEPTED)
15/10/23 19:13:24 INFO yarn.Client: Application report for application_1445627521793_0001 (state: RUNNING)
15/10/23 19:13:24 INFO yarn.Client:
         client token: N/A
         diagnostics: N/A
         ApplicationMaster host: 4b4780802318
         ApplicationMaster RPC port: 0
         queue: root.root
         start time: 1445627587658
         final status: UNDEFINED
         tracking URL: http://4b4780802318:8088/proxy/application_1445627521793_0001/
         user: root

```
15/10/23 19:13:25 INFO yarn.Client: Application report for application_1445627521793_0001
(state: RUNNING)
15/10/23 19:13:26 INFO yarn.Client: Application report for
15/10/23 19:13:51 INFO yarn.Client: Application report for application_1445627521793_0001
(state: FINISHED)
15/10/23 19:13:51 INFO yarn.Client:
         client token: N/A
         diagnostics: N/A
         ApplicationMaster host: 4b4780802318
         ApplicationMaster RPC port: 0
         queue: root.root
         start time: 1445627587658
         final status: SUCCEEDED
         tracking URL: http://4b4780802318:8088/proxy/application_1445627521793_0001/A
         user: root
```

In yarn-cluster mode, the Spark application result is not output to the console and has to be accessed from the YARN container logs accessible from the ResourceManager using the tracking URL http://4b4780802318:8088/proxy/application_1445627521793_0001/A in a browser if the final status is SUCCEEDED.

Running Apache Spark Job in yarn-client Mode

To submit the Spark application SparkPi in yarn-client mode using 1000 iterations, run the following spark-submit command with the --master parameter as yarn-client.

```
spark-submit
    --master yarn-client
    --class org.apache.spark.examples.SparkPi
    /usr/lib/spark/examples/lib/spark-examples-1.3.0-cdh5.4.7-hadoop2.6.0-cdh5.4.7.jar
    1000
```

The output from the spark-submit command is shown in Figure 14-6.

```
┌─────────────────────────────────────────────────────────────────────────┐
│ ⊠                          root@4b4780802318: /                  _ □ ✕   │
├─────────────────────────────────────────────────────────────────────────┤
│ File  Edit  View  Search  Terminal  Help                                 │
├─────────────────────────────────────────────────────────────────────────┤
│ dler{/jobs/json,null}                                                 ▲  │
│ 15/10/23 19:15:57 INFO handler.ContextHandler: stopped o.s.j.s.ServletContextHan│
│ dler{/jobs,null}                                                          │
│ 15/10/23 19:15:58 INFO ui.SparkUI: Stopped Spark web UI at http://4b4780802318:4│
│ 040                                                                      │
│ 15/10/23 19:15:58 INFO scheduler.DAGScheduler: Stopping DAGScheduler      │
│ 15/10/23 19:15:58 INFO cluster.YarnClientSchedulerBackend: Shutting down all exe│
│ cutors                                                                    │
│ 15/10/23 19:15:58 INFO cluster.YarnClientSchedulerBackend: Asking each executor  │
│ to shut down                                                              │
│ 15/10/23 19:15:58 INFO cluster.YarnClientSchedulerBackend: Stopped        │
│ 15/10/23 19:15:58 INFO scheduler.OutputCommitCoordinator$OutputCommitCoordinator │
│ Actor: OutputCommitCoordinator stopped!                                   │
│ 15/10/23 19:15:58 INFO spark.MapOutputTrackerMasterActor: MapOutputTrackerActor  │
│ stopped!                                                                  │
│ 15/10/23 19:15:58 INFO storage.MemoryStore: MemoryStore cleared           │
│ 15/10/23 19:15:58 INFO storage.BlockManager: BlockManager stopped         │
│ 15/10/23 19:15:58 INFO storage.BlockManagerMaster: BlockManagerMaster stopped    │
│ 15/10/23 19:15:58 INFO remote.RemoteActorRefProvider$RemotingTerminator: Shuttin │
│ g down remote daemon.                                                     │
│ 15/10/23 19:15:58 INFO remote.RemoteActorRefProvider$RemotingTerminator: Remote  │
│ daemon shut down; proceeding with flushing remote transports.            │
│ 15/10/23 19:15:58 INFO spark.SparkContext: Successfully stopped SparkContext ▒  │
│ root@4b4780802318:/# █                                                 ▼  │
└─────────────────────────────────────────────────────────────────────────┘
```

Figure 14-6. *Submitting Spark Application in yarn-client Mode*

A more detailed output from the Apache Spark application is as follows and includes the value of Pi calculated approximately.

```
spark-submit --master yarn-client --class org.apache.spark.examples.SparkPi
/usr/lib/spark/examples/lib/spark-examples-1.3.0-cdh5.4.7-hadoop2.6.0-cdh5.4.7.jar 1000
15/10/23 19:15:19 INFO spark.SparkContext: Running Spark version 1.3.0
15/10/23 19:15:43 INFO cluster.YarnScheduler: Adding task set 0.0 with 1000 tasks
15/10/23 19:15:43 INFO scheduler.TaskSetManager: Starting task 0.0 in stage 0.0
(TID 0, 4b4780802318, PROCESS_LOCAL, 1353 bytes)
15/10/23 19:15:43 INFO scheduler.TaskSetManager: Starting task 1.0 in stage 0.0
(TID 1, 4b4780802318, PROCESS_LOCAL, 1353 bytes)
15/10/23 19:15:57 INFO scheduler.TaskSetManager: Finished task 999.0 in stage 0.0 (TID 999)
in 22 ms on 4b4780802318 (999/1000)
15/10/23 19:15:57 INFO scheduler.TaskSetManager: Finished task 998.0 in stage 0.0 (TID 998)
in 28 ms on 4b4780802318 (1000/1000)
15/10/23 19:15:57 INFO cluster.YarnScheduler: Removed TaskSet 0.0, whose tasks have all
completed, from pool
15/10/23 19:15:57 INFO scheduler.DAGScheduler: Stage 0 (reduce at SparkPi.scala:35)
finished in 14.758 s
15/10/23 19:15:57 INFO scheduler.DAGScheduler: Job 0 finished: reduce at SparkPi.scala:35,
took 15.221643 s
```

Pi is roughly 3.14152984

Running the Apache Spark Shell

The Apache Spark shell is started in yarn-client mode as follows.

```
spark-shell --master yarn-client
```

The scala> command prompt gets displayed as shown in Figure 14-7. A Spark context gets created and becomes available as 'sc'. A SQL context also becomes available as 'sqlContext'.

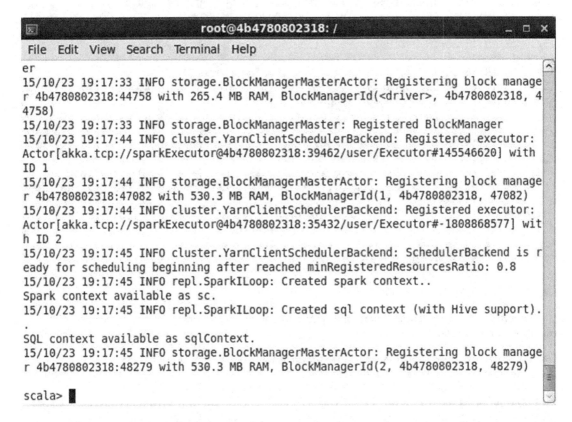

Figure 14-7. *The scala> Command Prompt*

A more detailed output from the spark-shell command is as follows.

```
root@4b4780802318:/# spark-shell --master yarn-client
15/10/23 19:17:16 WARN util.NativeCodeLoader: Unable to load native-hadoop library for your
platform... using builtin-java classes where applicable
15/10/23 19:17:16 INFO spark.SecurityManager: Changing view acls to: root
15/10/23 19:17:16 INFO spark.SecurityManager: Changing modify acls to: root
15/10/23 19:17:16 INFO spark.SecurityManager: SecurityManager: authentication disabled;
ui acls disabled; users with view permissions: Set(root); users with modify permissions:
Set(root)
15/10/23 19:17:16 INFO spark.HttpServer: Starting HTTP Server
15/10/23 19:17:16 INFO server.Server: jetty-8.y.z-SNAPSHOT
```

```
15/10/23 19:17:16 INFO server.AbstractConnector: Started SocketConnector@0.0.0.0:56899
15/10/23 19:17:16 INFO util.Utils: Successfully started service 'HTTP class server' on port
56899.
Welcome to


      / __/__  ___ _____/ /__
     _\ \/ _ \/ _ `/ __/  '_/
    /___/ .__/\_,_/_/ /_/\_\   version 1.3.0
       /_/

Using Scala version 2.10.4 (OpenJDK 64-Bit Server VM, Java 1.7.0_79)
Type in expressions to have them evaluated.
Type :help for more information.
15/10/23 19:17:22 INFO spark.SparkContext: Running Spark version 1.3.0
15/10/23 19:17:45 INFO repl.SparkILoop: Created spark context..
Spark context available as sc.
15/10/23 19:17:45 INFO repl.SparkILoop: Created sql context (with Hive support)..
SQL context available as sqlContext.
15/10/23 19:17:45 INFO storage.BlockManagerMasterActor: Registering block manager
4b4780802318:48279 with 530.3 MB RAM, BlockManagerId(2, 4b4780802318, 48279)
scala>
```

Run the following Scala script consisting of a HelloWorld module in the Spark shell for a Hello World program.

```
object HelloWorld {
    def main(args: Array[String]) {
      println("Hello, world!")
    }
}
HelloWorld.main(null)
```

The output from the Scala script is shown in Figure 14-8.

```
scala> object HelloWorld {
     |     def main(args: Array[String]) {
     |       println("Hello, world!")
     |     }
     |   }
defined module HelloWorld

scala> HelloWorld.main(null)
Hello, world!

scala>
```

Figure 14-8. Output from Scala Script

Summary

In this chapter, we ran Apache Spark applications on a YARN cluster in a Docker container using the spark-submit command. We submitted the example application in yarn-cluster and yarn-client modes. We also ran a HelloWorld Scala script in a Spark shell.

This chapter concludes the book on Docker. In addition to running some of the commonly used software on Docker, we discussed the main Docker administrative tasks such as installing Docker, downloading a Docker image, creating and running a Docker container, starting an interactive shell, running commands in an interactive shell, listing Docker containers, listing Docker container logs, stopping a Docker container, and removing a Docker container and a Docker image. Only a few of the software applications could be discussed in the scope of this book. Several more Docker images are available on the Docker hub at https://hub.docker.com/.

APPENDIX A

■ ■ ■

Using the Amazon EC2

Amazon Web Services (AWS) provides various services and Amazon Elastic Compute Cloud (Amazon EC2) is one of the services. Amazon EC2 may be used to create a virtual host server. Amazon EC2 provides a wide selection of instance AMIs (Amazon Machine Images) to choose from when creating a virtual server. In this Appendix we shall discuss creating and configuring Amazon EC2 instance/s for installing Docker and Docker images. Amazon EC2 instance is not a requirement to run Docker software and an alternative platform, local or remote, may be used instead.

> Creating an Amazon EC2 Instance
>
> Create a Key Pair
>
> Starting an Amazon EC2 Instance
>
> Connecting to an Amazon EC2 Instance
>
> Finding the Public IP Address
>
> Finding the Public DNS
>
> Adding the default Security Group
>
> Stopping an Amazon EC2 Instance
>
> Changing the Instance Type

Creating an Amazon EC2 Instance

We have used Amazon EC2 instances based on Linux for deploying Docker and Docker images. Amazon EC2 is not a requirement and an alternative such as a local Linux installation may be used instead. The Linux platform is required to support 64 bit software. We have made use of two different 64 bit (required) AMIs:

1. Ubuntu Server 14.04 LTS (HVM), SSD Volume Type - ami-d05e75b8 64 bit

2. Red Hat Enterprise Linux version 7.1 (HVM), EBS General Purpose (SSD) Volume Type (ami-12663b7a) 64 bit

To create an Amazon EC2 Instance, an Amazon Web Services Account is required, which may be created at https://aws.amazon.com/getting-started/?nc2=h_l2_cc. To create an Amazon EC2 instance, navigate to https://aws.amazon.com/ec2/ and click on Sign In to the Console. Select EC2 from the listed Amazon Web Services. Click on INSTANCES ➤ Instances to list the Amazon EC2 instances already created in the account. Click on Launch Instance to create a new Amazon EC2 instance as shown in Figure A-1.

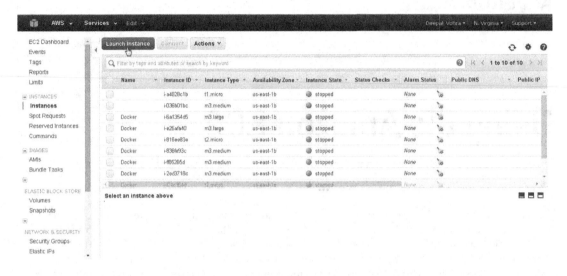

Figure A-1. *Launching an Amazon EC2 Instance*

Select an AMI to create a virtual server from. Some of the AMIs are eligible for the Free tier. For example, select the Ubuntu AMI as shown in Figure A-2.

Figure A-2. *Selecting an AMI*

In Choose an Instance Type different types are available differing by features such as supported capacity and virtual CPUs (vCPUs). Select one of the Instance Types, for example the General Purpose ➤ t2.micro and click on Review and Launch as shown in Figure A-3.

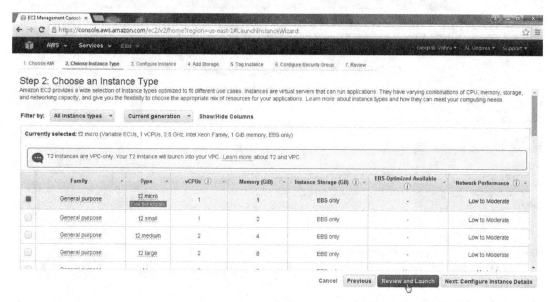

Figure A-3. *Review and Launch*

Click on Launch in Review Instance Launch as shown in Figure A-4.

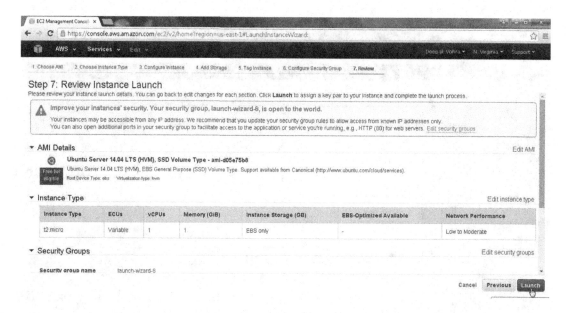

Figure A-4. *Launch*

A dialog gets displayed to create or select an existing key pair. A key pair is required for authorization. To create a new key pair, select the "Create a new key pair" option as shown in Figure A-5.

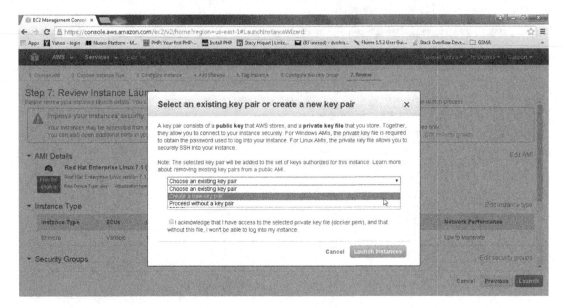

Figure A-5. *Selecting "Create a new key pair"*

Specify a Key pair name and click on Download Key Pair as shown in Figure A-6. The Key pair gets created and downloaded. The key pair selected for an Amazon EC2 instance when creating the instance is required when connecting to the instance, as is discussed later in this Appendix.

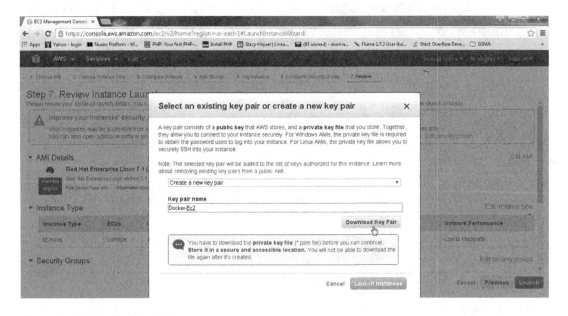

Figure A-6. *Download Key Pair*

Alternatively, select the option "Choose an existing key pair" and click on Launch Instances as shown in Figure A-7.

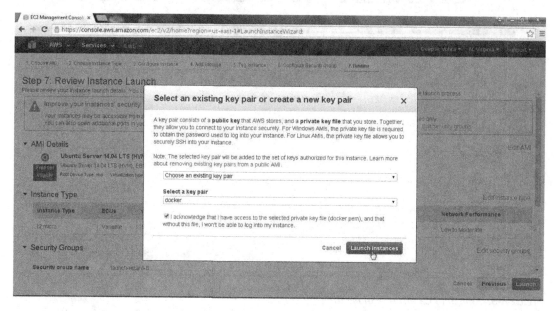

Figure A-7. *Choose an existing Key Pair*

The Launch Status gets displayed. Click on the instance id to display the instance as shown in Figure A-8.

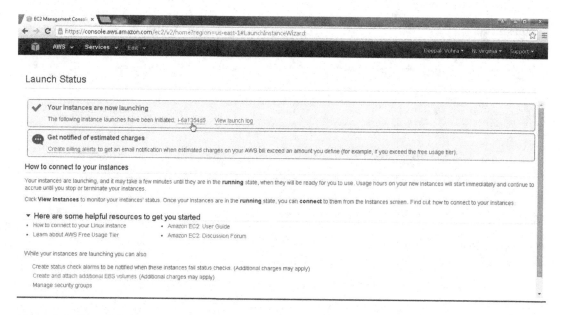

Figure A-8. *Launch Status*

The instance gets listed and is initially in the "pending" state as shown in Figure A-9.

Figure A-9. *Amazon EC2 Instance in Pending State*

When an instance has launched completely, the Instance State becomes "running" as shown in Figure A-10.

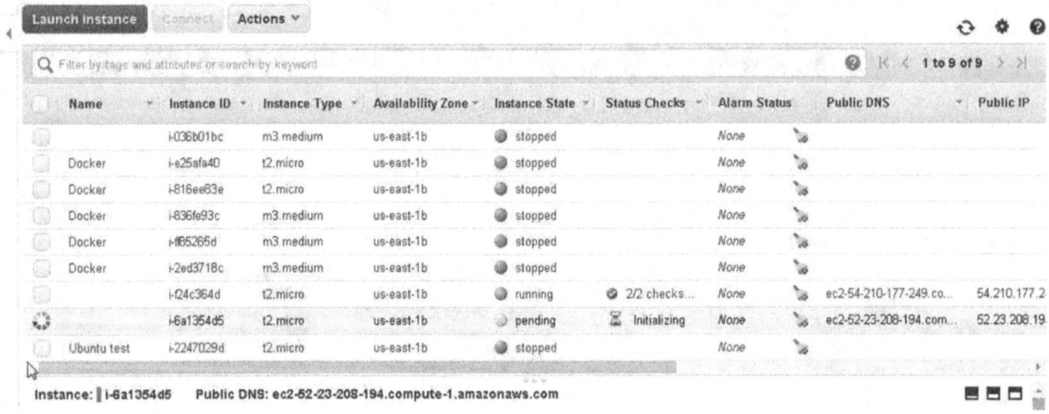

Figure A-10. *Running Instance*

Creating a Key Pair

As mentioned previously, a key pair is required to connect to a Amazon EC2 instance. A key pair may be created while creating an instance or separately. To create a key pair separately select Network & Security ➤ Key Pairs as shown in Figure A-11.

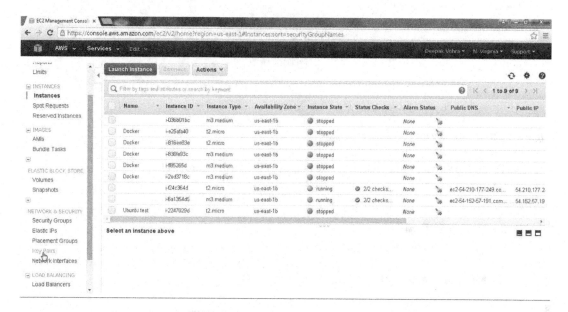

Figure A-11. *Network & Security ➤ Key Pairs*

The key pairs already created get listed. A key pair may be deleted by selecting the key pair and clicking on Delete. Click on Yes in the dialog as shown in Figure A-12.

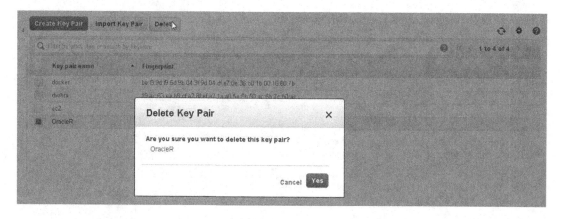

Figure A-12. *Delete Key Pair*

To create a new key pair, click on Create Key Pair as shown in Figure A-13.

Figure A-13. *Create Key Pair*

Specify a Key pair name and click on Create button as shown in Figure A-14.

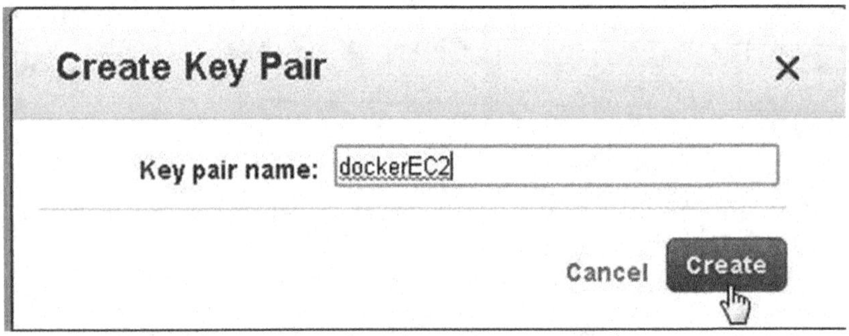

Create Key Pair   ✕

Key pair name: dockerEC2

Cancel   **Create**

Figure A-14. *Create Button*

A new key pair gets created as shown in Figure A-15.

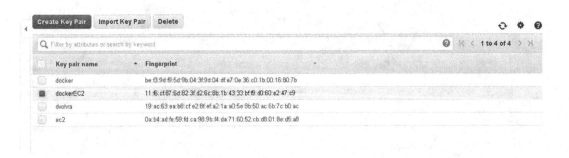

Figure A-15. *New Key Pair*

Starting an Amazon EC2 Instance

When a new Amazon EC2 instance is created and Launch is selected, the instance gets started. A stopped instance may be started by selecting the checkbox adjacent to the instance and selecting Actions ➤ Instance State ➤ Start as shown in Figure A-16.

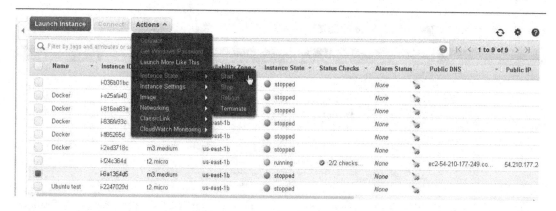

Figure A-16. *Actions ➤ Instance State ➤ Start*

In Start Instances dialog click on Yes, Start as shown in Figure A-17.

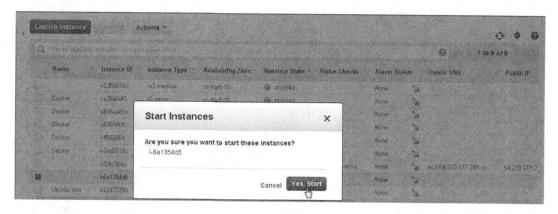

Figure A-17. *Starting an instance*

Connecting to an Amazon EC2 Instance

An instance that has been started may be connected to from a local machine such as a local Linux instance without as much RAM and a different Linux distribution than the instance being connected to. The ssh command to use to connect to a running instance may be obtained by clicking on Connect as shown in Figure A-18.

Figure A-18. *Connect*

In the Connect To Your Instance dialog, the ssh command is displayed. The "docker.pem" is the key pair used to create an instance and also downloaded to the local instance from which the Amazon EC2 instance is to be connected. The username for an Ubuntu instance is "ubuntu" as shown in Figure A-19 and for a Red Hat instance is "ec2-user".

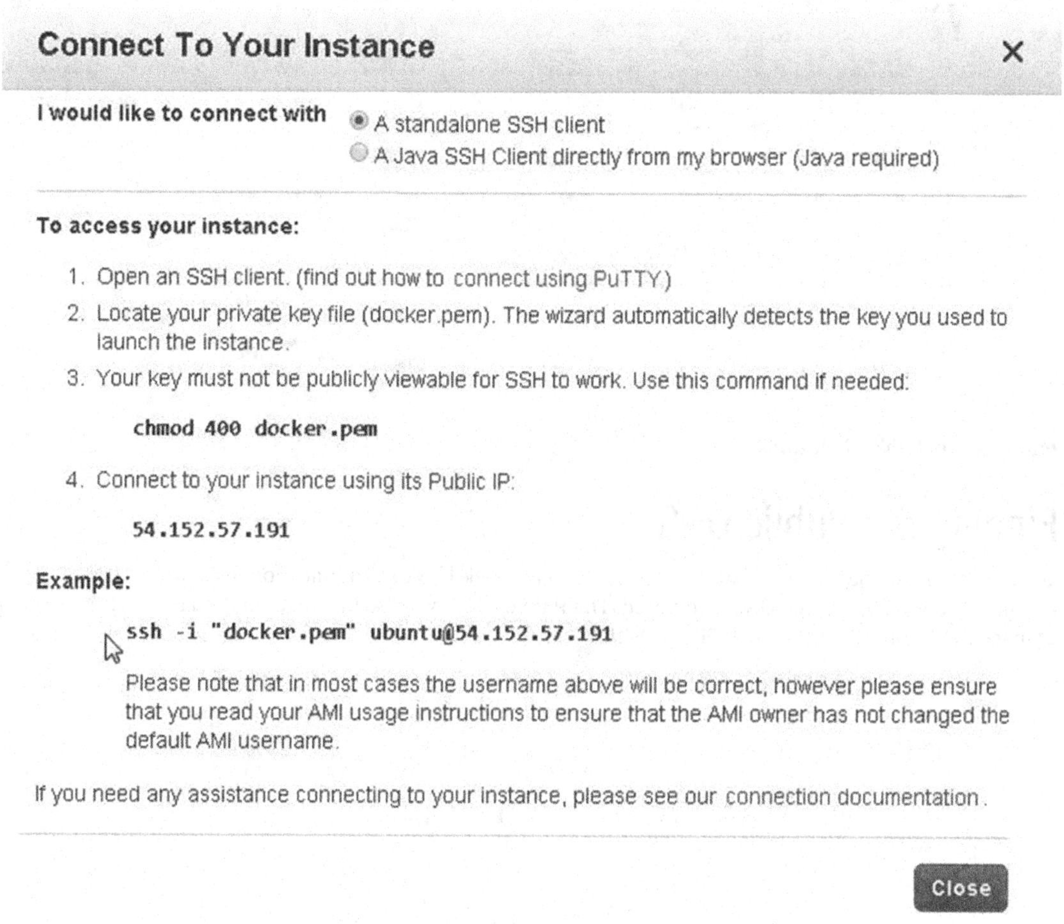

Connect To Your Instance ✕

I would like to connect with ● A standalone SSH client
○ A Java SSH Client directly from my browser (Java required)

To access your instance:

1. Open an SSH client. (find out how to connect using PuTTY.)
2. Locate your private key file (docker.pem). The wizard automatically detects the key you used to launch the instance.
3. Your key must not be publicly viewable for SSH to work. Use this command if needed:

   ```
   chmod 400 docker.pem
   ```

4. Connect to your instance using its Public IP:

   ```
   54.152.57.191
   ```

Example:

```
ssh -i "docker.pem" ubuntu@54.152.57.191
```

Please note that in most cases the username above will be correct, however please ensure that you read your AMI usage instructions to ensure that the AMI owner has not changed the default AMI username.

If you need any assistance connecting to your instance, please see our connection documentation.

Close

Figure A-19. *Connect To Your Instance dialog*

The IP Address shown in the ssh command is the Public IP Address of the Amazon EC2 instance.

Finding the Public IP Address

The Public IP Address may also be obtained from the EC2 Console as shown in Figure A-20.

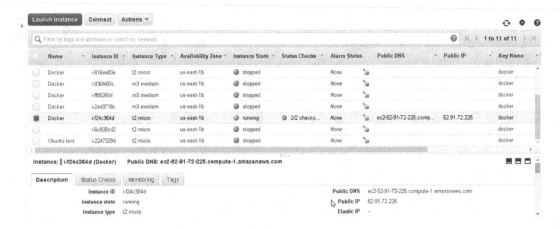

Figure A-20. *Public IP Address*

Finding the Public DNS

To connect to an Amazon EC2 instance process such as the HelloWorld application in Chapter 1 from a remote browser, the Public DNS is required. The Public DNS may also be obtained from the EC2 Management Console as shown in Figure A-21.

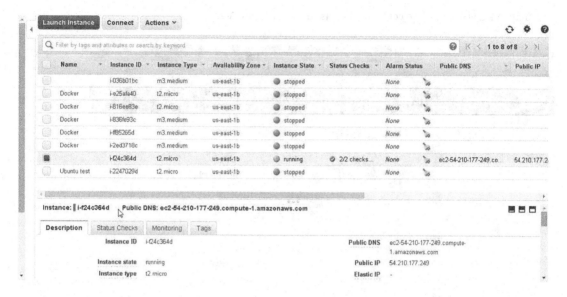

Figure A-21. Public DNS

The Public DNS may not get displayed initially. To display the Public DNS, select Services ➤ VPC in the EC2 Management Console as shown in Figure A-22. VPC is a virtual private cloud assigned to a user.

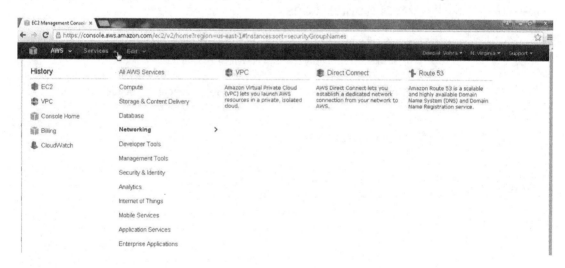

Figure A-22. Services ➤ VPC

In the VPC Dashboard, select Your VPCs as shown in Figure A-23.

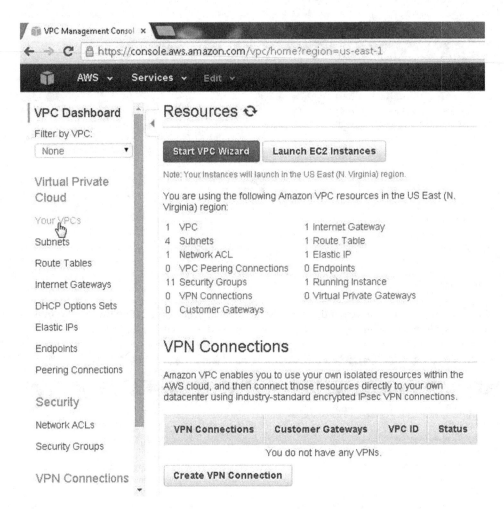

Figure A-23. *Your VPCs*

Select the VPC listed as shown in Figure A-24.

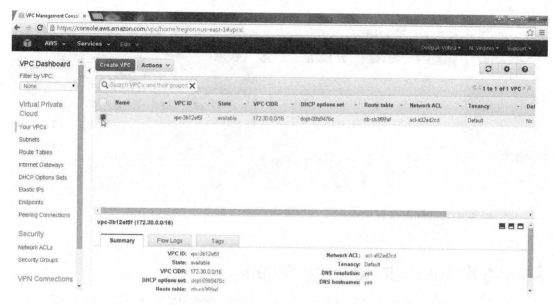

Figure A-24. *Selecting the VPC*

From Actions, select Edit DNS Hostnames as shown in Figure A-25.

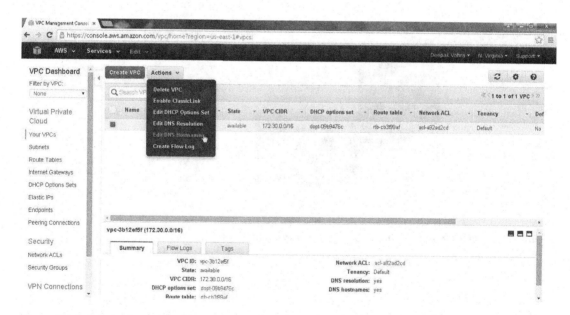

Figure A-25. *Edit DNS Hostnames*

In the Edit DNS Hostnames dialog, select Yes for the DNS Hostnames, and click on Save as shown in Figure A-26.

Figure A-26. *Edit DNS Hostnames Dialog*

Adding the default Security Group

To be able to connect from a remote browser, the Inbound and Outbound rules are required to be set to allow all traffic using any protocol on all ports in the range 0-65535 from any source. The "default" security group is configured by default to allow all traffic. We need to assign the "default" security group to the Amazon EC2 instance running Docker. Select the instance and select Actions ➤ Networking ➤ Change Security Groups as shown in Figure A-27.

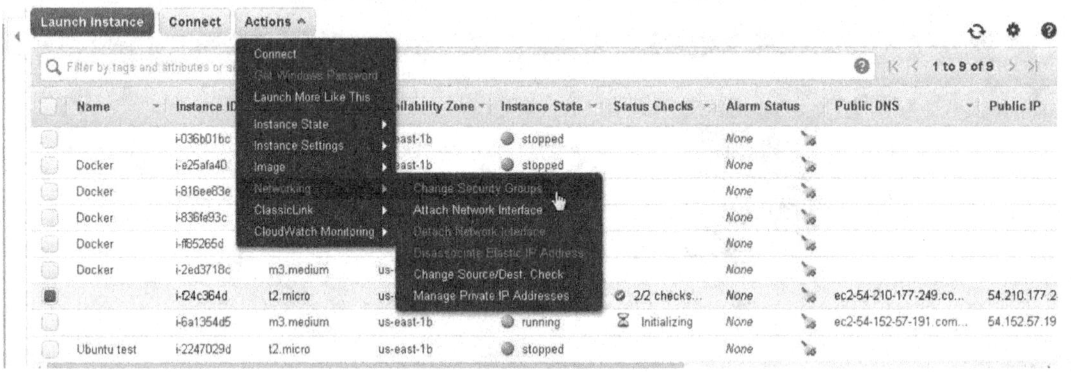

Figure A-27. *Actions ➤ Networking ➤ Change Security Groups*

In the Change Security Groups panel, the "default" group might not be selected as shown in Figure A-28.

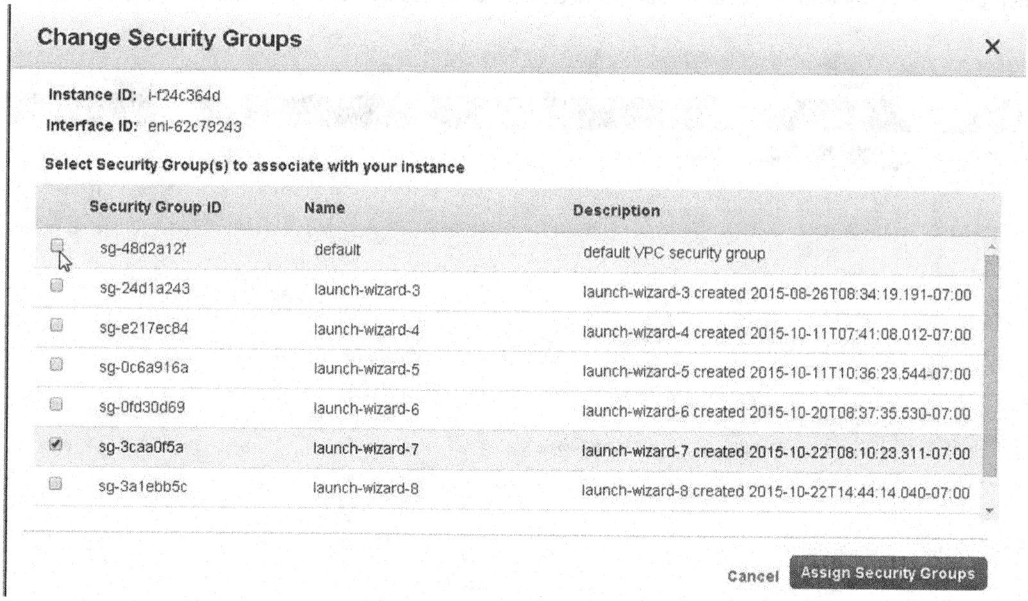

Figure A-28. *The "default" group not selected*

Select the checkbox for the "default" security group and click on Assign Security Groups as shown in Figure A-29.

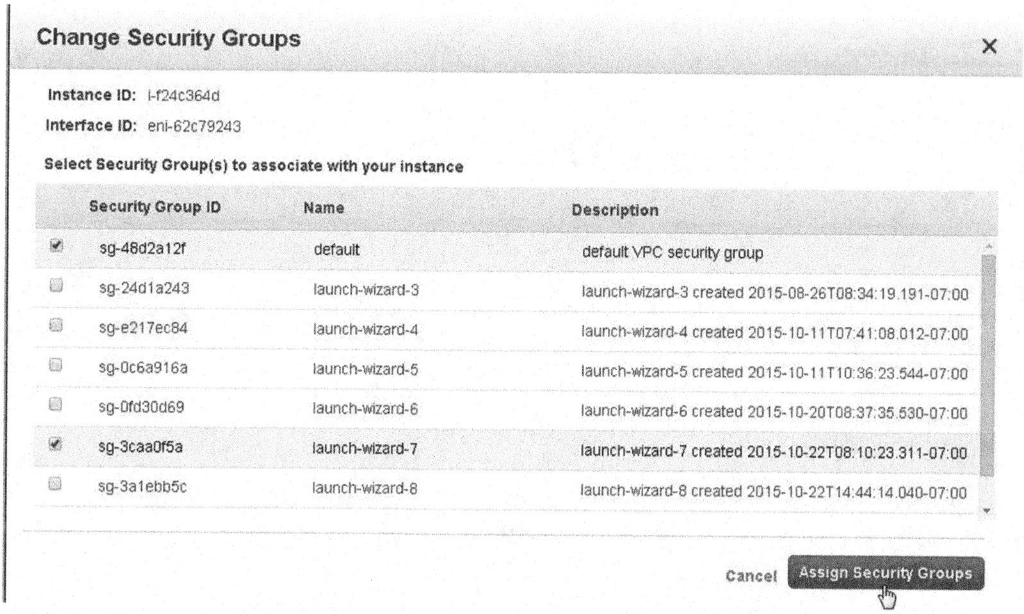

Figure A-29. *Assign Security Groups*

245

The default security group gets assigned to the Amazon EC2 instance. To find the available security groups and their inbound/outbound rules, click on Network & Security ➤ Security Groups as shown in Figure A-30.

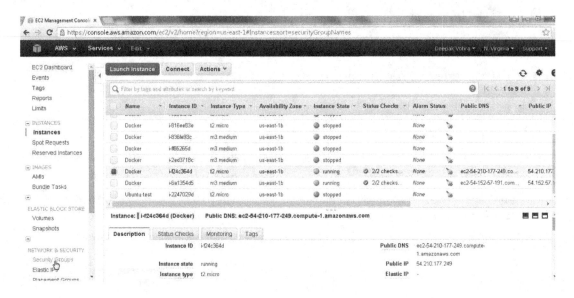

Figure A-30. *Network & Security ➤ Security Groups*

The "default" security group should be listed. Select the "default" group. Select the Inbound tab. The Type should be listed as "All Traffic", the Protocol as "All", the Port Range as All and Source as 0.0.0.0. To edit the inbound rules, click on Inbound ➤ Edit as shown in Figure A-31.

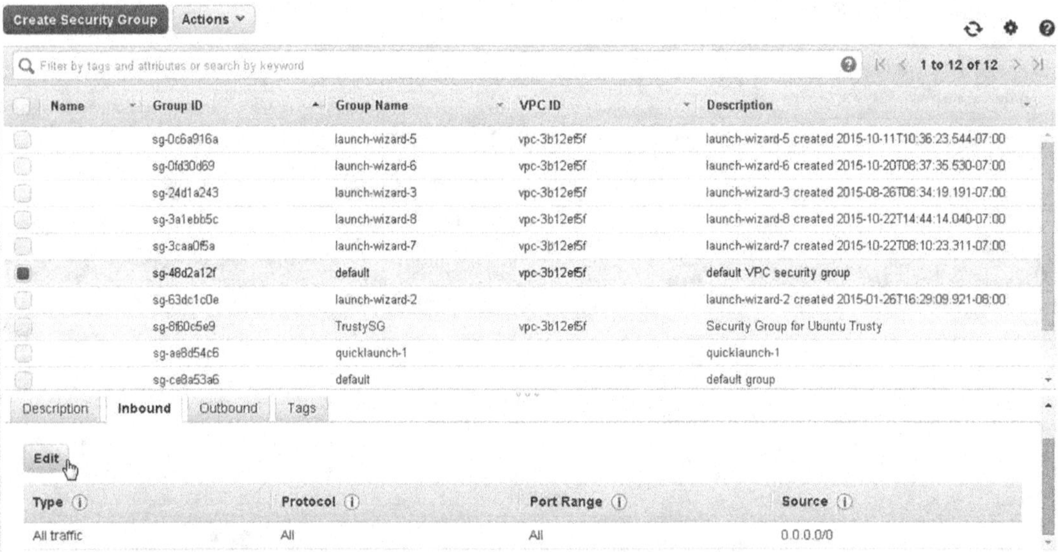

Figure A-31. *Inbound ➤ Edit*

The inbound rules get displayed and should be kept as the default settings as shown in Figure A-32. Click on Save.

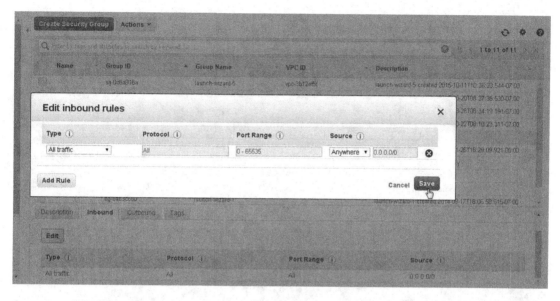

Figure A-32. *Edit inbound rules dialog*

Similarly, select the Outbound tab. The Type should be listed as "All Traffic", the Protocol as "All", the Port Range as All and Destination as 0.0.0.0. Click on Edit as shown in Figure A-33.

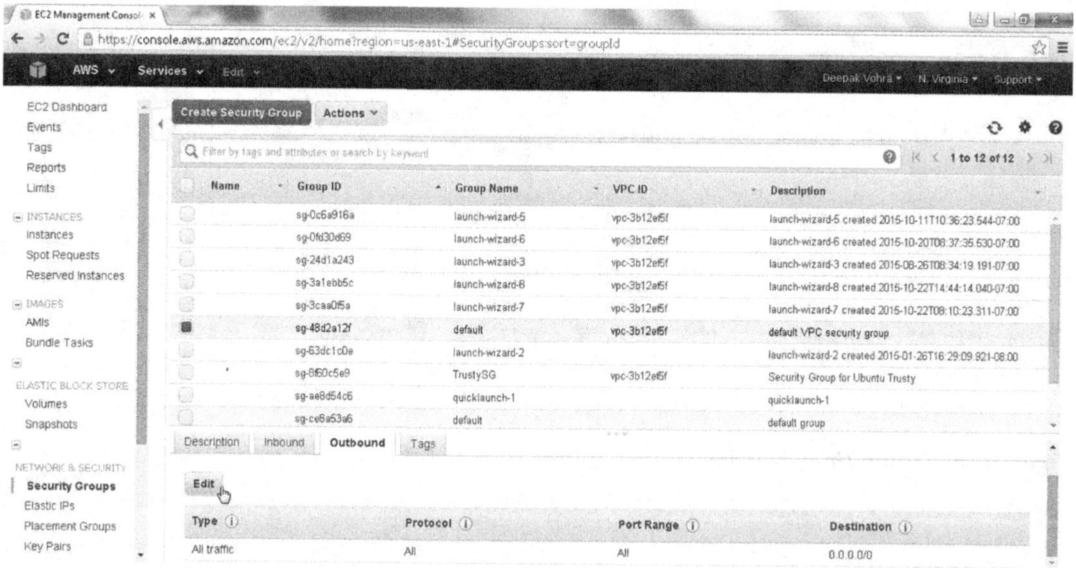

Figure A-33. *Outbound ➤ Edit*

The default settings for the Outbound rules get displayed and should be kept as the default as shown in Figure A-34. Click on Save.

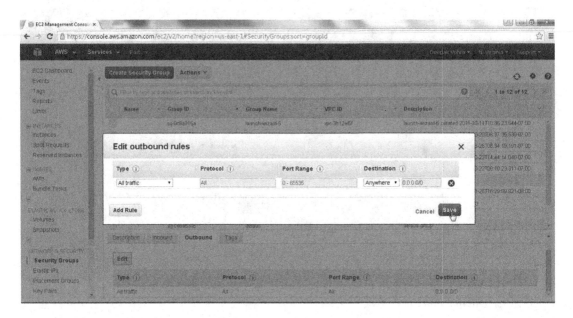

Figure A-34. *Edit outbound rules dialog*

The security groups assigned to an instance are listed in the Security Groups column as shown in Figure A-35.

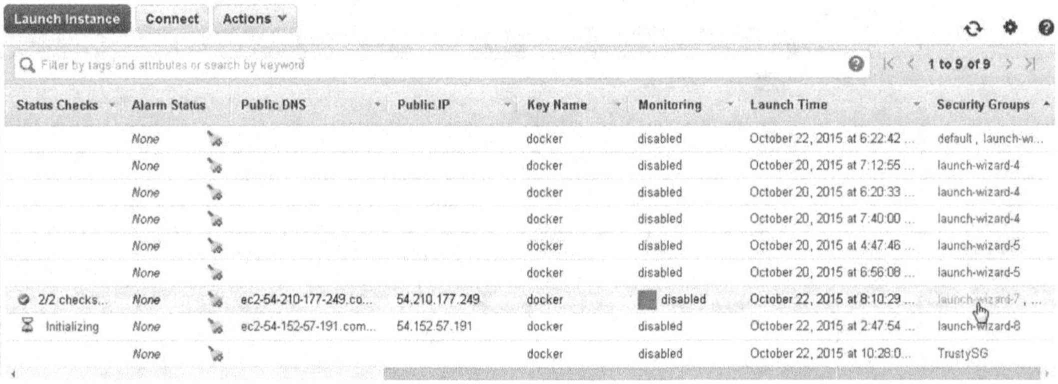

Figure A-35. *Security Groups column*

Stopping an Amazon EC2 Instance

To stop an Amazon EC2 instance select the instance and select Actions ➤ Instance State ➤ Stop as shown in Figure A-36.

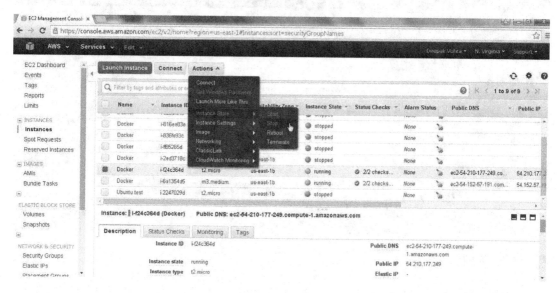

Figure A-36. *Actions ➤ Instance State ➤ Stop*

Multiple instances may be selected and stopped together as shown in Figure A-37.

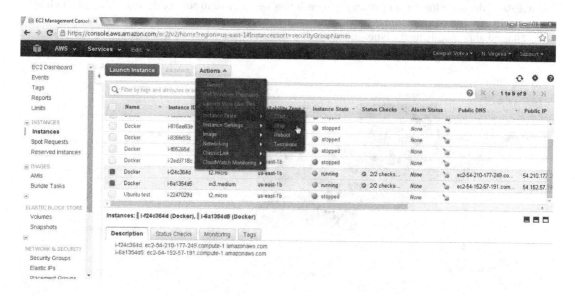

Figure A-37. *Stopping Multiple Instances*

In the Stop Instance dialog, click on Yes, Stop as shown in Figure A-38.

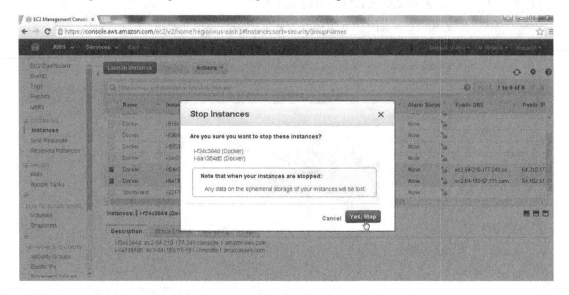

Figure 38. *Stop Instance dialog*

The instance/s get stopped.

Changing the Instance Type

To increase or decrease the capacity of an instance, it may be required to change the instance type, such as from a micro instance to a medium instance. An instance must first be stopped before changing its type and later restarted after modifying the type. To change the instance type, select the instance and select Actions ➤ Instance Settings ➤ Change Instance Type as shown in Figure A-39.

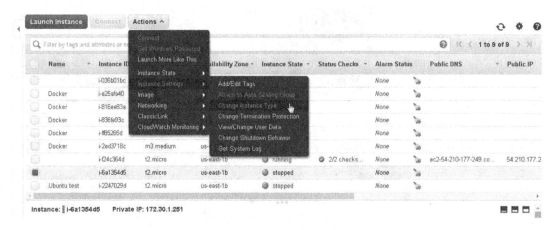

Figure 39. *Actions ➤ Instance Settings ➤ Change Instance Type*

In the Change Instance Type dialog, select the Instance Type to apply, for example, m3.medium as shown in Figure A-40.

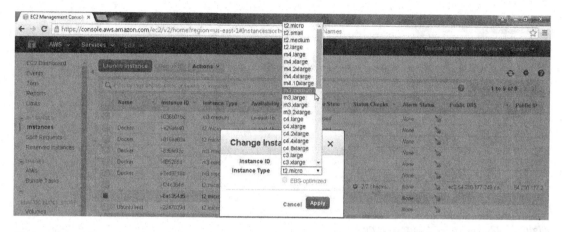

Figure A-40. *Change Instance Type dialog*

Click on Apply as shown in Figure A-41.

Figure A-41. *Applying a new Instance Type*

The instance type gets upgraded to m3.medium as shown in Figure A-42. Keep in consideration that upgrading an instance type could make the instance not eligible for the free tier.

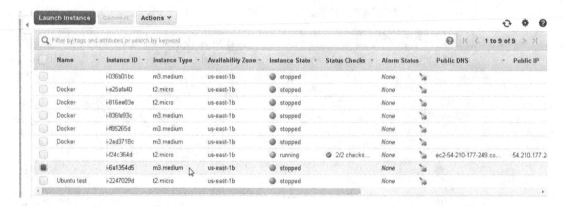

Figure A-42. *Upgraded Instance Type*

Summary

In Appendix A we discussed creating an Amazon EC2 instance based on an AMI, starting an instance, connecting to an instance, finding the Public IP Address, finding the Public DNS, changing the instance type and stopping an instance.

Index

■ O, P, Q, R, S, T, U, V, W, X, Y, Z

Get the eBook for only $5!

Why limit yourself?

Now you can take the weightless companion with you wherever you go and access your content on your PC, phone, tablet, or reader.

Since you've purchased this print book, we're happy to offer you the eBook in all 3 formats for just $5.

Convenient and fully searchable, the PDF version enables you to easily find and copy code—or perform examples by quickly toggling between instructions and applications. The MOBI format is ideal for your Kindle, while the ePUB can be utilized on a variety of mobile devices.

To learn more, go to www.apress.com/companion or contact support@apress.com.

Printed in the United States
By Bookmasters